www.wadsworth.com

wadsworth.com is the World Wide Web site for Wadsworth Publishing Company and is your direct source to dozens of online resources.

At *wadsworth.com* you can find out about supplements, demonstration software, and student resources. You can also send e-mail to many of our authors and preview new publications and exciting new technologies.

wadsworth.com
Changing the way the world learns®

Public Personnel Administration

Fourth Edition

N. Joseph Cayer
Arizona State University

THOMSON

™

WADSWORTH

Australia • Canada • Mexico • Singapore • Spain
United Kingdom • United States

THOMSON
™
WADSWORTH

Executive Editor, Political Science: David Tatom
Development Editor: Scott Spoolman
Editorial Assistant: Dianna Long
Technology Project Manager: Melinda Newfarmer
Marketing Manager: Janise Fry
Marketing Assistant: Mary Ho
Executive Advertising Project Manager: Nathaniel Bergson-Michelson
Project Manager, Editorial Production: Emily Smith

Print/Media Buyer: Doreen Suruki
Permissions Editor: Sarah Harkrader
Production Service and Compositor: Lachina Publishing Services
Copy Editor: Lachina Publishing Services
Illustrator: Lachina Publishing Services
Cover Designer: Brian Salisbury
Cover Image: © PhotoDisc; © Digital Vision/Getty Images; © PhotoDisc
Text and Cover Printer: Webcom

For more information about our products, contact us at:
Thomson Learning Academic Resource Center
1-800-423-0563

For permission to use material from this text, contact us by:
Phone: 1-800-730-2214 **Fax:** 1-800-730-2215
Web: http://www.thomsonrights.com

Library of Congress Control Number: 2003105407

ISBN 0-534-61866-9

Wadsworth/Thomson Learning
10 Davis Drive
Belmont, CA 94002-3098
USA

Asia
Thomson Learning
5 Shenton Way #01-01
UIC Building
Singapore 068808

Australia/New Zealand
Thomson Learning
102 Dodds Street
Southbank, Victoria 3006
Australia

Canada
Nelson
1120 Birchmount Road
Toronto, Ontario M1K 5G4
Canada

Europe/Middle East/Africa
Thomson Learning
High Holborn House
50/51 Bedford Row
London WC1R 4LR
United Kingdom

Latin America
Thomson Learning
Seneca, 53
Colonia Polanco
11560 Mexico D.F.
Mexico

Spain/Portugal
Paraninfo
Calle/Magallanes, 25
28015 Madrid, Spain

About the Author

N. Joseph Cayer is professor of public affairs at Arizona State University. He received the Ph.D. from the University of Massachusetts, Amherst and a B.A. and MPA from the University of Colorado, Boulder. He also has taught at Lamar University, the University of Maine—Orono, and Texas Tech University. He is the author or coauthor of seven books and numerous chapters and articles on public management and policy, with an emphasis on issues of human resources management in the public sector. Books he has authored or coauthored include *Public Administration: Social Change and Adaptive Management; American Public Policy: An Introduction; Managing Human Resources; Handbook of Training and Development for the Public Sector;* and *Supervision for Success in Government.* He also is active in academic and professional associations.

Contents

Preface

Since the publication of the third edition of *Public Personnel Administration* in 1996, many changes in society and government have affected the field. Many aspects of theory and practice have changed, but the basic themes and values of the field have remained consistent. This edition explores the themes and practices in light of changing environmental pressures and personnel practices. For example, the sustained pressures on government to reduce costs while increasing services have had implications for the practice of personnel administration. Similarly, issues of social equity and responsiveness of government affect the specifics of personnel management. Ethical issues have arisen in each of the national administrations since the publication of the last edition and continue to influence the image and expectations of public agencies and employees. Most recently, efforts to protect against terrorism have had direct impact on the lives of public employees and agencies.

Some specific issues explored more fully in this fourth edition include legal aspects of public personnel administration, controversies over affirmative action, sexual harassment, and the Americans with Disabilities Act and its enforcement. Also addressed are the implications of changing technology, controversies over sexual orientation and employment, privacy, and violence in the workplace. These and other issues lead government to constantly reform its approach to personnel administration. Readers will find examination of changing policies and laws as well as judicial decisions that affect personnel actions and decisions.

Clearly, public personnel administrators and all managers face constantly changing pressures and concerns. This book presents public personnel management in the context of changing times and forces. Among the most important are demographic changes and their impact on public agencies. Readers of this book should come to recognize that public personnel administration is a dynamic field of endeavor crucial to effective government.

This fourth edition contains exercises that provide opportunities for students to experience and apply what they learn. The mini cases of the third edition are incorporated into the exercises. Each chapter also lists Web sites appropriate to the subject matter of the chapter. The Web sites represent the organizations and government agencies most appropriate to the material. Internet users will find many more relevant sites.

The fourth edition of this book has benefited greatly from the comments and suggestions of many people who read the first three editions. Students who challenge the ideas presented have been particularly important in stimulating me to think about the issues. Thank you to my students at the University of Maine, Texas Tech University, and Arizona State University and others who have written or talked to me for your help in sharpening and clarifying my approach to the field. Faculty colleagues who have offered suggestions are too numerous to identify, but I would like to single out Sherry Dickerson, Lawrence Mankin, and Ronald Perry of Arizona State University for their questions, suggestions, and constant identification of new materials and ideas.

In preparing the manuscript, Loree Alvarez was very efficient in helping me prepare tables and figures. Matt Young did an incredible job of word processing of the manuscript. Without his tireless help, I would still be working on it. Manuscript reviewers—Sheilah Watson Bishop, University of Missouri-Columbia, Jason Jensen, University of North Dakota, William Parle, Oklahoma State University, Glenn W. Rainey, Jr., Eastern Kentucky University, and Zachary Smith, Northern Arizona University—offered valuable suggestions and insights for improving the book. To all, a heartfelt thank you!

The staff of Wadsworth was outstanding in their efforts. David Tatom, executive editor, encouraged me to do the new edition. I am especially indebted to Scott Spoolman, development editor, who demonstrated great patience and careful guidance. His efforts improved the work greatly. Lachina Publishing Services did an outstanding job of copyediting.

Without the help of these talented people, the fourth edition would not be a reality. Nonetheless, any shortcomings are entirely mine.

N. Joseph Cayer
Mesa, Arizona

1

The Environment of Public Personnel Administration

Personnel administration encompasses all activities related to people in organizations. It entails the utilization of human resources to accomplish an organization's objectives as efficiently and effectively as possible. Because the successful management of people is the key to organizations' effective operation, good personnel management is essential to good administration. In turn, good personnel administration requires both technical and interpersonal skills. Personnel managers must know how to recruit, select, evaluate, promote, train, discipline, and dismiss employees. They must be adept at motivating, counseling, and bargaining with workers. In addition, personnel managers are asked to classify positions, develop compensation plans, measure productivity, and handle grievances and complaints. In short, personnel management involves all aspects of managing an organization's human resources, and *public personnel administration* refers to that function in governmental entities.

Personnel administration also is a universal management activity. Every supervisor is in effect a personnel manager. Whereas personnel offices normally develop and monitor personnel policies, supervisors are responsible for carrying out those policies. Supervisors are the crucial links in the personnel process because they deal with employees daily. The organization's effectiveness in turn hinges in part on how well supervisors perform their personnel functions.

Those who perform personnel activities in the public sector do so in a political environment; therefore, political considerations shape their actions. First, interests that have anything to gain or lose from developments in public bureaucracies compete. Second, bureaucrats themselves have a stake in the process and engage in politics to maintain their status. The reactions to efforts in 2002 to create a homeland security department at the cabinet level attest to the political interests that personnel issues energize. One of the major controversies in creation of the cabinet position was the president's desire to exempt employees of the new department from many traditional personnel and labor relations policies. The employees and labor unions became energized very quickly, and the Democrats in Congress took up their cause, but President George W. Bush prevailed.

Finally, the political considerations include policy issues that are affected by public personnel administration. These include the following:

1. How collective bargaining and the merit concept can coexist
2. Whether the public service should be used to solve social problems, for example, by being the employer of last resort, taking the lead in affirmative action, or satisfying the demands of myriad special interests with convincing claims
3. How to reconcile continued demands for a higher level of services with demands for lower taxes and smaller budgets
4. How to maintain a politically responsive bureaucracy without endangering the concept of merit.

More generally, the public service itself is an issue. The support that political candidates receive for promising to reduce the size of the public bureaucracy indicates people's concerns about government service. Because public policy issues affect the public service, public employees can influence policy as they help shape and implement it.

In examining the personnel process in government, this book analyzes the specific personnel responsibilities of supervisors and personnel officers. In particular, it evaluates the effects each of these elements has on government's responsiveness and accountability and the ways in which alternative approaches affect the delivery of services.

The Field of Public Personnel Administration

Public personnel administration has been accused of not having a sense of identity, being too narrow in scope, and lacking a theoretical foundation.[1] These problems have resulted in large part from a slavish attachment to principles that seemed appropriate to developing civil service systems in an attempt to replace the abuses of the spoils systems of the nineteenth century. In a zealous effort to remove partisanship from the personnel process, administrators focused almost exclusively on techniques such as testing and selection methods that could be applied to personnel activities. Lost in the shuffle was a concern with serving the purposes of management generally. As a result, the rest of management came to perceive personnel administration as a nonpolitical, technical service rather than as management per se. Nineteenth-century reform established a foundation of moral fervor among personnelists that labeled politics as evil and devotion to "neutral" principles of personnel management, as defined by personnelists, as good. As Wallace Sayre noted, public personnel management became a "triumph of technique over purpose."[2]

Personnel management lost touch with its environment and became isolated. It assumed a policing role in which it seemed more interested in telling management what it could not do than in finding positive ways to assist management. It is little wonder that the personnel office became regarded with scorn.[3]

Contemporary personnel managers have come to realize that public personnel management is very closely connected with the environment in which it operates. For public personnel administrators, that environment is characterized first and foremost by politics. Whereas the reformers eschewed politics, contemporary personnelists recognize the political nature of the field and criticize traditionalists for ignoring the relevance of political concerns.

The environment of personnel managers also includes many other forces. Employer and employee values affect the personnel system. These values affect the types of personnel policies developed, the decision-making rules, and the results of processes. Conflicts over values to be represented are resolved through politics,[4] and the error of many personnel reformers has been in equating politics with partisan politics. By focusing on partisan politics, the reformers forgot that decisions were being made by compromising the differing values and interests of those participating in personnel decisions.[5]

Changes in society also affect public personnel management. As will be noted throughout the book, factors such as the civil rights movement, the women's movement, affirmative action and diversity efforts, cutback management and privatization of public services, and ever-changing technology have affected personnel management significantly. The terrorist attacks of September 11, 2001, also have had many effects on the public service. The culmination of these environmental changes has resulted in a change in the way the public service functions. Paul Light suggests that we have seen the end of government-centered public service and the beginning of a multicentered public service.[6] By this he means that government managers no longer can decide how to approach the public service from only their perspective. If government is to compete for employees, it must compete for talent and recognize that the diversity of the workforce requires focusing on what potential employees want from their jobs. Pay and security are no longer the only things potential employees seek. They now expect flexibility, interesting work, and the opportunity to grow.

Changes in management approaches also have had significant impact on the organization of the personnel function. It now is recognized that managing human resources is a partnership between the personnel departments (increasingly called *human resources departments*) and the department managers and supervisors.

Today, the civil service and merit concepts prevail in public personnel management. Nonetheless, there have been challenges to both concepts. Public sector labor unions enjoyed tremendous growth during the 1960s and

1970s. The public sector still is the major growth area for union membership; unions in the private sector have been on the decline for decades. Some positions of unions on the criteria for personnel decisions conflict with traditional merit concepts. Unions are examined in detail in Chapter 8. Civil service systems have been under attack in many jurisdictions. Georgia, for example, dissolved its merit system in 1996 and decentralized much of the personnel function to agencies;[7] Florida followed in 2000 with a similar approach. The fortunes of management, employees, elected public officials, citizens, and the bureaucracies themselves are affected by the changing manner in which personnel is managed.

Although traditional personnelists exhorted public personnel administrators to apply neutral principles, the presence of competing values makes such an approach impossible. Value judgments must be used to implement differing selection systems, affirmative action programs, performance evaluation, and all other elements of personnel systems. Someone will gain and someone will lose with each decision made. For example, how should an agency respond to a cut in its budget? Are the newly hired let go? Are older employees urged to retire early? Are those hired under affirmative action programs protected? Are all departments required to contribute equally to the reduction? Are private vendors used for service delivery? All these and many other concerns affect the final decision, and each involves a value judgment. Decisions regarding competing value judgments also are political decisions, so a modern personnel administrator is a participant in the political process.

Public versus Private Sector Personnel Administration

Public and private sector personnel administration have much in common. For instance, the technical processes used for selecting, interviewing, evaluating, and training employees can be the same in both public and private organizations. However, the administration of personnel in the public sector differs from that in the private sector in four important ways:

1. Public employees are subject to more legal restrictions.
2. Lines of authority are less clear in the public sector.
3. Labor-management relations have followed different paths.
4. The political environment affects public personnel to a greater extent than it does those in the private sector.

We shall examine these differences briefly; readers should keep in mind, however, that the differences are blurred by the public and private sectors' interaction and the constant changes in society. Also, people increasingly move back and forth between the public and private sectors; thus, they affect the way things are done in each sector. In the past, people tended to have one career and often stayed with the same organization for their entire careers. Today, people are likely to have several careers and move from organization to organization including moving between public and private employers.

LEGAL RESTRICTIONS

Public employees usually are governed by numerous legal limitations on their activities. Legislation or executive orders require employees to refrain from even the appearance of a conflict of interest, that is, the possibility that their official actions serve their self-interests, economically or otherwise, or that they favor family or friend. Personnel administrators and supervisors must monitor their employees' activities to make sure that they have no conflicts of interest.

Government employees often are prohibited from engaging in political activities. At the national level, the Hatch Act of 1939 prohibited most partisan political participation by federal employees until 1993, when the act was amended. State and local governments have their own rules, which sometimes prohibit participation even in nonpartisan elections. These restrictions are aimed at making the delivery of services nonpartisan and protecting employees and citizens from abuses typical of the spoils system.

After many years of relaxing regulations on personal appearance, dress, and residency, governmental units, especially at the local level, have been reinstituting some such rules. For example, police officers typically are prohibited from growing beards or long hair and employees may be required to live in the jurisdiction in which they are employed. Although employees have challenged such restrictions in the courts, the U.S. Supreme Court has been inclined to side with the employer.[8]

The national government tends to be less concerned with personal behavior as long as it does not affect job performance. Nevertheless, a stricter standard of behavior generally is applied to public employees compared with that for most private sector workers. Because citizens pay the taxes that pay government salaries, managers and personnel administrators are sensitive to the image public employees project, and their concerns have encouraged the administrators to curtail behavior that could create a negative public reaction. When public displeasure is aroused by employees who are intoxicated in public, have unorthodox lifestyles, or promote controversial causes, elected political leaders often put pressure on managers to do something about the "problem." The same pressures are not as likely to appear in the private sector.

While public employees can experience more legal restrictions than their private sector counterparts, they also enjoy more protections. In particular, public employees are protected by the U.S. Constitution, including the Bill of Rights. As a result, they are entitled to procedural due process in disciplinary actions. For example, public employees are entitled to a pretermination hearing when an employer wants to fire them. In the private sector, employees do not enjoy the same protection unless the employer decides to give it to them.

LINES OF AUTHORITY

The lines of authority for public employers tend to be more diffuse and much less clear than those for employers in private enterprise. Although the public agency organization chart can suggest a clear line of authority, it does not show all outside pressures brought to bear on public employees' activities. Theoretically, public employees must respond to the "public interest" and various representatives of the public and interested parties. As David Rosenbloom observed, the constitutional principle of separation of powers fragments political power and creates multiple command points for public employees.[9] Agency employees may be asked to do different things by the chief executive, an influential member of the legislature, a clientele group, and a consumer group. Such multiple command points often make it difficult for public employees to decide exactly what they should do in a given situation.

Public employees often face a dilemma regarding which authority to accord more attention. Should they respond to their clientele, their superiors, their legislators, or their interpretation of the public interest? The case of Bertrand Berube illustrates this difficulty. Berube was fired by the General Services Administration (GSA) in 1983 after revealing problems of neglect and deterioration in federal buildings in Washington, D.C. Ironically, his firing came from the same administration that had awarded him a $7,500 bonus for similar conduct in 1981: publicizing problems in the GSA under the previous administration.[10] The case illustrates the difficulty in knowing what to do in sensitive situations. What is in the public interest is never completely clear. Each participant in the political process can have a different interpretation. Thus, a public employee's action can precipitate a negative reaction from someone in a position to act against that employee. Finally, not only the employee but also the personnel system as a whole must respond to the confusion produced by these multiple commands. The response of both normally takes the form of personnel rules and regulations, codes of conduct, and the like. However, some of these restrictions severely limit administrators' flexibility in adapting to differing situations and the organization's differing needs.

LABOR-MANAGEMENT RELATIONS

The public sector traditionally has differed from the private sector in being almost totally management oriented. There have been exceptions in both sectors: Some governments such as those in New York City and Milwaukee, Wisconsin, have had long histories of public sector union activities, and many corporations, especially in the Sun Belt, are fervently antiunion. In general, however, the public sector has only gradually shared personnel decisions with employees through the bargaining process. The implications for public personnel management, which will be discussed in Chapter 8, have been and will continue to be manifold.

POLITICAL ENVIRONMENT AND SCRUTINY

Perhaps the most significant factor unique to public personnel administration is that citizens and their representatives closely watch the public service. Because taxpayers foot the bill for government, they are entitled to know what is being done with their money. Since the late 1960s, freedom of information and open meeting statutes also have become common across the country; thus, most agencies' activities have become subject to public examination, and personnel management must accommodate such a scrutiny. Although personnel actions involving individual employees are exempted from these "sunshine" laws, personnel policies are affected by them in many ways. The elements of the political environment important to public personnel management include the executive, legislative, and judicial bodies; the media; interest groups; political parties; and the general public.

Executive, Legislative, and Judicial Bodies.   The U.S. Constitution established the separation of executive, legislative, and judicial powers, a model that has been used by state and local governments. In theory, public employees generally are under the direction of the executive branch, although employees of the legislature and the judiciary report directly to those branches. In reality, the chief executive has very limited authority over the public bureaucracy. Because civil service regulations protect most public employees, the chief executive has little power to change the conditions of their employment or control their activities. In addition, because chief executives usually are elected for a fixed and relatively short term, the permanent bureaucracy generally finds it relatively easy to resist direct pressure. Chief executives usually control the appointment of upper-level officials in departments and hope to influence public employees through their power. However, the number of appointments is usually small in proportion to the total bureaucracy. In 2002, conflict over President George W. Bush's desire to have more appointment and removal authority over employees in the Homeland Security Department led to a delay in moving legislation creating the department through Congress. The president has direct appointment authority for approximately 4,000 persons in a civilian bureaucracy of about 2.5 million. Many of these appointive positions include judges and officers of regulatory agencies who, once appointed, are independent of the president, thus severely limiting the chief executive's ability to direct the bureaucracy through the power of appointment. The legislative body and the judiciary limit that authority even more through confirmation power and review of attempts to dismiss employees, respectively.

Through the budget process, the executive and legislative bodies have a great impact on the personnel system. Because the chief executive is responsible in most governments for developing budget recommendations, agencies must be aware of the administration's desires. The agencies work hard to ensure adequate funds for their personnel needs because a loss of funds normally means a reduction in the number of an agency's employees. Once the chief executive makes recommendations to the legislative body, the agency's attention turns to legislative politics. In the legislature, it is often possible to increase agency budgets through mobilization of clientele and good work by agency personnel, thus demonstrating the agency's needs to the legislative body. Of course, agencies often get caught up in a struggle between the executive and legislative branches. At the national level, for example, conflicts over the budget often lead to a temporary layoff and delay of paychecks for federal employees at the end of a fiscal year. Ordinarily, Congress then passes an emergency resolution authorizing the agencies to continue operating until a budget finally is adopted. Nonetheless, planning is difficult when the agency does not know whether it will have a budget for the next year.

The basic policy concerning public personnel generally is determined as a result of executive and legislative efforts. The Civil Service Reform Act (CSRA) of 1978 serves as the basic foundation of the national government's civil service. Most state and local governments have adopted similar systems. CSRA was the result of trade-offs among the executive branch and the legislature. Many interests—employees, managers, veteran's groups, political parties, unions, civil rights groups, and women's groups—participated in the process leading to the adoption of CSRA. President Jimmy Carter initiated the process with his proposal for reform, but many of his suggestions were modified in the political jockeying that determined the final outcome. The legislation states the broad policy, but its meaning results from actions of the Office of Personnel Management (OPM), the Merit Systems Protection Board (MSPB), and the Federal Labor Relations Authority (FLRA). Of course, the judicial branch participates by court decisions on litigation concerning the act's provisions and the agencies' implementation of them.

The three branches of government also affect the personnel system because all branches affect public employees. Personnel and agency managers must be aware of each branch's interests and decisions in order to carry out personnel policies. Missteps by public employees can be exploited by people in political office if doing so will work to their advantage. Thus, public managers and employees are under much pressure that does not apply to any great extent to private sector employees.

The Media.   It is difficult to imagine a force in the political environment with a greater potential for influencing public personnel administration than the communications media. Because of constitutional guarantees of freedom of the press and speech in the United States, the media can keep the public well informed about the public service and its activities and problems. Indeed, public and political actors depend on the media for much of their information. Even though the press often focuses on the negative aspects of the public service, it frequently is responsible for improvements. Many problems in the public service are spotlighted and scrutinized by the media, whereas the private sector rarely undergoes such close examination of its staff or personnel policies and practices. The media cannot, however, ensure that agency personnel continue to perform effectively. They are unlikely, for example, to expose unenthusiastic performance of duties, an important form of evaluation of the public service.

Interest Groups.   Many interest groups also exert pressure on public personnel operations. Among these are clientele groups, minority and women's groups, public interest groups, professional associations, civic groups, taxpayer associations, and public employee associations and unions. Although interest groups generally are most concerned about issues other than personnel management, they recognize that having some power over the people who make decisions will influence an agency's response to their concerns.

Some groups tend to concentrate on relatively narrow issues of self-interest. Thus, clientele, minority, women's, professional, and public employee groups are likely to seek policies that ensure that the agency will give their particular welfare as much consideration as possible. Public interest and civic groups such as civil service leagues, good government associations, the League of Women Voters, taxpayer reform associations, and the Center for the Study of Responsive Law take a more general approach. They pursue policies beneficial to the "public interest" and usually promote personnel systems that reduce the potential for partisan political influence. These groups also tend to favor policies that require public employees to disclose personal financial interest and control conflict of interest situations.

Political Parties.   Political parties and politicians always have had an interest in public personnel operations. Politicians often view patronage as a means of exerting control over and ensuring the responsiveness of public employees. Furthermore, politicians often find public bureaucrats easy targets for political rhetoric and thus exploit public service problems and inadequacies for political purposes. In fact, public personnel reform in 1883 and 1978 came about partly because politicians used corruption and inefficiency as issues; therefore, personal political gain is not always the overriding concern behind such appeals. Too often, however, criticism of the public service does little to improve it and serves merely to denigrate it.

Certainly, demagogic exploitation of the public service is not as extensive today as it once was, but many politicians still run their campaigns on platforms that include references to the "incompetent" or "oversized" public bureaucracy. Indeed, today most candidates for public office promise to reduce taxes and cite reducing the bureaucracy as one way to do so. The promise has obvious implications for personnel management and it is not surprising that once elected, the office holders often face some distrust from government employees.

Among personnel policies attracting attention in recent years have been affirmative action and nondiscrimination. Politicians and others have used strong opposition to these policies to change them. In California and Washington, for example, voters have adopted policies to outlaw much of affirmative action. Many members of Congress also have railed against affirmative action. Other policies that have direct impact on public employees are adopted directly through initiative and referendum. In Oregon, for example, voters changed policies on public pension systems to reduce contributions to public employee retirement systems and reduce the benefits given to retired public employees.[11] The National Performance Review led by Vice President Al Gore in the Clinton administration focused on reinvention of government and performance measures that had immense impacts on personnel in the national government.[12]

The political parties traditionally have depended on government jobs as a way of building party strength, but the pervasive adoption of merit systems greatly diminished this source of support. States such as Louisiana, Indiana, Illinois, and New Jersey, however, demonstrate that patronage is still alive and well in some state bureaucracies.[13] Some local governments still indulge in political favoritism. Court decisions and a public less attached to political parties, however, make much direct partisanship difficult to continue.

The General Public.   In a democracy, the public service is supposed to serve the interest of the general public. The problem lies in defining what the "public interest" is. Responsiveness to the public and its wishes, which are difficult to determine, is one aspect of serving the public. Some people consider that responsible public service is effective in achieving the system's long-range goals, although this approach sometimes runs counter to the public's short-term wishes.[14] What is important to the administration of public personnel is not that the public expects responsiveness, but many political leaders exploit this expectation by promising attractive but impractical solutions to problems. Other individuals and groups, particularly public interest groups, direct their attention to long-range objectives, and public administrators, including personnel administrators, are caught in the middle.

The public's view of bureaucracy is determined by society's general value system. People's assumptions about the work ethic, self-reliance, and individualism color their responses to the public service, especially as society weighs the effects that government programs and employees have on those values. The common impression is that the public service is composed of indolent, secure employees who have too much power over people's lives and consume tax money with little beneficial effect. These views, along with the idea that the bureaucracy is oversized and uncontrollable, sometimes make it difficult for the public service to recruit employees.

Relentless attacks on the bureaucracy certainly have an impact on the perception that people have of the public service. Even more damaging, however, are the lapses in ethics and behavior of public officials. Although most scandals involve elected officials and their political appointees rather than career public servants, the public does not make much distinction between the two. Thus, the trust in the efficacy and integrity of the public service generally suffers. The Watergate scandal during the Nixon administration, which was covered extensively on television, brought public misbehavior to people's living rooms. The many ethical lapses by numerous Reagan administration appointees and the scandalous personal behavior of President Clinton have contributed to people's disdain for the public service. The state and local levels have not fared much better. From Arizona, where one recent governor was impeached for boorish behavior and another resigned because of conviction on charges related to his business activities,[15] to the conviction of the mayor of Providence, Rhode Island, on corruption charges,[16] it is not surprising that citizens are cynical. Add to that the apparent ineptitude of Florida's Department of Children's Services and of the inability of the Florida Secretary of State's office to ensure smooth elections in the 2000 presidential election and the 2002 primary elections, which have caused people to become more cynical about the ability of government to perform competently and ethically.[17] Public employees are tainted by these situations, most of which they cannot control.

Summary

Public personnel management resides in a complex environment and is part of a larger governmental system. Because the system in the United States contains a variety of interests competing for position and power, the personnel system becomes entwined in the political process. The various political actors and forces outlined in this chapter obviously have different interests in the personnel system. The personnel function cannot be viewed as a neutral instrument of management; instead, it is at the center of the decision-making process and can easily become a pawn in the struggle for political power and influence. Although all actors, such as the president and members of Congress, insist that they want only the most efficient and responsive public service possible, they actually could be concerned primarily with maintaining or improving their political positions. Thus, expressions of outrage from either side regarding personnel actions often are calculated more for political advantage than for improving personnel practices. Similarly, other participants in the political environment have conflicting interests, which can lead to compromise and accommodation in public personnel management.

This chapter has identified the role of public personnel management in the governmental process and has introduced the major forces that affect public personnel management and the issues that are of concern to personnel managers. The remaining chapters elaborate on these topics. Chapters 2 and 3 focus on political considerations in the development of public personnel systems. Chapter 2 traces the evolution of public personnel management, and Chapter 3 examines some of the enduring political forces that shape the way the management of personnel is organized in government.

Chapters 4, 5, and 6 evaluate the technical tools and techniques used in managing personnel, and Chapters 7, 8, and 9 consider some challenges that contemporary personnel management faces. Finally, Chapter 10 discusses continuing challenges for public personnel administration.

NOTES

1. D. E. Klingner and J. Nalbandian, "Personnel Management by Whose Objectives?" *Public Administration Review,* 38 (July–August 1978), 366–372; H. B. Milward, "Politics, Personnel and Public Policy," *Public Administration Review,* 38 (July–August 1978), 391–396; and D. H. Rosenbloom, "Public Personnel Administration and Politics: Toward a New Public Personnel Administration," *Midwest Review of Public Administration,* 7 (April 1973), 98–110.

2. W. S. Sayre, "The Triumph of Technique over Purpose," *Public Administration Review,* 8 (Spring 1948), 134–137.

3. F. C. Mosher, *Democracy and the Public Service,* 3d ed. (New York: Oxford University Press, 1982); M. Morse, "We've Come a Long Way," *Public Personnel Management,* 5 (July–August 1976), 218–221; and F. J. Thompson, *Personnel Policy in the City* (Berkeley and Los Angeles: University of California Press, 1975).

4. T. J. Lowi, "Machine Politics—Old and New," *The Public Interest,* 9 (Fall 1967), 83–92; C. A. Newland, "Public Personnel Administration: Legalistic Reforms vs. Effectiveness, Efficiency, and Economy." *Public Administration Review,* 36 (September–October 1967), 529–537; W. C. Rich, *The Politics of Urban Policy: Reformers, Politicians and Bureaucrats* (Port Washington, N.Y.: Kennikat Press, 1982); and D. H. Rosenbloom, "The Sources of Continuing Conflict between the Constitution and Public Personnel Management," *Review of Public Personnel Administration,* 2 (1981), 3–18.

5. F. J. Thompson, "The Politics of Public Personnel Administration," in S. W. Hays and R. C. Kearney, eds., *Public Personnel Administration: Problems and Prospects,* 3d ed. (Englewood Cliffs, N.J.: Prentice-Hall, 1983), pp. 3–16.

6. P. C. Light, *The New Public Service* (Washington, D.C.: Brookings Institute Press, 1999).

7. S. E. Condrey, "Reinventing State Civil Service Systems: The Georgia Experience," *Review of Public Personnel Administration,* 22 (Summer 2002), 114–124; C. W. Gossett, "Civil Service Reform: The Case of Georgia," *Review of Public Personnel Administration,* 22 (Summer 2002), 94–113; L. G. Nigro and J. E. Kellough, "Civil Service Reform in Georgia," *Review of Public Personnel Administration,* 20 (Fall 2000), 41–54; and J. P. West, "Georgia on the Mind of Radical Civil Service Reformers," *Review of Public Personnel Administration,* 22 (Summer 2002), 79–93.

8. *Kelly v Johnson,* 425 U.S. 238 (1976); and *McCarthy v Philadelphia Civil Service Commission,* 424 U.S. 645 (1976).

9. D. H. Rosenbloom, "Public Policy in a Political Environment: A Symposium," *Policy Studies Journal,* 11 (December 1982), 245–254.

10. B. McAllister, "GSA Told to Reinstate Official Who Cited Perils at Buildings," *Washington Post,* July 20, 1988, p. a1.

11. http://bluebook.state.or.us/state/elections/elections21.htm

12. National Performance Review, *Creating a Government that Works Better and Costs Less* (Washington, D.C.: U.S. Government Printing Office, 1993).

13. A. Freedman, *Patronage: An American Tradition* (Chicago, Nelson-Hall, 1994); and D. K. Hamilton, "Is Patronage Dead?" *Review of Public Personnel Administration,* 22 (Spring 2002), 3–26.

14. F. E. Rourke, *Bureaucracy, Politics, and Public Policy* (Boston: Little, Brown, 1969).

15. D. Berman, *Arizona Politics and Government* (Lincoln, NE: University of Nebraska Press, 1998).

16. "Providence Mayor Guilty of Conspiracy," *NewsMax.com Wires,* June 25, 2002, accessed 3-11-03 at http://www.newsmax.com/archives/articles/2002/6/24/140658.shtml.

17. B. Cotterell, "State Task Force Digs into DCF Controversy," *Tallahassee Democrat,* May 10, 2002, p. A1; and A. Veiga, "After Two Big Foul-Ups, Florida's Election System Hopes to Get It Right This Time," *Government Technology,* November 1, 2002, accessed 3-11-03 at http://www.govtech.net/news/features/news_feature.phtml?docid=2002.11.01 -29593.

SUGGESTED READINGS

Ban, C., and N. M. Riccucci, eds. *Public Personnel Management: Current Concerns—Future Challenges,* 3rd ed. New York: Longman, 2002.

Condrey, S. E., ed. *Handbook of Human Resource Management in Government.* San Francisco: Jossey-Bass, 1998.

Freyss, S. F., ed. *Human Resource Management in Local Government: An Essential Guide.* Washington, D.C.: International City/County Management Association, 1999.

Hays, S. W., and R. C. Kearney, eds. *Public Personnel Administration: Problems and Prospects,* 4th ed. Englewood Cliffs, N.J.: Prentice-Hall, 2003.

Ingraham, P., and D. Kettl. *Agenda for Excellence: Public Service in America.* Chatham, N.J.: Chatham House, 1992.

Light, P. C. *The New Public Service.* Washington, D.C.: Brookings Institute Press, 1999.

McGregor, E. B. Jr. "The Great Paradox of Democratic Citizenship and Public Personnel Administration." *Public Administration Review,* 44 (March 1984), 126–132.

Mosher, F. C. *Democracy and the Public Service,* 2d ed. New York: Oxford University Press, 1982.

Rabin, J., T. Vocino, W. B. Hildreth, and G. J. Miller, eds. *Handbook of Public Personnel Administration.* New York: Marcel Dekker, 1995.

Thompson, F. J., ed. *Classics of Public Personnel Policy,* 2d ed. Pacific Grove, Calif.: Brooks Cole. 1991.

———. *Personnel Policy in the City.* Berkeley and Los Angeles: University of California Press, 1975.

SELECTED WEB SITES

International Personnel Management Association for Human Resources (IPMA). Membership organization of people employed and interested in public personnel administration. Publishes extensively on public personnel/human resources. www.ipma-hr.org

National Association of State Personnel Executives (NASPE). Membership organization of the state personnel directors/executives. Publishes a newsletter and reports. www .naspe.net

National Congress of American Indians (NCAI). Organization of more than 250 tribal governments that serves as a forum for policy development and provides governmental services among tribes. Web site includes tribal directory. www.ncai.org

Office of Personnel Management (OPM). Executive branch agency with responsibility for the personnel function in the national government. Works with federal departments/agencies in implementing policy. www.opm.gov

Public Management Committee and Public Management Service of the OECD. Web site focusing on human resources of the Organization for Economic Cooperation and Development (OECD) of the European Community. www.oecd.org/EN/home/0,,EN -home-308-no directorate-no-no-no-11,00.html

Partnership for Public Service. Nonpartisan organization to restore public confidence and prestige to the federal public service. www.ourpublicservice.org

Public Employees Roundtable (PER). Membership organization of individuals and organizations devoted to restoring the respect and honor of the public service. www .theroundtable.org

Section on Personnel and Labor Relations (SPALR). Section of the American Society for Public Administration that publishes the journal *Review of Public Personnel Administration;* also serves its membership by sponsoring conference panels and networking. www.aspanet.org/sections/sectionpages/spalr.html

Society for Human Resource Management (SHRM). Membership organization for those interested in and employed in personnel/human resources management with an emphasis on the private sector. www.shrm.org

University of Oklahoma Law Center—Native American Resources. Organization that conducts and disseminates research on tribal government issues including personnel matters; has links to tribal nation home pages. www.law.ou.edu/indian

---

Exercises

1. Access the Web site of the personnel/human resources office of a municipality, tribal government, county, or school district. Review the mission and structure of the office. Then interview the director of the office to find out how the office functions. Once you have gathered the information, explain what you think are the basic values represented by the office. Assess whether the values reflected in the mission statement appear to be the ones reflected in the director's explanation of the office's function.

2. Louisa Contalvo, director of the State Social Services Department, has just completed a well-deserved and badly needed vacation and is driving home from her mountain retreat. On the way home, her thoughts turn to work and the upcoming legislative hearings on her agency's budget. She knows that her staff has prepared the background material so that she will be well prepared to testify before the legislative committee. Nonetheless, she is concerned because the political climate and the most recent election have produced many calls for large reduc-

tions in the budget for social services. She knows it will be a tough sell but believes that a reasoned presentation will preserve what she considers to be needed services for the state's citizens.

As she nears home, she hears a radio news story concerning an employee of her agency. Carroll Spier is the director of Protective Services for Children (PSC), which is responsible among other things, for protecting children who are abused by family members. He and his wife are in a bitter divorce trial. Ordinarily, such a divorce would not be newsworthy, but his wife has charged him with sexual abuse of one of their children. Spier adamantly denies the charge.

When Contalvo arrives at the office, there are calls waiting for her from the governor, the chair of the legislative committee overseeing PSC, and many representatives of the news media. She returns the calls of the governor and the chair of the legislative oversight committee. The message from both is the same: "Spier is a political embarrassment and must be fired." Contalvo is in a difficult position because Spier is one of the best managers in the agency and has solved many of the problems that have plagued PSC for many years. She also knows that funding for her agency and even her job could be in jeopardy.

Place yourself in Louisa Contalvo's position. Before you return the other calls, think through the response you will give. Explain the options you have considered in dealing with this situation. Indicate your reasons for and against each one. What is your final decision, and why?

3. Sabina Crane is a career counselor at Maybridge High School. She has been with the school district for five years and each year has received outstanding evaluations for her performance as well as the maximum merit pay increases available to her. She also has been given awards from national organizations for her work with high school students.

To her surprise, Sabina was notified by the superintendent's office that her contract for the next year would not be renewed. Because renewal for the contracts for her position had been relatively automatic, nonrenewal meant essentially that she had been fired. When she asked the superintendent's office for an explanation, she was told that her personal lifestyle was not compatible with her work with high school students. After pressing further, she learned that the superintendent's office had been told that she was bisexual and had a female lover. She did not deny this but felt that it had nothing to do with her ability to do her job. As a result, she appealed the decision but was unsuccessful with the appeals board. Finally, she took her appeal to the school board.

The school board is made up of five elected members. Four members have made public their reaction to this case, and they are divided evenly, with two supporting and two opposing Crane's request to be renewed. You are the fifth member of the board. How will you vote?

Explain. Assume that the state has no legislation either protecting the right of gays and lesbians to hold jobs or prohibiting their employment.
4. Watch for the date of a city council or school district governing board meeting when a personnel-related issue is on the agenda. Attend the meeting. Explain what the issue was and how it was presented. Who spoke about it? What was the nature of the discussion? From your observation, did there appear to be any political undertones to the discussion? Who had a stake in the outcome? Explain your impression of the discussion and the decision about the personnel system of the jurisdiction.

2

Evolution of the Public Personnel System

All governments face the problem of determining how to staff and maintain a public service that must be consistent with political values and goals, competent, loyal to management, and responsive to the public. There has been constant conflict among these competing criteria for the establishment and operation of a personnel system, and there have been numerous dramatic changes in the public service in accommodating ever-changing political, social, and economic realities.

As noted earlier, this book's major premise is that public personnel administration can best be understood in terms of its relationship to political values and processes. Therefore, the brief historical overview of the public service presented in this chapter emphasizes the influence of political values on public personnel operation. There was the period of early development, 1789 to 1829; the period in which spoils predominated, 1829 to 1883, the period in which the merit system developed and dominated, 1883 to 1978; and finally, the period of contemporary reform, 1978 to present. During each of these time spans there were significant events that can be used to differentiate further the development of public personnel administration, but the periods suggested here break at the times when major new perspectives on the public service emerged. The last sections of this chapter evaluate the legacies of reforms through examination of legislative-executive conflicts, professionals-inheritors of the system, and spoils versus merit.

The Early Roots

President George Washington usually is credited with developing a competent public service. Because there was no established bureaucracy when he assumed the presidency, Washington was in the unique position of being able to build a public service from scratch. Although political considerations usually are not attributed to Washington in his personnel actions, he did make numerous concessions to political reality.[1] He was not, however, as politically partisan as many of his successors were.

One of the realities with which Washington had to contend was the fact that political power in the nation's early years was held almost exclusively by the aristocracy. Although Washington established fitness and ability as requirements for appointment to the public service, *fitness* usually meant social status or prestige rather than technical competence.[2] Washington was free to use such a definition because the tasks of the public bureaucracy were not highly specialized as they were later when our social and political systems became more complex. The important point is that Washington chose public servants from the politically powerful sectors of society.

Washington was influenced by other political considerations as well. He had the enormous task of integrating a new nation of previously independent-minded units, and to do this he had to plan and act carefully. A significant requirement for public service employment under Washington was support of the new federal political system. Although support for the political system does not seem radical today, it was a controversial issue at the time because many people hoped the new system of government would fail. Thus, oddly enough, a political position with which many citizens strongly disagreed was a requirement for holding a public job.

There were also regional considerations. President Washington wanted to ensure that local programs would be administered by members of each community and that all regions of the country would be represented in the high echelons of the public service. He thus hoped to gain nationwide support for and identification with the new political system.

Another political move by the new president was to defer to the wishes of Congress on many appointments. Recognizing that members of Congress could greatly affect his administration's success, Washington conferred with them, even though he was not legally required to do so in most instances. Indeed, presidents still consider congressional wishes in their appointments. Another group to whom Washington accorded special attention consisted of army officers from the Revolutionary War. They often were hired in preference to others, although Washington was careful to limit the extent of such appointments. Preferential treatments of veterans, now common in national as well as state and local merit systems, derives in part from Washington's policies.

The fact that Washington's decisions often were politically motivated should not come as a surprise. In a democratic system, it is expected that public officials will respond to political forces. As Van Riper noted, it is fortunate that these political considerations were consistent with the development of a highly competent public service[3] because many of these political accommodations left enduring marks on the staffing of public bureaucracies. Regional representation, partisan political support, loyalty, preference for veterans, and consultation with members of Congress have been and often still are significant concerns in filling public service positions.

Washington's immediate successors made few changes in his approach to staffing the public service. Partisan concerns became more important under

John Adams, but Thomas Jefferson made the most significant break with Washington's practices. Representing a new party in power, Jefferson wanted to reward his Republican followers with appointments. The long years of Federalist control, however, had resulted in the entrenchment of Federalists in public service positions. To obtain a bureaucracy more to his liking, therefore, Jefferson removed many government employees, justifying this policy by claiming a need for a balance of partisan viewpoints.[4] He believed that because the people had elected him president, they should have like-minded public servants to help him carry out his policies, a view that all modern presidents also have articulated. Political party affiliation was not Jefferson's only criterion; he also insisted on ability and fitness in the way Washington did. Jefferson was the real father of the spoils system in the sense of bowing to party pressure in appointments, yet he diligently resisted debasing the public service by making it strictly partisan.

Jefferson's successors followed much the same tradition. Although partisan politics became more important during his presidency, the character of the public service remained unchanged. Despite his Republican philosophy, Jefferson had to contend with a politically powerful elite. Consequently, the aristocracy retained its hold on public service positions through the administration of John Quincy Adams. Tests of loyalty, regional considerations, preference for veterans, and consultation with Congress remained factors in public service staffing.

Jacksonian Democracy

With a dramatic shift in the center of political power came an equally dramatic change in the public bureaucracy. The election of 1828 brought to a head the political frustrations that had been building in the populace. From 1800 to 1829, the U.S. political system became more democratic because new groups in society gained the opportunity to participate in politics. The addition of eleven states—nine in the West—brought a new flavor to politics and elections. Previously, only landowners and the aristocracy had the vote, but electoral reforms in the early nineteenth century and the admission of new states in which the common man ruled greatly broadened electoral participation. The western states led in extending suffrage, but by 1829 the right to vote was almost universally enjoyed by white males. The admission of western states to the union also changed the power relationship between the upper and lower classes in favor of the lower. Also, the egalitarianism of the frontier influenced national politics.

The extension of suffrage resulted from political considerations. With more voters, the parties could increase their ranks and thus saw the advantage of extending the right to vote. As the common man participated in the choice of elected political leaders, he also expected some of the fruits of politics, so it is not surprising that resentment toward the aristocracy's monopoly on public service positions developed. Astute political leaders could not ignore the expectations of their new constituents. Recognizing that political patronage could be used to build up their parties, politicians made the spoils system a standard feature of public service staffing in state and local governments.

The triumph of the common man extended to the national level with the election of President Andrew Jackson in 1828. His inauguration celebrations often are cited as examples of the dramatic change in the locus of political power. The social critics of the day were aghast at the antics and crudeness of Jackson's followers, many of whom descended on Washington in search of government employment.[5]

The expectations of Jackson's followers were high, and the genteel elements of Washington politics anticipated disaster. As it turned out, the expectations of both groups were exaggerated. Jackson was interested not only in realigning the public service's political makeup but also in reducing government activity and hence the size of the bureaucracy. Consequently, the hordes of office seekers found that Jackson meant to cut back on government jobs. However, and most important for our consideration, Jackson followed Jefferson's lead in insisting that the bureaucracy reflect the results of the election; accordingly, he removed many people from office and replaced them with his own followers.

Although Jackson did not turn out a significantly higher proportion of employees from the public service than Jefferson had, he is more closely identified with the spoils system because he was more openly partisan and proud of it. He saw his administration as one that revolutionized the U.S. political system. His administration broke the aristocracy's political power over both elective and appointive positions. The revolutionary character of Jackson's approach lay in the fact that the public service was democratized in response to the democratization of the electoral system.

The shift in political power caused intense criticism of Jackson's public personnel policies. However, despite his feeling that the government's work was so simple that anyone could do it (much more accurate then than today), Jackson insisted on competence and the judicious use of patronage. He would have been as uncomfortable as any of his predecessors to see the extent to which many of his successors used and abused patronage.

Weakening of Spoils

After Jackson's administration, the alternation of political party control of the presidency led to a revolving door for public servants, with the door turning every four years. Even though there were many carryovers from one administration to another, public servants usually were assigned to different positions by the new administration. Even the election of a president of the same party, as occurred when James Buchanan succeeded fellow Democrat Franklin Pierce, did not ensure the retention of the same public servants. Buchanan represented a different faction of the party and was pressured into changing the bureaucracy to reflect that fact.

The election of Abraham Lincoln in 1860 represents both the high point and the onset of the demise of the spoils system. Lincoln used the system to a greater extent than any other presistent had. Mobilizing the Union for the Civil War required a loyal public service, and Lincoln believed that the only way to create one was to use patronage.[6] Lincoln's sweep of people from office, the most extensive in U.S. history, was warranted by the political considerations of the time. His concern was to consolidate the Republican party, which had been in disarray, and conduct a major and controversial war. As the Union began to come apart, officeholders from the South were removed and those loyal to the Union were put in their places.

Despite his wide use of the spoils system, Lincoln also must be credited with initiating its gradual decline. After his election to a second term, he experienced a great deal of pressure to make a clean sweep of his appointees because his supporters had become accustomed to having a completely new team every four years. Lincoln's refusal to oblige gave hope to critics of the spoils system and led to an examination of the system that produced significant change in the next two decades. President Andrew Johnson, faced with internal political problems of his own, found it necessary to replace many of Lincoln's loyalists; however, the spoils system was marked for destruction, and in less than twenty years it was dealt a blow from which it never recovered. In the years between Lincoln's administration and 1883, political forces gradually chipped away at the patronage system. Much like the growth of democratic political participation from 1800 to 1829, the growth of discontent with the spoils system from 1865 to 1883 led to a revolution in the staffing of the U.S. government bureaucracy.

The Civil War greatly increased the power of the executive branch vis-à-vis Congress, and the end of the war brought an opportunity for Congress to attempt to regain some of its influence. With Andrew Johnson in office and plagued by internal party struggles, the stage was set. The area of greatest struggle and the immediate issue in the impeachment proceedings against Johnson was control over government personnel. The difficulties Johnson had with Congress and his party led him to drop many of Lincoln's supporters in favor of his own. Predictably, this action only heightened congressional opposition to him.

The Tenure of Office Act of 1867 symbolized Congress' attempt to gain control over patronage. This act limited the president's removal power to the extent that removal required Senate approval in cases involving officers who had been appointed with Senate confirmation. Defiance of Congress and the act led to Johnson's impeachment by the House of Representatives; the Senate acquitted him by only one vote. The power to appoint and remove was the immediate issue over which this momentous confrontation developed, but the political issues were much broader. For students of public personnel, however, it is a significant occasion because it signaled a movement away from presidential control over patronage and personnel policy issues. Congress subsequently consolidated its power over the general policy during the next decade and a half. Eventually, congressional interest led to the establishment of the merit system, although Congress's major interest at that point was in controlling spoils.[7]

President Andrew Johnson's lack of control and the weak administrations of Ulysses S. Grant and Rutherford B. Hayes produced even greater congressional interest in and control over the personnel process. At the same time, efforts for reform were being made. During Grant's administration, Congress passed the Civil Service Act of 1871, although its proponents had to attach it as a rider to an appropriations bill to get it passed.[8] Surprisingly, President Grant supported civil service reform and had actually proposed legislation similar to that which was passed in 1871. More important, to the surprise of many Republicans in Congress, he tried to institute a merit system. In effect, the act of 1871 reestablished presidential control over the personnel process by giving the president the authority to establish rules and regulations for employees in the public service and appoint advisers to help draw up and administer the rules and regulations. Grant did just that by appointing a seven-member civil service commission and issuing executive orders for a limited use of merit concepts.

However, political realities did not permit Grant's experiment with reform to endure. Congress was not willing to give up the control it had obtained. Fearing a loss of power through the loss of patronage, Congress refused to fund the system after 1873, so it was no longer able to operate, although some commissioners did work without compensation. Despite its short tenure, Grant's commission had lasting effects; its recommendations formed much of the basis of public personnel thought reflected in the 1883 reforms.[9]

Although the experiment had to be abandoned, it whetted the appetites of reformers, and the issue would not die. The ensuing scandals of the Grant administration helped make civil service reform a more vital political issue. Another supporter of merit, Rutherford B. Hayes, became president in 1877 and made some tentative moves toward reform. The controversy surrounding his election left him politically weak, however, and he was unable to accomplish much. Indications were that what he did to institute reform in some departments was more than offset by his lack of effort in others. Furthermore, Hayes's inconsistency in implementing executive orders against assessment (requiring employees to contribute a percentage of their salaries to their political parties) and partisan activity leads one to question the sincerity of his commitment to reform.[10]

Nonetheless, the issue of reform was attracting an ever-widening group of supporters. During the late 1870s and early 1880s, various associations favoring civil service reform organized and became more vocal. They attempted to pressure political leaders, but more important, they tried to educate the public about the evils of spoils. They portrayed the spoils system as one that undermines the work ethic and feeds the avarice of the bad citizen. Somehow the people still did not become intensely interested in the issue, although some public concern was manifested by the election of presidents committed to reform. With the aid of an increasingly interested press, however, the reformers made their mark on the public and politicians alike.[11]

The assassination of President James A. Garfield became a dramatic symbol of the evils of the spoils system: It could even lead to murder. The fact that Charles Guiteau, Garfield's assassin, had unsuccessfully sought patronage employment gave the reformers the impetus they needed, and the fact that Garfield supported reform only added to their sense of urgency.

Another political factor favoring reform was the Supreme Court's decision in *Ex Parte Curtis* in 1882.[12] Congress had passed a law in 1876 that prohibited the assessment of government workers. This practice involves a "contribution," or kickback, of a portion of an employee's salary to his or her political party organization or another benefactor. Obviously, when the patronage system operates, assessment could be enforced easily; an employee who refuses to "contribute," could be removed from his or her position. In any case, assessment became a scandal when Newton Curtis, a Treasury Department employee and treasurer of the New York Republican Party, was brought to trial for violating the 1876 law. The Supreme Court upheld his conviction and the law, and reform efforts could only gain from that decision.

In addition, the congressional elections of 1882 made the Republicans reflect on the political consequences of reform. Republican fortunes slipped badly in the elections, and a continuation of that trend would have meant the loss of the White House in 1884, the loss of power to appoint public servants, and possible large-scale purges of Republican officeholders. Congressional Republicans thus saw the wisdom of supporting reform.

As a result of these political forces and the persistent efforts of reformers, the Pendleton Civil Service Act became law on January 16, 1883. This act created a personnel system that was based on the merit concept and required the formulation of rules and regulations by which all personnel activities would be conducted. It had taken a long time and the assassination of a president, but Congress had acted. The character of the public service had undergone another revolution.

Consolidation of Reform Efforts

Passage of the Pendleton Act did not bring an end to the spoils system, however, nor did it mean that reform became a dead issue. The public servants covered by the act amounted to only about 10 percent of public employees in the national government, and so for that 10 percent, employment decisions were supposed to be based on merit. To implement the system, the president was authorized to appoint a bipartisan civil service commission. The basic elements of the civil service included competitive examinations, lateral entry, neutrality, and the prohibition of assessments of civil servants by political parties among many other features. Apparently, some supporters of reform expected the public service to become the domain of the aristocracy once again,[13] but this did not happen, partly because of the act's provisions and partly because of its gradual application. The increased attention to educational criteria for employment, though, gave an advantage to the upper socioeconomic groups.

In passing the Pendleton Act, Congress attempted to exert control over the personnel system of the U.S. government. Because the Constitution gives executive authority to the president, the constitutionality of congressional control was questioned. Consequently, Congress made the legislation permissive, meaning that the president could provide for the establishment of the merit system but was not directed to do so. Certainly the political squabbles between the president and Congress had an impact, but the realities of the constitutional provisions had to be accommodated.

Each of the act's major provisions had political implications. The first, authorizing rather than mandating presidential action on the matter, has been discussed in terms of the conflict between the president and Congress. Open competitive exams and lateral entry can be seen as adherence to the democratic tradition of equality. The reformers were actually interested in adopting the British system, requiring entry at the bottom and promotion from within. However, because the egalitarian tradition of the United States was inconsistent with that provision, the open system was adopted. Some suggest that the Democrats put the Republicans on the defensive and forced them to adopt the open system for fear of being branded as undemocratic by the press and the public.[14] Certainly this is true, although the Democrats were not entirely altruistic. They were concerned about being able to balance the public service in their favor if they won the presidency in 1884, as they did. It would be difficult to reward Democratic partisans if the current Republican president chose all high-level public servants. By contrast, with lateral entry, any vacancies at higher levels could be given to Democrats within the limits of the competitive system.

Apportionment of the positions in Washington offices among the states meant that the constituents of each member of Congress had a realistic chance to obtain employment. The South also was concerned about its inadequate representation in public service positions. In addition, apportionment helped further integrate the nation by ensuring participation by people from all parts of the country.

Both political parties realized the importance of the provisions regarding extending or reducing the extent of the merit system's coverage. Congress could hardly direct that all public employees be covered, given the constitutional question discussed earlier, so the extent of coverage was to be determined by the president. Because of the potential for abuse of this power, especially by a lame duck, the president also was authorized to roll back the coverage (or remove positions from civil service protection)—a power that has been used very infrequently. President William McKinley exercised this power in his first term, precipitating a bitter reaction, and others thus have been reluctant to try it. In contrast, presidents frequently have extended the coverage—particularly at the end of their terms—so that approximately 90 percent of federal government civilian employees are now under some sort of merit system.

It is clear that political considerations affected the decisions to reform the public service in 1883 and have been factors ever since in the system's evolution. David Rosenbloom has suggested that the 1883 reform was political in that its intent was to rescue government from the professional politicians.[15] The conflict between the values of professional politicians and of advocates of strict merit continue to be debated concerning how to make government personnel responsive.

Changing Concerns of the Merit System

Although the Civil Service System seemed to have a fairly broad grant of power under the Civil Service Act, it really exercised very little power, devoting most of its early years to screening applicants. Considering the political climate in which it was born, it is little wonder that the presidents and the commission moved cautiously. Remember that Congress created the new system more because of public sentiment and reformers' pressure than because it was committed to reform. Gradually, however, the commission gained prestige and influence and became the major force in public personnel policies. When Theodore Roosevelt became president in 1901, the civil service system had a friend in its chief executive. A former commissioner of civil service, Roosevelt did much to improve the service's image and increase its coverage. From that day on, with minor exceptions, the commission's position remained strong.

During the late nineteenth and early twentieth centuries, many changes in society and politics brought adaptive changes to the civil service system. In 1883, the jobs of public servants were still primarily clerkships, but the Industrial

Revolution had changed technology, and the post-Civil War era was characterized by a period of intensified development in the economy. Technological
advances and their consequences imposed new demands on the political system and resulted in an ever-larger public service. Jobs became more specialized, and with this development came the need for yet another specialty, the
personnel administrator.

The new system constantly faced changing political forces. Workers'
movements resulting in union organization had an early impact on the public
service; the National Association of Letter Carriers, for instance, was organized in 1889. Concern with employees' welfare became another issue to be
considered. As a result, there have been a gradual development and extension
of benefits so that today, federal government employees have one of the best
benefit packages available in the United States.

As noted earlier, the spoils system at the national level followed its development in state and local jurisdictions. When the federal government instituted reforms, however, most state and local governments were slow to follow
its lead.[16] In 1883, New York adopted the first civil service law, but only one
other state, Massachusetts, enacted such a law before the turn of the century.
In 1884, Albany, New York, became the first city to create a civil service system, and several other cities and one county (Cook County, Illinois) followed
suit during the 1880s and 1890s. Coverage usually applied to clerical workers
and the uniformed services of police officers and firefighters.

With the muckrakers' attention focused on corruption in municipal government in the early years of the twentieth century, the pressure for reform
increased. Similar exposure of patronage abuse in state governments had the
same effect. Many state and municipal governments therefore developed civil
service systems beginning in 1900 and continuing through the 1920s. Although
the scope of these reforms usually was limited, these actions did herald an era of
major change in state and local personnel practices. The Great Depression of
1929, however, brought a halt to most reform efforts. State and local governments reduced their funding of such programs as they attempted to cope with
other, more pressing problems relating to their citizens' physical well-being.

The national government was consolidating its reform effort, and the U.S.
Civil Service Commission gradually centralized its authority. Established to
protect the neutrality of the federal government service, the commission performed the major personnel functions and monitored agencies' activities to
ensure that they abided by the new civil service rules and regulations.

The Depression brought changes in the federal government service, just
as it did in state and local governments. President Franklin Roosevelt, in his
efforts to create programs to deal with the economic crisis, believed that the
already established bureaucracy was not flexible and adaptable enough to act
quickly and that speedy action was required if people were to receive the help
they needed to avoid total disaster. Convinced that the existing agencies were

not up to this task, Roosevelt persuaded Congress to create many agencies outside the civil service. Although most of the employees of those agencies eventually were "blanketed in" (given civil service coverage by executive order), they represented a loss of control by the Civil Service Commission.

Roosevelt also directed individual departments and agencies to create their own personnel units. These units eventually performed the majority of personnel actions for their agencies. Another factor leading to the decentralization of personnel activities was the World War II effort. The Civil Service Commission was unable to keep up with demands made by the new and rapidly growing agencies, resulting in relative independence for those departments.

Although there were efforts to reestablish the commission's authority, decentralization characterized the personnel function after the war. Individual departments became increasingly responsible for implementing personnel policies. The role of the Civil Service Commission also changed, becoming that of a policy maker, a provider of technical and support services, and a monitor of personnel activities. These changes in its role remain today, even though the old commission was abolished and a new organization was created in its place.

Other changes in personnel activities also occurred during this period. During the 1930s and 1940s, national government policy began to impose limits on the state and local level personnel practices. For example, the Social Security Act of 1935 created programs in which national government funding assisted state governments and required such programs to be efficiently administered, but it had no provisions for enforcing such a vague prescription. In 1940 the act was amended to permit specific federal personnel requirements in state and local programs utilizing federal monies under the Social Security Act. Over the years, Congress has provided for similar regulations requiring merit systems in other programs. Currently, a uniform set of merit principle guidelines exists for federally funded projects.

Another 1940 provision, an amendment to the 1939 Hatch Act, prohibited most political activity by employees of state and local government programs funded by federal monies. These provisions were repealed in 1974, but most states have their own statutes restricting partisan political activities; therefore, the federal repeal has not resulted in much change for most state and local employees.

During the 1930s and 1940s, there was a slow but steady growth in the number of states and municipalities adopting civil service systems. During the 1950s, however, the pace quickened, and, partly because of the federal government's grant-in-aid restrictions on personnel, all states adopted some form of merit requirement for their personnel systems; but, all did not cover every employee in one system. Although civil service protections were removed in Georgia and Florida in the 1990s, merit was supposed to govern. Some states, such as Texas, still have several different systems covering employees in particular departments and programs. Typically, public safety personnel are in separate systems as are public college and university employees. Municipalities tend to operate under merit systems, and counties (the last bastion of patronage) increasingly do so as well.

The federal government public service continued to change during the period of the 1930s to the 1950s. The Hatch Act of 1939 gave legislative force to the Civil Service Commission's prohibition on political activity, and the Ramspeck Act of 1940 prohibited discrimination in the personnel process. Preference was given to veterans in the Veteran's Preference Act of 1944, and the Government Employees Training Act of 1958 focused attention on the need for employees' continued personal growth.

In the 1960s and 1970s, personnel systems were challenged by developments in collective bargaining, antidiscrimination, and equal employment opportunity policies. In the 1980s and 1990s, performance and accountability became major issues. All of these issues continue as concerns for personnel systems in the twenty-first century.

Civil Service Reform Act of 1978 and Beyond

Ever since the Pendleton Civil Service Act was passed, its reform has been suggested. Although many changes have been made over the years, there was no comprehensive reform of civil service until the enactment of the Civil Service Reform Act of 1978. Fulfilling an election campaign promise to reform government to improve its efficiency, President Jimmy Carter pushed strongly for adoption of the reform. Along with the act, two reorganizations were approved by Congress to reorganize the Civil Service Commission and shift some of its responsibilities to the Equal Employment Opportunity Commission.[17] These reforms took effect in January 1979.

This 1978 legislation divided the Civil Service Commission (CSC) activities between the new Office of Personnel Management (OPM) and the Merit Systems Protection Board (MSPB). The Federal Labor Relations Authority (FLRA) also was created to monitor policies regarding federal employee labor-management relations. This division of responsibilities reflects the objections of many, especially employee organizations, to one organization having policy-making, implementation, and reviewing authority. Employees often viewed the CSC as representing management and did not feel comfortable approaching it with complaints or requests to review personnel actions.

The director and deputy director of OPM, appointed by the president, have responsibility for general personnel policy development for federal employees as well as for examinations, personnel investigations, evaluation of personnel programs, and training and development. OPM also offers techni-

cal assistance to departments and administers retirement and benefit programs for federal employees.

The independent MSPB was designed to protect federal employees
against unfair personnel actions and other abuses. It also must ensure that the
merit system is protected and makes annual reports to Congress on merit system operations. Federal employees are able to appeal personnel actions to the
MSPB, which has the authority to institute actions to correct abuses. An
important feature of the reform is that the special counsel established within
the MSPB has the power to investigate the activities of agencies and officials.
The special counsel also can ask the MSPB to take action against those who
violate merit system laws.

The FLRA monitors federal collective bargaining activity such as the
establishment of bargaining units and collective bargaining elections and works
with departments and agencies on activities that involve labor-management
relations. A general counsel in the FLRA investigates and prosecutes unfair
labor practices. The Federal Service Impasses Panel is an independent agency
that helps resolve negotiation impasses in the federal service.

Several features of the Reform Act of 1978 deal with personnel policy
issues. For example, OPM is authorized to delegate many of its functions to
operating departments, thus continuing the post-1933 trend toward decentralizing personnel functions. The Senior Executive Service (SES) created by
the act permits some high-level managers to be assigned as needed to maxi-
mize the use of their talents. These managers also are eligible for substantial
pay increases for meritorious service. Indeed, merit also became the basis for
pay increases for other managers in the federal service.

The 1978 legislation also streamlined the processing of incompetent
employees. In addition, whistle-blowers, that is, employees who expose illegal
activities or mismanagement in their agencies, are supposed to be protected
against reprisals by their superiors. One of the act's most important features is
that it put into law some terms that previously had existed only by executive
order or through Civil Service Commission policy. One provision spells out
and protects public employees' collective bargaining rights. Another lists specific merit principles and prohibited practices.

The Reform Act of 1978 was intended to improve the federal personnel
system in general and the performance of public employees in particular.
Many state and local governments were considering reform at the same time,
and many others acted after the national government passed this legislation.
The national law thus became a model for state and local governments.[18]

Numerous political issues, of which popular disenchantment with government and the willingness of a president to push for such legislation were
among the most important, combined to bring about the reform efforts.[19] Also
influential were the problems created by the Nixon administration's attempt to
politicize the public service and the changes in congressional leadership that

made the Congress more receptive to reform. The appointment of a prestigious task force to study the civil service system and make recommendations for change gave the effort additional credibility. Similar forces at the state and local levels, along with fiscal retrenchment, led to efforts to improve their public services.

The passage of the Civil Service Reform Act of 1978 did not end efforts for change or lead to a system that satisfied everyone. As rapid change continues in our society, calls for change arise at all levels of government. Distinguished task forces and commissions have studied the public services and called for changes. In 1989 the National Commission on the Public Service (commonly called the Volcker Commission) recommended far-reaching changes at every level of government to improve the effectiveness of the public service.[20] The recommendations stimulated much discussion among personnel professionals and public policy makers.

In 1993, two additional major reports were issued, again calling for significant changes. The Commission on the State and Local Public Service (the Winter Commission) covered numerous public policy issues with a major emphasis on improving state and local government performance.[21] Also in 1993, the National Performance Review (chaired by Vice President Al Gore) submitted its report to the president.[22] The National Performance Review based its recommendations on the theme of reinventing government. Many other less visible studies and reports have focused on the fact that no reform ever completely fixes the system and that constant effort is needed to adapt personnel systems to the ever-changing demands of the environment.

The political environment since the middle 1990s has resulted in new pressures for changes to personnel policies. Tax cut policies at all levels of government have put pressure on all public employers to find ways to reduce government spending and thus reduce the size of the workforce. Strong political reactions to affirmative action and set-aside programs in which minority- and female-owned firms must be included in projects funded with federal monies also have resulted in numerous lawsuits and policy changes. Continued pressures for evaluation of public programs also focus on performance of public employees and their agencies.

Many issues addressed by various reform efforts continue to provide challenges to public personnel management. Among the most prominent are the conflict between legislatures and executives to control the bureaucracy, the role of professionals, and spoils versus merit.[23] In 2002, The Brookings Institution announced creation of a second National Commission on the Public Service also chaired by Volcker. Its report in 2003 recommended comprehensive reform in the federal service. Issues addressed include recruitment, performance improvement, pay competitiveness, outsourcing, streamlining presidential appointments, leadership, and restoring trust in government.[24]

Legislative-Executive Conflicts

Legislators and elected executives constantly strive to control many aspects of the personnel function. Executives traditionally view government personnel as an instrument through which their policy perspectives can be translated into governmental action. In reality, most elected political executives complain that civil service personnel actually impede their efforts to deliver on campaign promises supposedly desired by the voters. Newly elected presidents, governors, and mayors customarily deplore the bureaucracy's lack of response to their policy directives. Thus, executives often view the merit system as decreasing their ability to control policy and the spoils system as augmenting that ability.[25]

Legislative bodies also wish to control policy. They see influence over the personnel system as one way to do this or at least to weaken the executive's ability to exercise such power. The close relationship of legislative committees to administrative agencies serves to ensure legislative influence over agency personnel. In addition, wedges often are driven between lower-level officials and their superiors by committees that insist on hearing employees' personal views in opposition to official policy.[26]

Lower-level bureaucrats often are protected by legislative committees or influential members of the legislative body. The State Department, for example, tried for years to change passport regulations, but Frances Knight, the director of the Passport Office, took a very cautious approach toward easing the restrictions. Furthermore, even a hint at replacing her invariably met pressure from conservative supporters in Congress who viewed her as a protector of U.S. security. Although Knight did institute some changes, she was able to withstand this pressure for most of the Cold War era and beyond because congressional support insulated her from her nominal superiors. J. Edgar Hoover, longtime director of the Federal Bureau of Investigation (FBI), also received such protection. The same situation existed for Louis Free, who was able to withstand accountability to the Clinton administration because he was a favorite of powerful members of Congress. Only after the September 11, 2001, terrorist bombings of the World Trade Center and the Pentagon did FBI mismanagement and ineptitude under Free's watch surface.

As noted in our discussion of the Civil Service Act of 1883, legislative and executive conflict over which should control the public service resulted in compromises in the establishment of the civil service system. A similar conflict arose in the consideration of the Civil Service Reform Act of 1978. President Jimmy Carter definitely was interested in exerting more control over the personnel function and wanted OPM to answer to the president. Congress, of course, was wary and built in some safeguards against too much presidential control. Thus, the creation of the MSPB was one way of allaying some fears of Congress.

The issue of control was highlighted again in 2002 as President George W. Bush and Congress disagreed on civil service coverage for employees in the proposed Homeland Security Department. The president wanted freedom from civil service and labor protections for employees in the federal government; many in Congress wanted to maintain the protections that exist. The president primarily supported his position with the argument that he needed the authority to ensure that the department would be responsive to the need for quick action in an emergency. After the elections of 2002, the president quickly prevailed. The differing concerns of executives and legislators will continue to be a source of conflict as public personnel systems evolve.

Professionals: Inheritors of the System

President Jackson characterized the work of government as being simple enough for any citizen to perform, which was not far from the truth because at that time, most government work consisted of simple clerical tasks. Today, however, even clerical work requires complex skills and responsibilities. More to the point, modern society requires government activities calling for a high degree of expertise in practically every field of endeavor. The challenge of creating a personnel system capable of satisfying those needs is great. As the public service has become more specialized, it also has had to deal with the professionalization of personnel activities.

Professionalization occurs with the development of specialized bodies of knowledge and standards for applying that expertise. Modern society has produced many new professions and professional associations that strive for the best possible performance of the specialty. These associations enable professionals to meet with and learn from fellow specialists and keep up with recent developments in the field. Professional groups also develop codes of ethics or conduct. The professionalization of public personnel thus has the potential to benefit the public service both by disseminating knowledge and establishing standards. However, there are costs as well.

Professionalism normally is characterized by (1) decision making on the basis of criteria that are universal rather than dependent on the particular situation, (2) specialization, (3) neutrality, (4) success as measured by performance, (5) elimination of self-interest from the decision-making process, and (6) self-control of professional activities.[27] The first five of these characteristics are beneficial to the public service and consistent with most of its features. The last, self-control of professional activities, is dramatically opposed to the principle that public personnel should be accountable to the public and its elected representatives.

Frederick Mosher has suggested that professionals have assumed control over the public agencies in which they work, developed an elite core within each agency to exercise that control, dominated many personnel policies, and provided protection for members of the profession.[28] Let us look at these and other effects.

As professionals became more numerous in public agencies, their efforts often turned from striving for the best performance to striving for power.[29] Thus, the emphasis is often on gaining policy control through domination of an agency. Professional groups tend to establish their own territorial jurisdiction in agencies and draw up operating procedures and approaches that are based on expertise.[30] For example, the biologists could compete for control with engineers in an environmental agency. Although the expertise of each is beneficial to the agency, there are problems in permitting each group's professional organization to have control. In such circumstances, an elite group not accountable to the general public is in control, so questions about the relationship of the public service to the rest of the political system arise. In public education, for instance, teachers' associations have been successful in establishing the criteria by which personnel decisions are made and persuading school districts and state education agencies to accept them. Many current criticisms of the quality of public education are directed at the professional associations that have so much influence over the system. Many critics believe that the professional education establishment seems more concerned about its own welfare than about the welfare of those it is supposed to be educating. Of course, the associations reply that they support their criteria and standards precisely because these elements lead to the best education of students.

Personnel systems are affected to the extent that professional associations dominate various personnel policies as they gain effective control over agency activities. A professional association can influence recruitment or selection in agency employment by dominating the process of establishing qualifications for applicants. Thus, the recognition or certification of programs and projects as meeting professional standards normally requires, in part, an agency's hiring of personnel with recognized professional training or experience. Such efforts restrict the flexibility and weaken the authority of personnel agencies and administrators.

Professional associations also emphasize a profession's status and autonomy. Professionals tend to respond to the pressure of the professional organization and their professional peers rather than to the agency's authority structure. The effect can be to undermine the agency's hierarchical lines of authority. In many ways, professional associations become protective shields for their members and theoretically ward off formal and legal control.[31]

Related to the issue of control is employees' loyalty to their agencies. The more highly professionalized people are, they become less loyal to their employers and more loyal to professional associations and standards.[32] Often such employees view the employing organization as an instrument for advancement and move from one organization to another as they advance professionally. In such cases, employees also could pursue their personal interests at the expense of the public and the public service. Nonetheless, their professional development is encouraged because it also brings the latest expertise to the agency. Intense specialization also often produces a very narrow view on the part of individual employees. They become so preoccupied with their particular fields of interest that the organization's work can suffer from a lack of coordination and interchange among different specialties. Such circumstances make personnel activities, particularly effective supervision, more challenging.

With its emphasis on performance and merit, professionalization is antithetical to spoils and patronage and thus helps further insulate the personnel system from partisan politics. Similarly, professionalization conflicts with the preferential treatment of individuals on bases other than merit. For example, policies that give preference to veterans are inconsistent with basic professional standards.

Professionalization of the public service has improved performance of public employees. Governments increase professionalization of their employees through training and development programs. Such programs expose employees to the best practices and equip them with the skills to use the most up-to-date technology, thus contributing to the quality of the public service. Personnel administrators have their own professional associations and thus see firsthand some effects of professionalization.

Spoils versus Merit

Another issue that affects the personnel function is the conflict between spoils and merit as bases for personnel actions. The main distinction between the two systems is that the spoils approach emphasizes loyalty and the merit concept stresses competence or expertise. Each system needs both attributes, however, to be effective.

Because the abuses of the spoils system led to political corruption, that system is viewed as an evil and there is little appreciation for its positive contributions. Yet the spoils system was largely responsible for democratizing the public service. By breaking the aristocracy's hold on government jobs, the system brought people from all walks of life and all areas of the nation into the public service. It provided a mechanism for integrating and unifying the political system. The epitome of this functional role was Lincoln's use of patronage during the Civil War when partisan appointments were instrumental in gaining support for a controversial cause.

The spoils system also helped build and unify political parties in the United States. Voters were attracted by the prospect of patronage rewards, and party finances were strengthened by employee assessments. In addition, with the buildup of party machines, the spoils system aided in the political socialization of various ethnic groups in large cities and provided many of the social services now performed by governmental agencies.

Jacksonian Democracy's focus on egalitarianism somehow became obscured in the quest for patronage positions, and in an ironic twist, egalitarianism also became an important issue in the reform movement's arguments. The abuse of the spoils system pointed up some of its costs. The constantly changing bureaucracy led to gross inefficiencies, some incompetence, and even chaos and insecurity for public employees. In addition, the president and members of Congress found themselves constantly at odds over appointments, meaning that government was often at a standstill. More important, the president squandered much time and energy worrying about whom to appoint to what position. Office seekers arrived in never-ending streams, and whether or not jobs were available, the president wasted valuable time dealing with these individuals. The quality of social services provided by political machines was undermined by corruption and partiality of the political and administrative processes.

The spoils system inevitably led to favoritism and inequity in the treatment of the public, so the reformers tried to neutralize and democratize the public service. The civil service system was heralded as the savior of our political order, and it created a neutral public service that chooses and relates to employees on the basis of competence and ability to perform. The merit system also was supposed to foster egalitarianism in that everyone—not just those who happened to support political leaders—would have a chance to compete.

A major concern of the reformers was to bring morality back to the public service. The merit system would free public servants from the control of evil politicians and machines and permit the bureaucracy to focus on the job of serving the public. The merit system led to vast changes in bureaucracy and aided in reviving the prestige of the public service. Ultimately, however, problems with it were found.

One of the unintended consequences of the merit system is that it weakens a supervisor's authority. Because a supervisor does not completely control the selection and removal process and protection for employee job security increases, employees gain a degree of independence. This fact frequently leads to exaggerated criticism of merit systems, but it is worth considering. An allied criticism is that under a merit system, bureaucracy is not so responsive to the people because their representatives have less control when they must consider factors other than loyalty in making appointments. Of course, others argue that the bureaucracy is more responsive because it is more competent and better able to serve the "real" needs of the people.

A major criticism of the merit system is that it has strayed from the egalitarian concept, just as the spoils system did. The examination process obviously eliminates some people from consideration and is seen as a positive instrument for selecting the most qualified, but questions about the appropriateness of the exams have been raised. Do they measure the qualities required for successful performance? Similarly, questions are raised about the appropriateness of the credentials required for positions. These issues are central to a merit system and are the cause of many conflicts.

It is an extreme oversimplification to characterize the distinction between spoils and merit as the difference between evil and good, but many people unfortunately do just that. In reality, each system is a product of particular political and social forces. Neither can provide an effective bureaucracy without some cost. Although all levels of government have moved to a neutral bureaucracy, patronage is still important. The use of patronage has adapted to changing conditions and demands, just as the merit system has adapted.[33] Some argue that the merit system has created a politics of its own that seeks support for its programs, agency autonomy, professional association interests, and clientele interests.[34] These interests and groups play the game of politics and insist that the spoils be theirs rather than the political party's. However, regardless of how the system is perceived, it is certain to change in response to demands and pressures in the political environment.

Summary

The conflict between spoils and merit principles has been an enduring issue in the public service. Merit systems were developed originally to rid public personnel of political patronage. Consequently, the primary emphasis of merit systems has been on policing personnel actions. Traditionally, most personnel departments spend much of their time making sure that others comply with personnel policies, rules, and regulations. Although there has been much change, such policing still is prominent in the activities of personnel administrators, particularly at the state and local levels.

The role of personnel administration has changed. Currently, the most common model teams central personnel agencies with line department managers so that departments can comply with personnel policies and regulations and improve the quality of public service. Central personnel agencies offer technical assistance, training programs, services in compliance with legal requirements, and labor-management relations, among other areas. Through such activities, personnel administrators can reduce the tension between themselves and department managers so that they can work together to accomplish the government's objectives. Cooperation seems to be more evident as the central personnel agency has focused on policy development, review, and technical assistance, and individual agencies have been performing more day-to-day personnel functions. The Civil Service Reform Act of 1978 and its progeny at the state and local levels have accentuated this trend.

The remainder of this book considers this trend and other challenges facing the public personnel function.

NOTES

1. H. Kaufman, "The Growth of the Federal Personnel Service," in W. Sayre, ed., *The Federal Government Service: Its Character, Prestige, and Problems*, 2d ed. (Englewood Cliffs, N.J.: Prentice-Hall, 1965); F. C. Mosher, *Democracy and the Public Service* (New York: Oxford University Press, 1982); and P. P. Van Riper, *History of the United States Civil Service* (New York: Harper and Row, 1958).

2. L. D. White, *The Federalists: A Study in Administrative History* (New York: Macmillan, 1948).

3. Van Riper, *History of the United States Civil Service,* 27.

4. L. D. White, *The Jeffersonians: A Study in Administrative History 1801–1829* (New York: Macmillan, 1961).

5. C. R. Fish, *The Civil Service and the Patronage* (New York: Russell & Russell, 1963); and A. Hoogenboom, *Outlawing the Spoils: A History of the Civil Service Reform Movement 1865–1883* (Urbana: University of Illinois Press, 1961).

6. Fish, *The Civil Service and the Patronage,* 213.

7. Hoogenboom, *Outlining the Spoils.*

8. Fish, *The Civil Service and the Patronage,* 213.

9. L. V. Murphy, "The First Federal Civil Service Commission: 1871–1875," *Public Personnel Review,* 3 (January, July, October 1942), 29–39, 218–231, and 299–323.

10. Hoogenboom, *Outlawing the Spoils,* 143–178.

11. A. Hoogenboom, ed. *Spoilsmen and Reformers* (Chicago: Rand McNally, 1964); and C. J. Nelson, "The Press and Civil Service Reform," *Civil Service Journal,* 13 (April–June 1964), 1–3.

12. 106 U.S. 371 (1882).

13. A. Hoogenboom, "The Pendleton Act and the Civil Service," *American Historical Review,* 64 (1958–59), 301–318; and Hoogenboom, *Outlawing the Spoils.*

14. Hoogenboom, *Outlawing the Spoils;* and Van Riper, *History of the U.S. Civil Service.*

15. D. H. Rosenbloom, "Politics and Public Personnel Administration: The Legacy of 1883," in D. H. Rosenbloom, ed., *Centenary Issues of the Pendelton Act of 1883: The Problematic Legacy of Civil Service Reform.* New York: Marcel Dekker, 1982.

16. A. H. Aronson, "State and Local Personnel Administration," in F. J. Thompson, ed., *Classics of Public Personnel Policy* (Oak Park, Ill: Moore, 1979), 102–111.

17. U.S. Civil Service Commission, *Introducing the Civil Service Reform Act* (Washington, D.C.: U.S. Government Printing Office, 1978).

18. N. J. Cayer, "Merit Reform in the States," in S. Hays and R. Kearney, eds., *Public Personnel Administration: Problems and Prospects,* 3d ed. (Englewood Cliffs, N.J.: Prentice-Hall, 1995), 291–305; and K. S. Chi, "State Civil Service Systems," in S. E. Condrey, ed., *Handbook of Human Resource Management in Government* (San Francisco: Jossey-Bass, 1998), 35–55.

19. S. Knudsen, L. Jakus, and M. Metz, "The Civil Service Reform Act of 1978," *Public Personnel Management,* 8 (1979), 170–181.

20. National Commission on the Public Service, *Leadership for the Public Service* (Washington, D.C.: National Commission on the Public Service, 1989).

21. National Commission on the State and Local Public Service, *Hard Truths/Tough Choices: An Agenda for State and Local Reform* (Albany, N.Y.: Rockefeller Institute of Government, 1993).

22. National Performance Review, *From Red Tape to Results: Creating a Government That Works Better and Costs Less* (Washington, D.C.: U.S. Government Printing Office, 1993).

23. P. W. Ingraham, B. S. Romzek, and Associates, *New Paradigms for Government: Issues for the Changing Public Service* (San Francisco: Jossey-Bass, 1994); L. M. Lane and J. Wolf, *The Human Resource Crisis in the Public Sector* (New York: Quorum Books, 1990); P. C. Light, *The New Public Service* (Washington, D.C.: Brookings Institution Press, 1999); and C. A. Newland, "Critical Issues for Public Personnel Professionals," *Public Personnel Management,* 13 (Spring 1984), 15–46.

24. National Commission on the Public Service, *Urgent Business for America* (Washington, D.C.: The Brookings Institution, 2003).

25. H. C. Mansfield, "Political Parties, Patronage, and the Federal Government Service," in Sayre, ed., *The Federal Government Service,* 114–162; and H. M. Somers, "The President, Congress, and the Federal Government Service," in Sayre, ed. *The Federal Government Service,* 70–113.

26. Somers, "The President, Congress, and the Federal Government Service."

27. P. M. Blau and W. R. Scott, *Formal Organizations: A Comparative Approach* (San Francisco: Chandler, 1962).

28. Mosher, *Democracy and the Public Service.*

29. D. Schuman, *Bureaucracies, Organization, and Administration: A Political Primer* (New York: Macmillan, 1976).

30. S. Seidman, *Politics, Position, and Power: The Dynamics of Federal Organization,* 4th ed. (New York: Oxford University Press, 1986).

31. G. F. Goerl, "Cybernetics, Professionalization, and Knowledge Management: An Exercise in Assumptive Theory," *Public Administration Review,* 35 (November–December 1975), 581–588; and Schuman, *Bureaucracies, Organization, and Administration.*

32. Blau and Scott, *Formal Organizations,* 64–67

33. A. Freedman, *Patronage: An American Tradition* (Chicago: Nelson Hall, 1994); and F. J. Sorauf, "The Silent Revolution in Patronage." *Public Administration Review,* 20 (Winter 1960), 28–34.

34. Kaufman, "The Growth of the Federal Personnel Service." 59–69.

SUGGESTED READINGS

Cainevale, D. S., S. W. Housel, and N. Riley. *Merit System Reform in the States: Partnership for Change.* Norman, Okla.: Programs in Public Administration, University of Oklahoma, 1995.

Condrey, S. E., and R. Maranto. *Radical Reform of the Civil Service.* New York: Lexington Books, 2001.

Hoogenboom, A. *Outlawing the Spoils: A History of the Civil Service Reform Movement 1865–1883.* Urbana: University of Illinois Press, 1961.

Kettl, D. F., P. W. Ingraham, R. P. Sanders, and C. Horner. *Civil Service Reform: Building a Government That Works.* Washington, D.C: The Brookings Institution Press, 1996.

Lane, L. M., and J. F. Wolf. *The Human Resource Crisis in the Public Sector: Rebuilding the Capacity to Govern.* New York: Quorum, 1990.

Mosher, F. C. *Democracy and the Public Service,* 2d ed. New York: Oxford University Press, 1982.

Nalbandian, J., and D. Klingner. "The Politics of Public Personnel Administration: Towards Theoretical Understanding." *Public Administration Review,* 41 (1982), 541–549.

National Academy of Public Administration. *The Case for Transforming Public Sector Human Resources Management.* Washington, D.C.: National Academy of Public Administration, 2000.

Pfiffner, J. P., and D. A. Brook. *The Future of Merit: Twenty Years after the Civil Service Reform Act*. Baltimore, Md.: The Johns Hopkins University Press, 2000.

Rosenbloom, D. H., ed. *Centenary Issues of the Pendleton Act of 1883: The Problematic Legacy of Civil Service Reform*. New York: Marcel Dekker, 1982.

Sayre, W., ed. *The Federal Government Service: Its Character, Prestige, and Problems*, 2d ed. Englewood Cliffs, N.J.: Prentice-Hall, 1965.

Sorauf, F. J. "The Silent Revolution in Patronage." *Public Administration Review*, 20 (1960), 28–30.

Thompson, F. J., ed. "Symposium: The Winter Commission Report: Is Deregulation the Answer for Public Personnel Management?" *Review of Public Personnel Administration*, 13 (1994), 5–90.

Titlow, R. E. *Americans Import Merit: Origins of the United States Civil Service and the Influence of the British Model*. Washington, D.C.: University Press of America, 1979.

U.S. Office of Personnel Management. *Human Resource Management: Aligning with the Mission*. Washington D.C.: U.S. Office of Personnel Management, Office of Merit Systems Oversight and Effectiveness, 1999.

Van Riper, P. P. *History of the United States Civil Service*. New York: Harper & Row, 1958.

SELECTED WEB SITES

Brookings Institution. A think tank focusing on government and public policy issues, especially at the federal level. Many of its publications focus on the public service. www.brookings.org

National Academy of Public Administration (NAPA). Organization that conducts and publishes research on various public administration issues including human resource management with a focus on the federal public service. www.napawash.org

National Institute for Government Innovation (NIGI). Institute that studies cutting-edge ideas in public service at all levels, publishes reports, and conducts seminars and workshops to disseminate information on and promote innovations in government. www.nigi.org

U.S. Congress, Congressional Budget Office (CBO). Entity that publishes reports on many issues including human resource management. www.cbo.gov

U.S. General Accounting Office (GAO). Office that publishes reports on agencies and programs at the request of congressional committees and members, many of which deal with personnel issues; issues a monthly list of reports. www.gao.gov

U.S. Merit Systems Protection Board (MSPB). Organization that publishes an annual report on its activities and special reports on managing the federal workplace. www.mspb.gov

U.S. Office of Management and Budget (OMB). Entity that publishes analyses of the use of resources by federal agencies, including utilization of personnel. www.omb.gov

U.S. Office of Personnel Management (OPM). Body that oversees the federal government personnel function and publishes materials to help agencies implement policies; also publishes many analyses of public personnel and labor relations issues. www.opm.gov

Exercises

1. Find the Web site for your city, county, or state government. Investigate the historical development of the personnel/human resource management function in that government. Explain what type of system it is. Have the basic values on which it is based changed? For example, is

there a merit system? If so, when was it developed? What stimulated its development? The answer to some of these questions could require a library search and/or interview with persons responsible for managing the personnel function.

2. Contact your local city manager or county executive/manager. Interview the manager concerning his or her view of the appropriate role of the personnel/human resources department in that government. Ask that manager about the role that the personnel department performs. Then ask the personnel/human resources director for the same information. Do the two interviews lead to the same or different views about the role of personnel? Explain.

3. Governor Sy Littlejohn won reelection after a tough race, although he won by a surprisingly large margin. His political party also took control of both houses of the state legislature. As he mapped out plans for his second administration, Littlejohn thought about the people he would appoint to various boards and commissions. His thoughts turned to some of the appointments he had made in his first administration, and he vowed to correct some of his earlier mistakes. Some of his appointees, especially to environmental and business regulatory boards, had surprised him by often taking positions contrary to his ardent probusiness stance. He believed that there should be virtually no constraints on business activity, but these boards were enforcing previous legislatures' environmental and consumer laws that Littlejohn considered burdensome to business.

   One of the governor's ideas was to seek legislation that would permit him to remove members of boards and commissions. Currently, the governor has the authority to appoint members, but to remove them only for cause.

   You are a personnel consultant called in by Governor Littlejohn to offer suggestions on a variety of issues involving human resources management. He shares his idea of seeking removal authority over board and commission members and asks for your advice. How would you advise him? What are the strengths and weaknesses of the governor's idea?

4. John Scurry assumed the job as director of the state prison system amid a great deal of concern about the problems associated with it. With the state's tough stance against crime, the prison population was increasing at a rapid rate, but the facilities remained the same. The result was a major overcrowding problem that was leading to many other problems.

   In appointing Scurry, Governor Cantu praised him as a progressive administrator who could solve the corrections problem for the state. When he was hired, the governor promised Scurry to strongly support his efforts to develop innovative programs to rehabilitate inmates who demonstrated the ability to change. The governor also voiced strong support of new facilities to ease the crowding problem.

Governor Cantu's support was important to the new director, who had a reputation for inmate-oriented programs that worked. As the next election neared, the state legislature, in which the governor's party was the minority, focused considerable attention on the prison system and its many problems. Because no new funds had been made available for constructing new facilities, the overcrowding problem had become increasingly worse, as had the discipline problems. There had also been several escapes from the prison. The general public became alarmed, and the prison problem promised to become a major issue in the state election campaign.

The state legislative committee on law and justice held highly publicized hearings on the problems in state prisons. Scurry testified at them and was berated by several majority party members. The committee's message was clear: Scurry had better clean up the mess in the state prisons and stop creating programs to coddle prisoners, or the prison system could forget about any increase in appropriations in the next legislative session. Governor Cantu, seeking reelection, had conveniently avoided the issue of prisons to that point.

You are John Scurry. What are your alternatives? What will you choose to do? Why?

3

Personnel System Design

A lthough everyone in an organization, especially the managers and supervisors, has personnel responsibilities, certain individuals or units have the primary function of developing and implementing personnel policies. The personnel function can rest with the chief executive officer or a personnel office ranging from a few people to a large complex bureaucracy. This chapter analyzes the various bases on which personnel activities can be organized and the alternatives for structuring the personnel function. First the chapter explores the function of the personnel office.

Personnel Office Roles

Personnel offices often are seen as negative policing agencies that make sure that operating departments obey rigid rules and procedures.[1] As a result, many department managers view personnel units with suspicion and hostility rather than as a source of support and assistance. This attitude, though, is changing. The personnel office is supposed to be a service office for the rest of the organization. It performs what normally is referred to as a *staff function* as it helps line departments deliver their services to the public by supporting the departments in staffing and managing their workforces. In contemporary views of personnel offices, they perform policing and monitoring roles and provide service to line departments. Personnel offices also are expected to take a leadership role on personnel issues with the rest of the organization.[2]

The personnel office's main service traditionally has been the recruitment of employees. The operating department notified personnel of its need for persons to fill vacancies. The personnel office then advertised and screened applicants and administered the appropriate exams to certify candidates for selection. Along with these duties, the personnel office updated position classification and compensation systems. Its audit and review functions meant policing departmental activities and often finding problems that had to be corrected. Any review of activities from outside the departments tended to produce anxiety and suspicion, and personnel offices created both, partly because they often emphasized abiding by "good" rules and regulations while ignoring the need to be flexible and get things done, which is important to department managers.[3]

However, the role of personnel offices has changed and expanded greatly in recent years. One change is that the personnel function is now viewed as supporting all aspects of management. Public sector jurisdictions recognized the need to make personnel part of general management and emulated the private sector by integrating personnel into the overall management function. The ever-present fiscal constraints since the late 1970s have prodded public managers to include personnel administration in decisions involving the largest resource expenditure, the government employees (human resources). The 1978 Civil Service Reform Act was predicated in large part on President Carter's promise to revamp management at all levels of the federal government. State and local government reforms were stimulated by similar concerns.

Because of the evolution in views of the personnel function, many more activities have become the province of the personnel office. Now it must deal with issues of equity and discrimination, labor-management relations, retention and development of good employees, training, and accommodation to disabilities and family leave, to mention only a few. Reform efforts since 1978 have decentralized many personnel functions, leading to conflicts over the proper role of the central personnel agency and departmental personnel offices. In addition, concerns over the political responsiveness of public servants have created new issues. Especially important is the maintenance of effective services in times of fiscal constraint, including borrowing practices from the private sector and contracting out services. The reinventing government and quality management movements also have focused attention on the role and processes of personnel management. As a result, personnel offices increasingly are playing strategic roles in overall management.

Types of Personnel Systems

Public personnel systems vary based on the size and type of jurisdiction as well as the values important to the jurisdiction. For very small jurisdictions, the personnel function can be combined with other functions. For example, in villages, towns, or townships, the manager of the jurisdiction can perform all management functions including personnel. As the size of the jurisdiction increases, personnel can be the responsibility of a manager who also has budgeting and finance or other responsibilities. As size increases, personnel specialists are likely, and in large jurisdictions, full-fledged personnel (or human resources) staff are common. Very large jurisdictions have separate divisions or departments dealing with different aspects of personnel administration. Thus, there could be a human resources department, a labor-management relations authority, a training department, and an equal employment opportunity office.

The organization for personnel management also depends on the dominant values of the governmental jurisdiction. Most personnel systems in the United States value merit and competence; thus, merit principles are at the core of the systems. Nonetheless, other values also are important and can affect the way the function is organized. Fairness and equity are strong values of the U.S. political system and are reflected in governmental personnel systems. Governments in settings that have strong unions and collective bargaining reflect that fact, and the personnel system likely permits public sector bargaining and could have a separate organization to do it. The civil rights and women's movements have had significant impact on most public personnel systems as reflected in the creation of programs and organizational units to deal with equality and nondiscrimination.

Historically, public bureaucracies have been conceptualized as guardian, caste, patronage/spoils, merit, welfare, affirmative action, and labor-management dominated.[4] Each of these approaches supports different societal values and illustrates how the personnel function can be organized to serve the values.

The guardian bureaucracy is based on a predetermined selection process in which the guardians protect the good and right. Plato's *Republic* presents an example of the guardian approach to bureaucracy. The rulers' bureaucracy maintains the system, which reflects the good society. However, determining who is born to rule is not easy. The caste bureaucracy, by contrast, offers a simpler method of choosing the members of the bureaucracy. People are born into a social caste, and only those in the higher caste can rule. Thus, the system normally reflects society's structure. Traditional societies and monarchies reflect these values.

The patronage, or spoils, system of personnel management stems from the model associated with Jacksonian Democracy, but its value underpinnings were part of administration from the beginning of our nation. All systems use it to some extent. In this system, a political leader or another patron rewards supporters by giving them jobs. Although merit can be taken into account, the primary consideration is whether the potential employee has worked or will work for the interests of those in power. Loyalty is the overriding value in this system. As explained in Chapter 2, many employees in the U.S. public service still are selected on the basis of patronage. Cabinet members and other high-level officials are chosen through patronage as are members of regulatory and other independent agencies as well as the judiciary in many jurisdictions. Spoils systems still operate in many state and local governments.

Merit personnel systems are predominant in the United States, at least in theory. Under the merit system, personnel decisions are based on specified standards, qualifications, and performance. Although most civil service systems are justified as merit systems, merit and civil service systems are not synonymous. The major premises of Weberian bureaucracy (developed by the nineteenth-century German sociologist Max Weber) form the bases of merit personnel systems, especially as a career service with fixed salaries, specified selection and training procedures, rules and regulations for all program activities, and evaluation of performance as parts of the personnel function.

Welfare and affirmative action personnel systems are founded, in part, on government employment as the answer to social problems. In the welfare-based approach, government serves as the employer of last resort for people who would not otherwise have jobs, lack skills, or are among the hard-core unemployed. The public service training employment programs such as the Job Training Partnership Act (JTPA) and Americorp are examples of such a system.

Similarly, affirmative action personnel systems are based on accomplishing a social purpose. Equal employment and affirmative action policies require that personnel policies consider people who previously experienced discrimination. Affirmative action implies some preference for target groups, just as veterans' preference accords advantages to those with military service. Systems based on preferential treatment require that a person's membership in a specified group be taken into account in the employment decision. Other preferential considerations could involve citizenship and residency.

Labor-management–dominated systems are those in which personnel activities reflect values negotiated by labor and management. The labor agreement or contract can specify criteria for selection of employees, promotion, and discipline. The agreement also establishes procedures for conducting many of the personnel functions, particularly discipline and employee appeal procedures.

All of the values and systems except guardian and caste can be found in most U.S. public personnel systems. Thus, it is unusual to find a system that reflects only one of the approaches. Which values or systems dominate are choices made by each governmental unit. Merit and spoils dominate the discussion of this book because they are the two most commonly found in U.S. public personnel administration. The others are discussed as appropriate.

Organizing Personnel Activities

The basic structure of the personnel system in every jurisdiction is based on a legal framework. In many cases, state constitutions or local government charters spell out the major requirements for personnel operation. Commonly, such provisions indicate that the public service must be based on merit and provide for policy-making and implementation organizations. Whether a civil service commission, a single personnel or human resources director, or any other arrangement will be used is stated, as are the powers and duties of such organizations. In the absence of or in addition to constitutional or charter provisions, laws or ordinances establish the system's legal foundation. Executive officers and civil service commissioners or the like also may issue rules and regulations that affect the personnel system structure. All these bases for establishing the system are related. Normally, the constitutional or charter provision grants authority to the legislative body that then authorizes the personnel or civil service commission to issue rules and regulations. Thus, the various elements of the process complement one another in organizing the personnel activities.

Three key organizational questions must be considered in establishing a personnel system:

1. Is an independent personnel board or commission desirable? If so, what are its powers and functions?
2. Will a central personnel office carry out the personnel activities, or should each department perform its own personnel activities?
3. Should the final personnel authority rest with the chief executive, the legislature, or an independent personnel board or commission?

The answers to these questions depend on the needs of individual jurisdictions. Naturally, the needs of a very small unit of government will not be the same as those of one with a large employee force. Similarly, jurisdictions with partisan political elections have expectations different from those of jurisdictions with nonpartisan elections. Each jurisdiction must determine what will work best for it.

A bipartisan or nonpartisan civil service commission or personnel board is the model that dominated public personnel administration at all levels of government in the United States after the adoption of such a system at the national level in 1883. Such agencies generally are responsible for personnel policy development and its implementation. Furthermore, the civil service commission often serves as the appeals board of last resort for employees who claim to have been mistreated by their supervisors and managers. Although the commission commonly has overall responsibility for personnel functions, it is impossible for it to carry on day-to-day activities. Instead, an executive director usually is employed for that purpose. However, some systems, such as that in New York State, designate one member of the commission as chairperson or president responsible for implementing personnel policies.

The main alternative to the independent commission is to create a central personnel office directly responsible to the chief executive and thus closely connected to the administration's management. The Civil Service Reform Act of 1978 created such an arrangement at the national level, with the Office of Personnel Management reporting to the president. Many state and local governments instituted similar reforms both before and after the national government did. This arrangement permits the personnel function to be a strategic player in the management of the organization. When a personnel office reports to the chief executive and supervises personnel administration, an appeals board normally is created to review employee appeals. The Merit Systems Protection Board at the national level serves this function. In some cases, a personnel board provides advisory services to the chief executive or legislative body and approves personnel rules and regulations. New York City, Chicago, and Mesa, Arizona, use this approach, which is common in state and local government.

Another aspect of personnel organization pertains to whether the function is centralized in one department of personnel or decentralized among the agencies in the jurisdiction. Most systems combine both approaches. In a few places, such as Texas, individual departments still have a great deal of autonomy over most of their personnel activities.

The reform movement stimulated by the 1883 Civil Service Act led to the creation of central personnel offices in most large jurisdictions. After World War II, however, the trend was toward decentralizing implementation functions. Legislation such as the 1978 Civil Service Reform Act at the national level institutionalized this decentralization. Although central personnel agencies (for example, Office of Personnel Management) were created to make policy, develop programs, ensure compliance with policy, and provide technical assistance, operating departments have the day-to-day personnel responsibilities.

Centralizing the personnel function has many advantages. It provides for uniformity in dealing with personnel activities and permits a high degree of specialization in the technical aspects of these activities. Economies of scale also result when recruiting, examining, and the like are performed for a jurisdiction as a whole. With the influence of labor organizations in many jurisdictions, uniformity of policy and procedures also offers support to management because a lack of uniformity could lower employee morale and productivity if individuals compare their positions with those of others in the organization.

There also are disadvantages when a central office has all personnel responsibilities. Critics cite the distance of the personnel office from the operating agencies. Indeed, many managers view the central personnel office as an outside force, not as a support service. The personnel office also tends to deal with problems in a generic sense, not from the perspective of the operating department and its needs. It is difficult for it to adapt decisions to the particular situation of each department.

Under a decentralized system, each department has its own personnel officer and staff. The personnel policies and activities are likely to reflect the particular circumstances of the department or unit and are not likely to be uniform across the jurisdiction. When each department is permitted to adapt policies and actions to its own needs, the personnel function tends to be integrated with the management of the department. The principal problems of the departmental personnel office model are the lack of uniformity among departments, the cost of duplicating activities in numerous agencies, fewer opportunities for specialization, and the absence of objectivity in handling personnel problems.

In most large jurisdictions, the extremes represented by the centralized and decentralized systems are ameliorated by combining the approaches. The central office has certain responsibilities, and officials in each department are responsible for daily personnel activities. Thus, the central office can focus on policy development, specialized expertise, monitoring, and review, and the departmental office can concentrate on carrying out the policy in the relevant setting. The departmental office can ask the central office specialist for help when it is needed. Central personnel offices now are likely to have liaisons to individual departments and actually station a personnel staff person in large departments. With such an arrangement, the operating departments are more likely to see personnel policy as a support of their activities.

The quality management and reinventing government movements of the 1980s and 1990s stimulated reforms in many personnel activities at all levels of government. Results include efforts to empower employees, increase labor-management cooperation, shift the focus from inputs to results, and better align personnel with organizational mission. At the national level, these movements have also led to reduction in the size of the federal workforce. Florida and Georgia went so far as to abolish their civil service systems. Clearly, reform strikes a chord with many critics of government performance, and the popular themes of reinvention and accountability provide a strong foundation for many reform efforts.

As personnel policies have evolved, many new agencies have developed to deal with specialized human resources management. As noted, labor-management relations activities led to the creation of a separate agency, the Federal Labor Relations Authority, to manage labor relations at the national level. Similar organizations, usually called *public employee relations boards,* exist at the state and local levels (for example, Maine, Minnesota, and Los Angeles). Similarly, equal employment opportunity and affirmative action produced agencies in most jurisdictions to administer these policies. Training and development are other functions often found in separately created units. Although these activities can take place outside the personnel office, they are still personnel functions and will be examined later in this book.

Career Systems

Different types of systems operate within the varied personnel structures. Certainly political appointees and career civil servants represent two different systems that interact within the organization. Typically, political appointees oversee the career service employees. During the early part of every administration, the top-level political appointees promise major shake-ups in the career bureaucracy, but usually little changes. The career bureaucrats provide the information and support needed for the programs desired by the agency or department head appointed by the elected chief executive. In most departments, the top administrator cannot risk the opposition of career civil servants. Accommodations are made, and the administrator usually follows the career servant's recommendations. When this does not happen, career servants often lobby for their positions before sympathetic legislative committees.[5]

A political executive's career pattern differs from that of a career service executive in that the former's tenure in a position depends on the election cycle. If a new party wins the presidency, governorship, or mayoralty, for example, the political appointees normally change. Even if a party or administration is reelected, changes in emphasis and thus changes in personnel are likely. Loyalty to the current administration and its policy positions also are obligatory for political executives, and dismissal for disagreement is common.

Even more difficult for political executives is the fact that they could have the confidence of the chief executive but become a liability because of political considerations. For example, Securities and Exchange Commission Chair Harvey Pitt became an embarrassment to President George W. Bush. While the president claimed Pitt had his full support even as Pitt seemed to be allowing the industry to influence his decisions and withholding important information from other commission members, the president dumped him after the 2002 elections. Pitt was generating too much controversy. Of course, top political executives usually have no difficulty finding alternative work and fade into the background for a while only to reappear in a new administration. The administration of George W. Bush brought back a number of high-level appointees from the previous Bush and Reagan administrations, including William Ruckelshaus and Donald Rumsfeld. Even people discredited in one administration can show up later in another.

Career civil servants, of course, have protected tenure and thus continue from one administration to another. Within that career system, however, are what are referred to as *open* and *closed career systems.* Closed career systems are those in which high-level positions are filled entirely through promotion from below. To become a high-level official within the organization, a person must begin at the bottom and advance up through the hierarchical ladder. The military, FBI, Foreign Service, police and fire departments, and British civil service use such a system. The military is the strictest; with some exceptions, the others usually require experience at a lower level of the organization to attain a higher rank.

An open system means that positions are filled through competition from both inside and outside the organization. Sometimes called *lateral entry,* the open system allows employees to enter an organization at any level.

Open systems are supposed to make an organization more dynamic by bringing in people with fresh ideas and approaches and thus eliminating the stagnation often created by the culture and socialization processes within the organization. However, in practice, most systems that are technically open—as in the case of most government jurisdictions—usually lean more toward the closed system approach. Employees and employee organizations often prefer closed systems because many collective bargaining agreements call for promotion on the basis of seniority, which is a closed system approach. High-level managers often are more comfortable with a closed system because it allows them to deal with known quantities in selecting staff. People from below can be chosen according to how well they get along in the organization, whereas someone from outside the organization is an unknown quantity.

Closed systems also usually include an up-or-out feature. *Up-or-out,* or *selection-out,* refers to the situation in which a person is expected to qualify for promotion within a certain period of time or must achieve a particular performance level. If the promotion or performance level is not attained, the person is asked to resign or is dismissed from the organization. The military and foreign service use this process, and academic departments in most colleges and universities employ a less strict version. The Senior Executive Service (SES) in the federal service requires achievement of a particular performance level to remain in the service.

The Senior Executive Service represents another type of personnel system. Although the national government's SES, formalized in law by the Civil Service Reform Act of 1978, is the most visible, several states actually preceded the national government in experimenting with this concept. The basic purpose of the SES is to permit flexibility in using the talents of high-ranking administrators. The objectives of such programs are to

1. Offer managers opportunities to use talented administrators where they can contribute the most
2. Offer talented administrators opportunities to broaden their perspectives through wider experiences
3. Improve communication across organizational units
4. Improve the image of the public service and thus make the recruitment and retention of competent administrators easier
5. Improve administrators' performance by rewarding them for outstanding performance.

The success of SES is debatable. Evaluative studies differ in their conclusions concerning its effectiveness.

Another way of structuring the personnel system is by choosing between rank-in-person or rank-in-job. *Rank-in-person* means that the individual is evaluated and ranked according to his or her performance. Compensation and other benefits are based on the person's rank, regardless of the duties performed. Qualifications such as education and experience also help determine the rank. Military, police, and fire departments use rank-in-person systems as do academic faculties. Personnel at different ranks can perform similar activities, but they are paid differently because of their ranks. Thus, for example, an assistant professor and a full professor perform the same basic functions (i.e., teaching, research, and public service), but they receive very different levels of pay. Of course, performance expectations within each of these ranks also tend to be different. The Senior Executive Service is a variation of the rank-in-person system.

The *rank-in-job system* means that the organization is structured around the work to be done and the basic structural unit is the position. Thus, position classification is a key aspect of rank-in-job systems. Jobs (positions) are arranged in a hierarchy, and compensation is based on where the job fits in the organization's hierarchy. Most public sector organizations are based on the rank-in-job concept. Thus, no matter the education, experience, or seniority of the individual, the compensation for that individual is based on the position she or he holds.

The rank-in-job and the closed system often produce problems in dealing with good employees because the only way to advance in salary and prestige and acquire other badges of success is to move up through the hierarchy. People are thus rewarded for effective service by promotion to supervisory and managerial positions. These jobs, however, require different skills, and often those good at doing the organization's tasks are not good at managing or supervising others. As a result, some people suggest that a dual-track or multi-track career system would permit rewarding individuals for good technical performance and provide for promotion within the managerial ranks for those with management skills. Dual and multitrack systems have not caught on to a great extent in the public service, but they represent a way to alleviate the problems created by the pressures for promotion common in our society.

Since the 1970s, government increasingly has partnered with private sector organizations, both for profit and nonprofit, to deliver public services. The result is another twist on the organization of the public personnel function. Government agencies, sometimes the personnel agencies, have become managers and monitors of contracts. One part of managing the contracts has been monitoring aspects of their personnel activities. Government partnership agreements and contracts usually include some provisions regarding personnel activities. Provisions commonly include equal employment policies and labor protections for those employed by the partner or contractor. In recent years, some jurisdictions have required a minimum level of benefits for employees of partners or contractors as well. Personnel functions themselves can be outsourced.[6] These arrangements raise issues of differential treatment of public employees and the employees of the partners and contractors.

Intergovernmental Personnel Issues

One of the most significant factors affecting the development of state and local government personnel systems has been the variety of federal government requirements imposed on jurisdictions receiving federal funds. Stemming from the Social Security Act of 1935 through the proliferation of categorical grant-in-aid programs during the 1950s, 1960s, and 1970s, state and local governments have been prodded to use merit principles for programs funded by federal monies. State and local officials often criticized federal government requirements as being onerous and costly, but the requirements also have been credited with improving many personnel systems across the country.[7] At present, all states except Texas have statewide systems, most of which are direct results of the federal government's requirements although some agencies can be exempted. In 1981, the Reagan administration succeeded in ending many federal government personnel conditions associated with grants, but general requirements related to equal employment opportunity, nondiscrimination, and employee rights still exist or have been broadened through nonfunded federal mandates.

If left to the states and local governments, policies protecting equal employment opportunity, older workers, people with disabilities, and other groups would be difficult to ensure in all places. Thus, affected groups still look to the federal government for protection.

Summary

The personnel function requires that jurisdictions develop structures appropriate to their needs and resources. Systems vary according to the concerns and values important to the particular governmental jurisdiction. Thus, in organizing personnel activities, governments must consider whether they wish to base the system on merit, patronage, or a social purpose. Questions about who should have the authority for personnel activities also must be addressed. In the main, a jurisdiction must develop a structure and policies that best keep the system responsive to the public while finding and using the best talent available. All of these concerns also depend on resource availability.

NOTES

1. A. K. Campbell, "Revitalizing the Federal Personnel System," *Public Personnel Management,* 7 (1978), 58–63; J. Nalbandian, "From Compliance to Consultation: The Changing Role of the Public Personnel Administrator," *Review of Public Personnel Administration,* 1 (1981), 37–51; and E. B. Staats, "Personnel Management: The Starting Place," *Public Personnel Management,* 5 (1976), 424–441.

2. C. Ban, "The Changing Role of the Personnel Office," in C. Ban and N. M. Ric-cucci, eds., *Public Personnel Management: Current Concerns, Future Challenges* (New York: Longman, 2002), 8–25; and W. J. Rothwell, R. K. Prescott, and M. W. Taylor, *Strategic Human Resource Leader: How to Prepare Your Organization for the Six Trends Shaping Your Future* (Palo Alto, Calif.: Davies-Black Publishing, 2000).

3. C. Ban, "How Do Public Managers Manage?" *Bureaucratic Constraints, Organizational Culture, and the Potential for Reform* (San Francisco: Jossey-Bass, 1995); J. D. Cogburn, "Deregulating the Public Personnel Function," in S. W. Hays and R. C. Kearney, eds., *Public Personnel Administration: Problems and Prospects,* 4th ed. (Upper Saddle River, N.J.: Prentice-Hall, 2003) 75–90; and M. M. Morse, "We've Come a Long Way," *Public Personnel Management,* 5 (1976), 218–224.

4. D. E. Klingner, "Competing Perspectives on Public Personnel Administration," in S. W. Hays and R. C. Kearney, eds., *Public Personnel Administration: Problems and Prospects,* 4th ed. (Upper Saddle River, N.J.: Prentice-Hall, 2003), 16–28; M. M. Morse, in a presentation at the Center for Public Service, Texas Tech University, April 18, 1979; and F. Morstein Marx, *The Administrative State* (Chicago: University of Chicago Press, 1957).

5. M. M. Golden, "What Motivates Bureaucrats?" *Politics and Administration during the Reagan Years* (New York: Columbia University Press, 2000); and L. Reed, "The Bureaucracy: The Cleverest Lobby of Them All, *Washington Monthly,* 10 (April 1978), 49–54.

6. S. Fernandez, C. E. Lowman, and H. G. Rainey, *Privatization and Human Resources Management,* in C. Ban and N. M. Riccucci, eds., *Public Personnel Management: Current Concerns, Future Challenges,* 3d ed. (New York: Longman, 2002), 225–242; W. C. Lawther, "Privatizing Personnel: Outsourcing Public Sector Functions," in S. Hays and R. C. Kearney, eds., *Public Personnel Administration: Problems and Prospects* (Upper Saddle River, N.J.: Prentice-Hall, 2003), 196–208; and G. B. Siegel, "Outsourcing Personnel Functions," *Public Personnel Management,* 29 (2002), 225–236.

7. L. D. Greene, "Federal Merit Requirements: A Retrospective Look," *Public Personnel Management,* 11 (1982), 39–54.

SUGGESTED READINGS

Buford, J. A., and J. R. Lindner. *Human Resources in Local Government.* Dallas, Tex: South-Western Publishing 2002.

Carnevale, D., S. W. Housel, and N. Riley. *Merit System Reform in the States: Partnership for Change.* Norman: University of Oklahoma Programs in Public Administration, 1995.

Douglas, J. M. "State Civil Service and Collective Bargaining: Systems in Conflict." *Public Administration Review,* 52 (1992), 162–172.

Dresang, D. L. "Diffusion of Civil Service Reform: The Federal and State Governments." *Review of Public Administration,* 2 (1982), 35–47.

Greene, L. D. "Federal Merit Requirements: A Retrospective Look." *Public Personnel Management,* 11 (1982), 39–54.

Harper, K. "The Senior Executive Service after One Decade." In P. W. Ingraham and D. H. Rosenbloom, eds., *The Promise and Paradox of Civil Service Reform.* Pittsburgh: University of Pittsburgh Press, 1992, 267–282.

Ingraham, P. W., and S. C. Selden, "Human Resource Management and Capacity in the States." In C. Ban and N. M. Riccucci, eds., *Public Personnel Management: Current Concerns, Future Challenges.* New York: Longman, 2002, 210–224.

Lane, L. M. "The Office of Personnel Management: Values, Policies, and Consequences." In P. W. Ingraham and D. H. Rosenbloom, eds., *The Promise and Paradox of Civil Service Reform.* Pittsburgh: University of Pittsburgh Press, 1992, 97–119.

National Academy of Public Administration. *The Case for Transforming Public Sector Human Resources Management.* Washington, D.C.: National Academy of Public Administration, 2000.

_____. *Strategies and Alternatives for Transforming Human Resources Management.* Washington, D.C.: National Academy of Public Administration, 1995.

Newland, C. A. "The Politics of Civil Service Reform." In P. W. Ingraham and D. H. Rosenbloom, eds., *The Promise and Paradox of Civil Service Reform.* Pittsburgh: University of Pittsburgh Press, 1992, 97–119.

Peters, B. G., and D. J. Savoie. "Civil Service Reform: Misdiagnosing the Patient." *Public Administration Review,* 54 (1994), 418–424.

Sanders, R. P. "Reinventing the Senior Executive Service." In P. W. Ingraham, B. S. Romzek, and Associates, *New Pardigms for Government: Issues for the Changing Public Service.* San Francisco: Jossey-Bass, 1994, 215–238.

Wecshler, B. "Reinventing Florida's Civil Service System." *Review of Public Personnel Administration,* 14 (1994), 64–76.

Wise, L. R. "Rethinking Public Employment Structures and Strategies." In P. W. Ingraham, B. S. Romzek, and Associates, *New Paradigms for Government: Issues for the Changing Public Service.* San Francisco: Jossey-Bass, 1994, 239–258.

SELECTED WEB SITES

International City/County Management Association (ICMA). Membership organization of local governments with council manager forms that publishes materials on best forms and practices in local government. www.icma.org

National Academy of Public Administration (NAPA). Organization that researches and publishes reports on improving government including the public service. www.napawash.org

National Association of State Personnel Executives (NASPE). Membership organization of state managers responsible for personnel administration. Publishes a newsletter and reports dealing with structure and processes of personnel management. Focuses on innovative policies and practices. www.naspe.net

National League of Cities (NLC). Membership organization of local governments that publishes materials on and assists local governments in providing quality services to their citizens including human resources issues. www.nlc.org/nls_org/site/

Office of Personnel Management (OPM). Agency responsible for managing human resources for the national government. Publishes guides and information on personnel practices and organization. www.opm.gov

---

Exercises

1. Interview the director of a department in city, county, state, or tribal government. In your interview, ask about the director's perceptions of how much the central personnel office of the government focuses on monitoring, customer service, and leading and educating departments about personnel issues. Also ask what the department manager would

like to see changed about the central personnel office's function. Based on the interview, write your assessment of whether the central personnel office takes a traditional or a strategic approach to personnel administration.

2. Blue Creek is a newly formed municipality of 100,000 in a large, fast-growing urban area. The charter gives the city council the responsibility to create the administrative structure, and the council has contracted with you to develop a proposal for how to handle personnel administration. How would you approach developing your recommendations? What values would you base the recommendations on and why? Provide a basic outline of how the function would be organized.

3. Pert County has a personnel system in which each county supervisor has the authority to appoint employees who provide many services in their individual supervisory districts or precincts. As a result, some districts have large turnover because the supervisors never win reelection; in other districts, the staff remains the same because the same supervisors are returned to office regularly. In addition, several county officers (for example, county sheriff, county attorney, county assessor) are elected independently and have their own personnel rules and procedures for their offices.

   The voters have elected to create a task force on county reform, and it has hired you to help with recommendations on personnel reform since you are a national expert on county personnel matters.

   What issues would you want to consider in developing the recommendations? What are the political realities you would have to consider? What would be the basic outline of your recommendations? Provide a justification for them.

4. The inauguration of Governor Wellerson was an exciting event for Jeff East, the new governor's chief of staff. Being the campaign manager for Wellerson in an uphill election campaign had been the thrill of a lifetime. Now it is time to get to work to implement the new governor's promises. Among the major themes of the Wellerson campaign was the view that the public bureaucracy had become too big and too concerned about its own welfare rather than the public's problems. Wellerson promised to bring about change and root out all "incompetent lazy bureaucrats feeding at the public trough." East knew that the electorate had responded positively to that theme, but he also knew that it was rhetoric. He was well aware of the dedication of most public servants and knew that it would be difficult to accomplish much without their support. He thus was worried that the campaign had created a great deal of distrust of the new governor by the very bureaucracy that would be needed to get things done.

   Because of the concerns East has about being able to work with the public service, which is covered under the state's comprehensive civil service system, he hires you as a consultant to help him devise a means of working with the bureaucracy and to have the governor's program carried out efficiently.

What advice do you give East about how to proceed? How do you gain the trust of the public service? What is the best way to implement the new governor's program?

4

Techniques of Personnel Administration

Various instruments, procedures, and techniques are used to carry out personnel functions. These activities represent the mainstream of traditional personnel management and remain important components of public personnel administration. Among the instruments are workforce planning, classification, compensation, recruitment, selection, promotion, evaluation, and discipline. Other concerns include reductions-in-force (RIFs), training and development, benefits management, and special issues such as job sharing, dual-career couples, and counseling and employee assistance programs. This chapter and Chapter 5 briefly review the contributions and challenges of each instrument, procedure, and technique.

Human Resources Planning

Planning has become a mainstay of public sector organizations, and human resource systems play an integral part in the planning process. Strategic planning, which focuses on how an organization relates to its environment, has emerged as a basic tool for government. Strategic planning requires an organization to identify its goals clearly and examine alternative means for achieving them. Then, after considering the internal and external environments, the organization chooses appropriate methods and establishes processes for accomplishing its goals. A major consideration must be the resources needed and available for the effort, among which human resources are a critical component.

Human resources planning (also referred to as *human capital planning*) is critical for agencies to understand what their human resources needs are and how they can attain those resources.[1] Thus, agencies need to assess what types of employees they need to accomplish their goals and objectives and then assess their workforces to see how they fit those needs. Thus, it is necessary to know what future needs are likely to be and what the labor market is like. Once human resources managers understand these things, they need to do some action planning to guide them in actually doing the things that will get them where they want to be. For example, if managers find that they are going to need highly skilled information technology specialists and that there is a shortage of them in their own workforces and in the labor market generally, the managers need to plan ways to overcome these shortages. The action plans can include ways to train their own workers to fill the need, or the plans can direct change in the recruitment approach, adapt the compensation packages, or restructure the jobs to attract suitable employees. The concept of strategic planning and management is to identify needs and to take action to meet those needs. Public human resources management traditionally did little long-range planning. Instead, it reacted to crises or just depended on the labor market to meet its needs. The traditional view was that there was appropriate labor in the market to meet the needs of the public employer. With the rapid changes in technology and occasional labor shortages, human resources managers have had to become much more proactive.

Contemporary concerns challenge employers to plan for large numbers of retirements from the public service. How to replace those retirees without interruption to organizational activities is a major concern. Some projections suggest that many public employers will lose as much as 50 percent of their workforces to retirement by 2010. The aging of the workforce and early retirement incentives are causing potential problems in keeping positions filled. On the other side of the coin, cutbacks in the late 1970s and again in the early 2000s have created the need for the opposite type of planning. How does an organization plan its reductions-in-force? Do employers use reverse seniority, or do they use performance criteria? These are the situations that call for careful planning.

Faced with the need to determine the wisest use of human capital, personnel professionals and line managers have had to engage in continuous human resource planning. In the planning process, they consider forecasts of personnel needs in terms of both the numbers and the knowledge and skills needed. In addition to personnel capacity, financial resources are critical. Depending on the availability of needed knowledge and skills in the labor market, planning for training and development is necessary. Planning for human resource development also is essential to ensure that the existing workforce remains up to date. In reality, human resource planning contributes to the effectiveness of all aspects of the personnel process. Without knowing the organization's personnel needs, managers cannot anticipate and plan for all the other decisions and processes associated with maintaining a competent and effective workforce.

Although the need for planning seems obvious, public managers often find it difficult to do. Of course, political and other considerations could constrain the amount of planning that can be done. Sudden shifts in political values or priorities also can destroy plans. During the 1960s and early 1970s, for example, government employment increased dramatically, especially at the state and local levels. As a result, continued growth and a need for more employees were expected. Most jurisdictions therefore were unprepared for the radical change that came with the tax revolts and the passage of tax reduction and limitation laws inspired by Proposition 13 in California in 1978. With financial resources suddenly and drastically reduced, governments had to start planning how to reduce payrolls rather than increase them. Similarly, the economic boom of the 1990s left state and local governments with surpluses, but by 2001 with the economy in distress, tax revenues dropped. Most state and local levels faced increasing demands for social services but dwindling revenues. Budget cuts led to cuts in human resources, and planning once again had to reverse directions to accommodate reductions-in-force yet maintain or increase service levels.

Workforce planning usually is not a priority for public managers when they have to face the daily demands of citizens and others interested in their activities. Indeed, planning of any kind in government is often difficult because of the lack of stability in tenure of elected officials; when elected leaders change, so do many of the system's priorities. Thus, plans can become obsolete very quickly. Government cutbacks have not produced significant evidence that planning is now a larger part of public personnel management than it had been.[2] Clearly, planning could be a significant aspect of all personnel management activities, but very few constituencies among public managers support much planning.

Position Classification

Position classification is a cornerstone of the traditional approach to personnel management and is still the basis on which most public personnel systems are built. In their efforts to make the system fair and just, civil service advocates need to be able to compare all jobs in an organization. Position classification provides that mechanism and helps managers determine the pay level of any position in accordance with its relative importance. The process describes the duties and responsibilities of each position in the organization and groups the positions into classes in accordance with their similarities.

The classification system's main objective is to permit management to make the most rational decisions about the relationship of duties and responsibilities to the other concerns of personnel administration. For instance, a fair compensation plan requires an understanding of the demands of each position, effective examination and recruiting require knowing what the agency is examining and recruiting for, and determining the qualifications necessary for performing a job requires understanding what the job entails. Position classification evolved as a convenient and useful tool and an extension of the Scientific Management School's focus on efficiency and economy; it offered a rational approach to organizing activities in a hierarchy resulting in efficient coordination.

The reaction to spoils and the creation of the Civil Service Commission in 1883 aided the development of position classification, which offered a method of making personnel decisions on the basis of objective considerations rather than personal and political factors. For the Civil Service Commission to establish practical examinations, it needed to have some idea of position duties and responsibilities. In addition, the chaotic federal pay system of the late nineteenth and early twentieth centuries led to pressure for reform. In democratic societies, equal pay for equal work is a readily accepted slogan, at least in the abstract. To apply the principle, positions must be evaluated and classified to establish a basis for comparison. Thus, the movement toward comprehensive position classification arose from the desire for equality and was reinforced by the increasing complexity of technology and specialization. The fact that the classification also facilitated management's task in managing positions and people enhanced its appeal.

Position classification originated in the United States and is used more extensively in this country than in other nations. Partly as a response to good government movements and partly from a concern for fairness and equity, the city of Chicago created position classification in 1909, and many state and local governments followed suit.[3] The national government initiated position classification in the federal service with the passage of the Classification Act of 1923. The Civil Service Commission acquired responsibility for the process in 1932, and the Classification Act of 1949 authorized the delegation of responsibility for classification to operating departments and agencies. The commission (now the Office of Personnel Management) retained monitoring authority to ensure uniformity in the process.

To develop the position classification system, it is necessary to perform a *job analysis,* the process of collecting information about the tasks a job requires to be performed and the knowledge, skills, and abilities necessary to perform those tasks. The analysis identifies the exact activities of the job and the conditions under which the job is performed. It also identifies the qualifications necessary for successful performance.

Job analysis is performed in various ways. The incumbent of the job could be asked to describe its duties and responsibilities. The employee could be asked to fill out a questionnaire, be interviewed by the job analyst, or both. A variation on this process is to ask the employee to keep a diary of her activities over a two- or three-week period. In this process, the incumbent employee has the opportunity to explain exactly what she does and how much time she typically spends on each activity. The employee also is asked to explain the level of independence and supervision involved in the job as well as dealings with other personnel, parts of the organization, or clientele. It is important to have the employee involved because she knows best the specific activities. However, sometimes the employee could think that particular activities are unimportant or exaggerate the importance of other activities. Thus, it is important to include the supervisor's views in the collection of information.

The same information can be collected from the incumbent's supervisor. The supervisor could review the employee's description of activities or be asked to explain independently what the subordinate does and what levels of independence and supervision she has. Similarly, the supervisor is asked to explain how the position or job fits with the rest of the organization. Again, this information can be collected through a questionnaire or interview or both. The supervisor's perspective is important, but supervisors are not always aware of some activities or the extent to which some activities dominate the job.

The job analyst can also directly observe the incumbent employee in performance of the duties, which is common in reclassification requests. Direct observation allows the analyst to see how the job actually is done and to gauge the relationship among the various tasks. It also has limitations, however, because the employee could be affected by the presence of the analyst and perform differently. Additionally, no employee is likely to perform all tasks of a job in a specified period of time. Some tasks come at particular times of the day, week, or year, so direct observation will miss some of them.

Job analysis can also involve collecting information from other organizations that perform the same functions and tasks. This is especially true when new agencies or departments are created. Reviewing how other jurisdictions and agencies do the same things can be helpful in understanding jobs.

Effective job analysis requires a combination of these approaches. By using all of them, the analyst can capitalize on the strengths of each and reduce the effects of the weaknesses of each. Relying on the varying techniques for collecting the information lends balance to the data.

The *position description* results from the job analysis. The position description is the basic building block of the position classification system. A position is described in terms of its duties, responsibilities, complexity, working conditions, and skills requirements, called *job factors*. Functions are divided into essential functions and other functions. In traditional position classification systems—variously called *whole job ranking* and *grade description*—positions are described according to the degree to which each factor is present. The rankings of positions within the system are then determined on the basis of the differences among positions. A panel of classifiers or a classification specialist in the personnel agency or operating department can make the rankings. Grades and classes are established to differentiate positions within similar groupings of positions. For example, word processor represents a class of positions and Word Processor I, Word Processor II, Word Processor III, and so on, represent grades within a class.

Another method of differentiating positions, the *point-factor comparison system,* relies on quantification. The same job factors can be used, but points are assigned to each factor in each job description. Then the points for each factor are weighted according to how dominant they are in the job, and the points for all factors totaled. The total points represent the point-factor comparisons for each position. The points then are used to distinguish among positions within a class or throughout the organization. The point-factor comparison method is attractive to those who believe that quantification reduces subjectivity. The problem is that subjectivity is only transferred; the subjectivity rests in the points assigned to each factor rather than in the decision about the relative place of the position in the organizational hierarchy. Nonetheless, using panels for rating factors helps validate the ranking system.

Whichever approach is used, the result is the position classification system. It is important that the operating agency or department be closely involved in the classification because it knows its unit's tasks best. However, it also is necessary to monitor the classification process to ensure that there are no abuses, especially to protect against overclassification.[4] For example, classification could inflate the importance of a position or unit to the organization. Supervisors and managers gain status according to the number and level of positions they supervise. Thus, they could have an incentive to upgrade the classification of their subordinates' positions to inflate the importance of the unit and their own jobs. Another problem is that people often become locked into a level of pay, and the only way to increase their pay is to upgrade their positions. Although the position classification is not supposed to be used for this purpose, frustrated managers often see no other way to reward good and loyal employees.

Regardless of the reasons for overclassification, the problem requires some form of remedial action. Central personnel offices generally monitor the classification process. In most cases, the positions can be reviewed at any time, but most audits are performed in response to an agency or employee request. Most personnel systems perform a periodic review. The typical approach is to review each agency's classification plan at regular intervals, but some systems review occupation groups across all agencies. Reviewing a complete plan aids the comparison of the different positions in an agency, and reviewing similar positions across departments helps standardize classes of positions. In reviewing occupational groups, the importance of any type of position can be exaggerated because it is the focus of evaluation, and its relationship to other positions often is neglected.

Monitoring position classification places personnel administrators in a difficult spot. The internal political considerations of agency behavior and the concerns of individual employees make downgrading a position classification particularly problematic.[5] Monitors who attempt to lower a classification are viewed as indifferent to the individual's welfare and as a threat to the agency manager's ability to control his operation. Moreover, the employee union or association is likely to become involved. Given the alignment of opposition to downgrading classifications, it is no surprise that classification auditors tread lightly.

Position classification comes under attack from many quarters and often represents the policing role that personnel agencies are perceived to play. Managers of operating departments often see the classification process as inhibiting them. Traditional personnel offices' attention to classification as an end in itself rather than as a support of management also leads to opposition. Similarly, the strategic planning process, with its focus on mission and goals, seems to be inconsistent with traditional position classification, which focuses on the position as the building block. The strategic planning process puts pressure on classification systems to be more flexible and to continually examine how the positions and classifications relate to the purpose for which the organization exists.

One attempt to deal with the tendency of department managers to want to overclassify positions is the *average grade approach.* In such a system, all positions in an organization are assigned points according to their class, grade, and salary level.[6] The sum of points for all positions in the organization then becomes a base for the organization. When an employee leaves a position, the points assigned to that position can be reallocated among other positions in the unit. Thus, a Data Entry Operator I may be assigned 3 points, a Data Entry Operator II, 7 points, and a Data Entry Operator III, 10 points. If a Data Entry Operator III resigns, the unit has 10 points to redistribute. There are several possibilities for this redistribution. Depending on financial resources available, a new Data Entry Operator I and a new Data Entry Operator II could be hired, or, the Data Entry Operator II could be promoted a grade, using 3 of the points, and then another II could be appointed, using the remaining 7 points. Of course, the department manager has other positions with other point values within the organization and could distribute the points among them. The advantage is that the manager has flexibility in recognizing contributions of employees and using the points to reward them and realign positions in the organization to adapt to its changing needs.

The position classification system described here also is known as the *rank-in-job approach* to organizing positions. An alternative is the *rank-in-person approach* that differentiates jobs on the basis of incumbent employees. The rank-in-person system uses the individual employee's abilities, credentials, and experience as the basis for making personnel decisions, particularly on compensation. Personnel decisions in this system tend to be more subjective than are those in rank-in-job systems. Moreover, subordinates find it difficult to accept comparisons with other employees when they cannot see the whole picture. The criteria for making decisions are much less clear than they are in the rank-in-job position classification approach. In contemporary results-oriented public administration, the rank-in-person approach is viewed as holding managers more accountable because they have to justify their personnel decisions based on outcomes. Employees do not always see it that way and fear favoritism.

Rank-in-person systems appear to be more appropriate for professional personnel who are accustomed to being evaluated on the basis of their expertise, education, and other credentials. The military, police and fire departments, and academic departments typically use rank-in-person systems. The rank goes with the individual regardless of what particular tasks she is doing.

In reality, the position classification (rank-in-job) and rank-in-person approaches tend to be combined. Conceiving of a position classification system in which the incumbent does not influence the classification is almost impossible. Some of the abuses of the system, such as overclassification, result from supervisors' consideration of the needs and qualities of the incumbent in the position. Each employee brings different capabilities to the position, and each can expand or contract the scope of its duties and responsibilities. The average grade approach is an example of intentionally mixing the two systems.

Critics of the traditional classification system abound.[7] The system is rigid, they contend, making it slow to adapt to the changing environment and changing personnel needs. In addition, critics say that money is wasted on maintaining and monitoring the system, depriving managers of the flexibility to deploy those resources where they can be used most effectively for the organization.

Broadbanding is an alternative to the traditional classification system that combines similar jobs at various levels into broader groupings called *bands*. In some systems, the groups are referred to as *job families*. Figure 4.1 is a recommendation by the National Academy of Public Administration (NAPA) resulting from its study of the national government classification system. NAPA recommended broadbanding the federal government's classification system of 459 occupational groupings into 22 categories in 10 occupational families.[8] The model shifts the focus from the work of the individuals to the work of the organization. The occupational families are grouped on the basis of similarities in "career progression, basic skills, recruitment, training, and performance management."[9] As Figure 4.1 indicates, the families are (1) Office Services, (2) General Support, (3) Technical, (4) Administration, (5) Analysis, (6) Engineering, (7) Sciences, (8) Health, (9) Law enforcement, and (10) Other. Within the families, agencies could adapt to the uniqueness of particular occupations by developing more specific series. The figure also demonstrates another feature, the fact that the bands cover broader pay ranges than typical position classes as discussed later. The broadbanding approach permits agency managers more flexibility in assigning specific tasks and managing the financial resources of the agency assigned to personnel functions. NAPA has continued to recommend reform in the classification system at the national level, but so far with little effect.[10]

Although alternative approaches continue to be suggested, position classification is likely to retain its hold on most public personnel systems. Most

Figure 4.1 Broadbanded Classification Model Overview

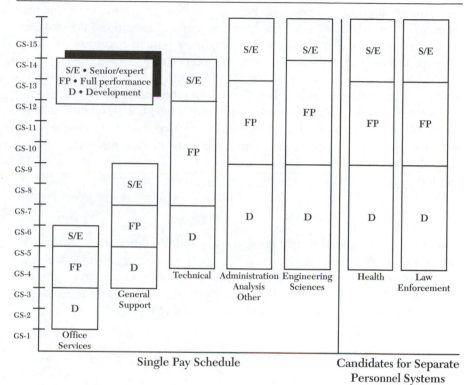

Source: National Academy of Public Administration, *Modernizing Federal Classification: An Opportunity for Excellence* (Washington, D.C.: NAPA, 1991), 45.

bureaucracies still are organized according to the traditional hierarchy, and position classification is a natural complement to that form of organization. Personnel administrators and department managers are likely to resist innovations that require less convenient criteria for making personnel decisions.

JOB DESIGN

Job design is the process of deciding how to structure the job factors that are included in a particular job. It is closely related to position description but is more than that. Position description merely explains what the position is. Job design is the actual creation of the content of the position. It is important to the discussion of classification because it can have an impact on the effectiveness of the whole system. Job design is particularly important to the interest and motivation that employees maintain in their jobs. Narrowly defined positions often become repetitive, boring, and demotivating. Effective job design can eliminate such problems by making a job challenging and giving employees as much discretion as possible. Recognizing that behavioral concerns such as employee needs, motivation, and environment are as important to job performance as are assigned duties, contemporary human resource managers attempt to incorporate these concerns into job design.

Consider an office responsible for monitoring the receipt of sales tax monies. If one position deals only with receiving monies, another with recording receipts, a third with checking records, and a fourth with follow-up investigations, employees are likely to become bored with their repetitive tasks. If, however, they are assigned to particular accounts and are responsible for all the activities associated with those accounts, they are likely to find their jobs more interesting and challenging.

QUALIFICATION STANDARDS

A direct result of the classification and job design processes is the development of qualification standards. These are the qualities an individual must possess to perform the duties and meet the responsibilities of a given position. Because qualification standards are pertinent to the recruitment process, they will be discussed more fully in our treatment of that topic.

Compensation

Compensation is the financial reward individuals receive for their work in an organization. It consists of direct salary and wages (pay) and benefits such as vacation, sick leave, retirement pension, and health insurance. In the public sector, compensation is always a major issue because taxpayers want to make sure that their tax money is not wasted. Public employee compensation represents a major expense to taxpayers and is an easy target when citizens become upset with government. Public managers are concerned with compensation because it affects their ability to recruit and retain employees and to influence employee behavior in the organization through the distribution of rewards. Employees are concerned for obvious reasons. Compensation, especially direct pay, becomes a sensitive issue if any of these groups perceives it to be unfairly distributed. Employee morale, in particular, is affected to the extent that employees believe that their pay is not equitable and appropriate.

As with all other features of the personnel system, a jurisdiction's basic policy normally establishes guidelines for compensation. For example, legislatures usually have the authority to set compensation. However, because they always are pressed for time and generally prefer not to get into the details of pay scales, legislatures usually delegate the authority to someone else, normally the civil service board or personnel agency. Thus, the executive branch commonly proposes compensation plans and makes recommendations to the legislative body for its final approval. Of course, in state and local governments that bargain over pay, compensation levels are established through negotiation between management and employee representatives.

Political leaders and citizens tend to focus on the costs of public personnel. Because personnel costs typically make up three quarters or more of government expenditures, it is easy to single out the public bureaucrat as the culprit in government spending. Given the image of the public bureaucracy, taxpayers are easily led by politicians who rail against the bureaucracy. In the past, public employees were perceived as underpaid compared to their counterparts in the private sector. Now, however, many public employees seem to fare well when compared with those in the private sector, especially if benefits are included in the comparison. Although top managers in the public sector lag far behind their private sector counterparts, employees in the middle and lower levels often do better than comparable employees in the private sector. There is great variation from jurisdiction to jurisdiction, with many trailing far behind the private sector and others paying their employees comparatively well.

COMPENSATION PLANS

Compensation or *pay plans* follow classification plans. As jobs are designed and organized, they are priced or put in the compensation plan. Using the differences established by describing and ranking positions, the pay plan establishes a pay rate on the basis of the position's classification. Theoretically, the resulting compensation plan reflects the relative value of positions to the organization. As explained later in this chapter, that assumption is not necessarily well founded.

The pay plan typically has several ranges and steps within ranges, as illustrated by Table 4.1. Positions are placed in a specified pay range or ranges. Specific placement depends on factors such as the skill levels, education, and experience required. Over time, with satisfactory performance, the employee moves up steps in the pay range. Differentials between ranges and between

Table 4.1 A Sample Compensation Plan (Monthly Pay)

Range	Step					
	1	2	3	4	5	6
PR1	$2000	$2100	$2205	$2315	$2430	$2551
PR2	2200	2310	2425	2546	2673	2806
PR3	2420	2541	2668	2801	2942	3088
PR4	2662	2795	3114	3269	3432	3603
PR5	2928	3047	3227	3388	3557	3734

steps within ranges normally are fixed at some percentage such as 3.5, 5.0, or 10.0 percent. Table 4.1 uses a 10.0 percent differential between ranges and a 5.0 percent differential between steps.

Once employees reach the maximum pay for a position, many jurisdictions provide longevity pay, called *loyalty pay* in some places. *Longevity pay* is a reward for employees who stay in a position for many years. They are valued by the organization because of their experience. Longevity pay provides an increase typically after five, ten, fifteen and more years. In some instances, the employee receives a bonus every year based on longevity. Employees must maintain satisfactory performance to receive longevity pay. Because public sector organizations have focused more on performance and results, longevity pay has decreased in popularity.

Most formal compensation plans tend to be inflexible and can lead to abuses. In particular, supervisors try to reclassify positions as a way to increase the pay of good employees who reach the top of their pay range and have no other way to receive increases. The problem is exacerbated by fiscal stress, which often precludes or leads to very small pay increases. Of course, promotions also lead to movement into new pay ranges for individual employees.

To overcome some of the problems associated with the inflexibility of pay plans that use the range and step system, some employers have experimented with pay banding.[11] As Figure 4.1 indicates, suggestions by NAPA provide a system in which most positions span multiple pay grades. Managers would have discretion in placing people at different stages in the pay band. Combined with effective performance reviews, this system could be used to pay individuals on the basis of performance as well.

The International Personnel Management Association (IPMA) and National Association of State Personnel Executives (NASPE) conducted a study during 2000–2001 of public sector pay and found that 45 percent of the respondents to their survey use some form of variable pay.[12] Thus, jurisdictions are not slavishly adhering to formal compensation plans. Instead, they are using pay for performance, skill-based pay, competency-based pay, and gainsharing. These approaches are explained later in this chapter as we consider adjusting pay. Numerous factors including comparability, collective bargaining, equity, and performance go into setting pay levels.

COMPARABILITY PAY

As noted previously, the pay for a particular position is based in part on the value of that position to the organization. Realistically, however, the labor market and collective bargaining also tend to play significant roles. The labor market plays its role through what is called *comparability pay* as well as through union bargaining strength. *Comparability* refers to the pay similar positions command in the relevant labor market. To determine the level of pay in the market, comparability studies are conducted. The federal government uses a very formal system that employs a nationwide survey to provide data for establishing appropriate pay rates in the General Schedule. Most levels of government use some form of comparability, but the sophistication of the systems varies greatly. Some conduct formal surveys, but commonly, Department of Labor data and review of pay plans in other jurisdictions serve as the basis for initially setting the pay and making decisions on the level of pay increases.

In some cases, especially in the federal government, comparability pay could reflect differences among regions. Different employees doing the same job in Eloy, Arizona, and Boston, Massachusetts, find that the same rate of pay has dramatically different buying power because of the differential in the cost of living in the two places. Therefore, with the Federal Employees Pay Comparability Act of 1990, the federal government adopted locality pay, which makes adjustments to compensate for the higher cost of living in some places. The Wage Board System for blue-collar workers in the federal government historically has employed local variations. Some large states also differentiate between large urban and rural areas.

Comparability also has the potential to bring more equity between the public and private sectors. The benefits for lower- and middle-level public employees in large jurisdictions generally have been better than those for their private sector counterparts although top-level managers in the private sector normally have many more benefits and perquisites than do comparable employees in the public sector. Past comparability studies excluded benefits from the comparability formula. By focusing only on direct salary and wages, public employees have generally improved their status relative to that of private sector employees because their salaries have become more comparable to private sector salaries and their better than private sector benefits packages have remained. However, these inequities have been disappearing because governments now include benefits in their comparability studies. Some critics suggest that comparability pay leads to never-ending increases in compensation costs.

COLLECTIVE BARGAINING

In organizations where collective bargaining exists, pay often is determined by negotiations. The federal government and many other jurisdictions preclude compensation from the formal bargaining process although pay certainly is discussed. Collective bargaining is used to establish pay for approximately two-thirds of public employees, as described in Chapter 8. In the collective bargaining process, prevailing wages for similar positions clearly are important to the negotiators. Other factors, such as the cost of living and availability of skills in the labor market, also affect the negotiations as does the relative political power of the parties to the negotiations.

ADJUSTMENT PAY

Adjustments to compensation usually are made on a regular basis. Employees usually expect annual increases, but there is no assurance that this will happen. In most jurisdictions the legislative body makes the basic policy decision on adjustments, but the details are left to administrators. Increases usually are across the board or based on merit or performance or a combination of the two. Increasingly, increments also are based on skills, competency, gainsharing, or other factors.[13]

Across-the-Board Adjustments. Across-the-board pay adjustments involve adding a certain percentage or fixed amount to the base pay of all employees. Such an adjustment often is called a *cost-of-living adjustment (COLA)* because it tends to be based at least in part on increases in the cost of living, but these adjustments usually fall short of the actual increases in cost of living. Across-the-board increases are easy to implement and require no discretion on the part of supervisors and managers in distributing pay increases. Generally, only employees with satisfactory performance are eligible for the increase. The downside of this system is that it does not recognize differences in the level of performance. Consequently, high performers can be demoralized by the fact that their pay increase is the same as that for employees who merely perform at the satisfactory level.

Merit/Performance Pay. *Merit pay* (often called *performance pay* or *pay-for-performance*) achieved prominence in the public sector during the 1990s. It has been used in many places but seldom lives up to expectations. Elected public officials tend to like the concept and often hail it in election campaigns as a way to make sure public employees are productive and accountable.

Although it is difficult to find people opposed to the concept of paying on the basis of merit or performance, there are serious problems with the system such as who is to define merit, what criteria are to be used, and how the merit money is to be distributed. Employees and especially their unions are concerned that if management determines the criteria and decides who will receive merit pay, the abuse of discretion is likely to lead to favoritism and inequity. Legitimate concerns often become politicized. Some jurisdictions' policies allow only half of the employees (or fewer) to receive merit increases; thus, inequities are inevitable. A unit with very productive employees would be penalized, because only a portion of its employees could receive merit increases while others in an unproductive unit could qualify for such increases. Good employees also become demoralized because merit money is not available every year and employees with very productive years do not receive the increase when there is no merit money. Obviously, the inequities result from the policy particulars, not from the concept itself. However, the mechanisms for implementing merit pay and the resistance to it by many employees have been problems.

Merit pay can come in the form of an adjustment to an individual's base pay or as a one-time bonus for high-level performance. When it is added to the base, it becomes a permanent reward for past performance and can be very costly because the employee's pay is permanently increased. The federal government and state and local governments use a one-time bonus. The advantages of the one-time bonus are that the merit pay is attached to a specific performance and for individuals to receive it again, they must continue to perform at a high level. Thus, if merit pay is supposed to be a motivator, the bonus or reward system seems to be the type of system that most closely ties pay to performance.

Research on merit pay and pay-for performance indicates that the concept retains strong support among governmental jurisdictions but has failed consistently to live up to expectations.[14] The reasons for the failure are many including the lack of adequate planning and design of systems, the lack of money to make rewards significant, and the difficulties in designing specific performance criteria to differentiate individuals. Pay-for-performance became prominent when most governments were experiencing fiscal stress and were forced to streamline and cut workforces; thus, morale was very fragile. As governments have continued to cut taxes and expenditures, the morale problems persist.

Gainsharing.   *Gainsharing* is another form of performance-based pay, but it is group based. Thus, members of high-performing groups share in the rewards, which generally come from the increased productivity of the group or the gains made from savings produced by the group's activities. Gainsharing is relatively rare in the public sector, but it is used in places such as Baltimore County, Maryland; Charlotte, North Carolina; and Virginia Beach, Virginia.

Skill-Based Pay.   *Skill-based pay* is another alternative that some organizations in the public sector have adopted.[15] In this system, pay increases are based on the level, breadth, and types of skills of employees. Thus, they are paid according to what they *can* do, not necessarily on the basis of what they *actually* do on a regular basis. Such an approach is most appropriate in a team-based work unit and when individuals are called on to deal with a wide range of tasks and engage in problem solving. In times of tight resources and taxpayer scrutiny of government, it is difficult to get legislative bodies to adopt skill-based pay. They are more interested in paying according to what employees actually do, however imperfect efforts are to measure what they do.

GENDER EQUITY IN PAY

A persistent problem in compensation is inequity in pay between jobs dominated by men and those dominated by women. Since the 1980s, efforts have been made to reduce these inequities. Often called comparable worth, the efforts have called attention to the value placed on different jobs and noted that discriminatory criteria often are incorporated into job evaluation systems.[16] As a result, classes of positions that are dominated by women or minorities usually are valued at a lower pay rate than those dominated by white males. From the time of the passage of the Equal Pay Act of 1963 until the early 1980s, the median salary for women hovered at around 60 percent of that for men. Pressure has been brought to bear on personnel systems to rectify discriminatory practices through legislative efforts, litigation, and collective bargaining with modest results. Today, on average, women earn approximately 75 percent of what men earn.[17]

The U.S. Supreme Court ruled in 1981 that the courts could not mandate comparable worth (equal pay for jobs of equal value) but that legislation could do so.[18] Legislative bodies in some jurisdictions, such as Colorado Springs, Colorado, and the state of Minnesota, have adopted comparable worth. In using this criterion to establish pay, a jurisdiction must determine the value of each type of position to the organization. Job analysis, as described earlier, is the process used for doing this, but discriminatory gender criteria must be purged from it.

Benefits

Employee benefits constitute an important part of the compensation of public employees. Benefits include those that are mandated by national or state law (Social Security, unemployment compensation, worker's compensation, family leave) and those that an employer may choose to provide, called *discretionary benefits* (health care coverage, vacation leave, dependent care, retirement pensions). These benefits usually are available to all the employees in an organization and represent a significant and increasing cost to employers. From 1929 to 2002, for example, benefits increased from representing 3 percent to representing more than 30 percent of total payroll for U.S. employers.

The public sector historically has had a more generous employee benefits package than has the private sector in part because it is easier politically to increase benefits than to increase pay.[19] Especially with retirement benefits, decision makers can put off paying until people actually retire; therefore, the current policy makers do not have to take much political heat for improving a benefit. The better benefits packages in the public sector often have been justified as being important in recruiting and retaining good employees, especially because pay in the public sector is often not as high as in the private sector.

MANDATED BENEFITS

Mandated benefits are provided to all employees (public and private sectors) because the federal government requires them. States may require some benefits for all employers in their states as well. Some of these benefits arose from the New Deal legislation of the 1920s. Social Security, for example, is a mandatory benefit including Medicare that provides pensions to retirees. Originally, state and local governments were not required to include their employees in the Social Security system, but a 1981 law requires that employees hired or rehired after March 31, 1986, be covered under Medicare. The law was changed in 1991 to require that any state and local government employees not covered by a public retirement system be included in Social Security. Every year, legislation is proposed in Congress to make Social Security mandatory for everyone, but the state and local officials have so far been successful in keeping it from passing.

As parts of the Social Security Act programs, worker's compensation and unemployment compensation also are mandated benefits. Employees who are unable to work because of job-related injuries are eligible for worker's compensation, which pays a portion of a disabled worker's wages and provides medical and rehabilitation benefits. Unemployment compensation provides benefits in the form of a fixed level of pay for employees who were laid off or quit their jobs under certain circumstances and are actively seeking work. Worker's compensation is funded through employer contributions, and unemployment compensation is funded by a combination of federal funds and employer contributions. Public employees are covered by both of these programs.

The Family and Medical Leave Act of 1993 (FMLA) established the newest mandated benefit. All employers with at least fifty employees must permit employees to take up to twelve weeks of unpaid family and medical leave during any twelve-month period. The leave may be used for the birth or adoption of a child, foster care placement, care of a family member, or one's own care. There has been much litigation concerning the appropriate circumstances for the leave. In what many hope will be a nationwide model, California adopted the first paid family leave in 2002 providing employees 55 percent of their pay for up to six weeks. The program is funded through a payroll tax paid by employees.

DISCRETIONARY BENEFITS

Public employers provide many different kinds of benefits at their own discretion. These optional benefits often are heralded as being important in attracting and retaining good employees. Almost universally, public employers grant vacation and sick leave. Commonly, they also allow for educational leave and reimburse employees for the cost of job-related courses and training programs. Day care services for children often are subsidized, and support for elder care programs increasingly has become an important benefit to employees with elderly parents or other relatives for whom they are responsible. Flexible work hours and job sharing are offered increasingly as incentives for employees to stay with an organization. Additionally, legal services are subsidized or provided in many benefits packages. The changing demographics of the workforce, especially the large presence of women with dependent care responsibilities, is changing the array of benefits needed and provided.

Health care benefits are among the most common discretionary benefits. They also are among the most costly with the costs rising at a very rapid rate. Because of the rising costs and importance of health care, the nation has been engaged in a debate about a national health care system for several decades. Many people support universal health care through either a nationalized system or the requirement that employers provide it for their employees (thus making it a mandated benefit). Neither is likely to occur soon, but changes related to health care are likely. Oregon voters, for example, considered universal coverage as state policy in 2002, although they voted against it. The irony is that as costs increase, many employers are either reducing or dropping coverage or increasing costs to the employee. Public employers also have experienced the rising costs. The result is that many public employers who previously paid all premiums for employee coverage now require employees to share part of the cost. Those who earlier shared costs are increasing the amount employees have to pay. Health care coverage has shifted from indemnity plans that give patients a choice in the selection of health care providers to health maintenance organizations (HMOs) and preferred provider organizations (PPOs) that limit the choice of providers. These plans also require patients to pay a fee (copayment) each time they visit a provider.

Typically, health care plans include a wide variety of coverages including physical health, medication, and hospitalization to maintain physical health and treat medical conditions. Gradually mental health coverage has been included, and dental benefits have become common. To stem increasing costs of coverage, many employers encourage preventive measures including physical examinations on a regular basis. Wellness programs to keep people healthy focus on nutrition, diet, nonsmoking, and exercise as well as stress reduction techniques that can help people avoid health problems.

Retirement benefits represent the other major benefit cost. Public employee retirement systems enroll some 18 million employees and have assets of more than a trillion dollars.[20] During the 1960s, public pension systems increased rapidly in numbers covered partly in response to the growth of collective bargaining and partly because pensions represented a benefit that public policy makers could grant while passing on the costs to future policy makers. During the late 1970s and 1980s, many of the systems experienced tremendous strain because they had not been prefunded but employees were retiring. Government generally responded by prefunding plans and establishing a two-tiered system in which new employees receive less generous benefits. Public pension systems became solvent and with the strong economy during the 1990s now have more than adequate funds. Ironically, the financial health of the systems have made them targets for raiding by governors and legislators to fund other programs as state and local resources took a major dip after 2001 and remained constrained through 2003.

One reason that government pension plans developed funding problems is that many were what is known as *defined benefits plans.* In these plans, the employee is guaranteed a specific benefit level (usually with cost-of-living adjustments) upon retirement, and public employees could often retire as early as age fifty-five. As people live longer and the cost of living increases, the cost of pensions often have outstripped the funds designated for them. Because most government pensions systems had been on a pay-as-you-go basis, operating budgets had to include funds for retirement pensions. Now most systems fund for the future, thus relieving some of the problem.

Increasingly, governments are using defined contribution systems, which are commonly provided by private industry. *Defined contribution plans* are those in which the employer and employee each contribute a specified amount, usually a specified percentage of the employee's pay, to an account in the individual employee's name. When the employee retires, the benefit is a function of what was placed in the account and how well the investment of funds has fared. Thus, the system is funded up front and pension fund managers are responsible for investing the money and managing the retirement systems.

ADAPTATION TO THE CHANGING WORKFORCE

Because the demographics of the workforce are changing constantly, public employee benefits programs adapt to these changes. Because the needs of all employees are not the same, flexible, or cafeteria-style, benefit plans are becoming more common. With flexible plans, employees can choose which benefits they want, although there usually are restrictions. For example, health services and retirement must be covered through the employee's benefits or a spouse's plan. In such a system, a fixed amount of money is set aside for each employee. The employee then can distribute the money across benefits most meaningful to him or her. Thus, one employee may choose child care services and another may choose to fund a legal services plan.

Domestic partnership policies emerged as a very controversial issue during the 1990s.[21] Eight states, California, Connecticut, Maine, New York, Oregon, Rhode Island, Vermont, and Washington, offered domestic partnership benefits in 2002.[22] Many municipalities also do so. After meeting the criteria established by the policy, unmarried domestic partners of employees are accorded the same benefits as are spouses of married employees. Some jurisdictions limit the domestic partnership benefits to same-sex couples on the basis that by law they cannot acquire the benefits that heterosexual couples can through marriage.

As health care has improved and people enjoy longer lives, elder care has become an increasingly important issue. As a result, employers face the increasing need to accommodate the requirements of those responsible for eldercare. Many employees have responsibility for both children and elder parents or other relatives. Called the "sandwich generation," these employees face particular challenges. To address their concerns, many employers develop benefits to allow time and resources for such care. The issue is particularly acute for women because they are more likely than men to have eldercare responsibilities.[23]

Strategies for Controlling Compensation Costs

In times of tight resources, public employers need to contain compensation costs. Several strategies are available, and most employers use a combination of them. The typical strategies include pay freezes, layoffs, attrition, privatization, and cutting the costs of benefits. Pay freezes usually are used as short-term measures and tend to be politically popular. The downside of pay freezes is that they create employee morale problems and often lead to higher recruitment and training costs as good employees leave for other opportunities. Layoffs also help in the short run and can help reduce costs quickly. *Attrition* means not filling positions as employees leave. Layoffs and attrition can lead to increased workloads and stress for employees who remain and to reduced morale and productivity. In the long run, all of these strategies could be counterproductive because of the problems they create.

Privatization (such as contracting for fire protection as many cities do) has been heralded by many as a way to increase efficiency and productivity of the public service by introducing business practices and strategies. The Reagan administration's Grace Commission on reducing the costs of government and increasing productivity and the reinventing government movement of the 1980s and early 1990s suggested privatization as one way to accomplish their goals. Similar efforts emerged in most state and large local governments. Privatization can reduce personnel costs initially and help the governmental jurisdiction avoid encumbering benefits costs, but there is scant evidence that long-run costs are reduced. New costs arise for the administration of privatized services in the form of preparing requests for proposals, handling the bidding and contract negotiations, and monitoring the contract after it is consummated.[24]

Cutting benefits costs has become the most recent approach to cutting compensation costs. As noted, benefits costs can be reduced by requiring increased employee contributions to the programs. Employees may be required to pay part of (or more of) their health care premiums and to pay larger copayments for services they access, thus reducing the cost of the contract for the employer. The Bureau of Labor Statistics reported in 2002 that the costs of benefits actually outstripped the increase in salaries with health care costs being the most significant part of the increase.[25] Small jurisdictions use consortia to help reduce costs. By joining a consortium, public employers can increase the number of employees for whom they bargain and thus enjoy some economies of scale to use as leverage in their negotiations with service providers. Consortia are used particularly for health care coverage, but the same principle applies to retirement systems as local jurisdictions join state-wide systems rather than form their own in many places. Another strategy to reduce benefits costs is to reduce the number of people eligible for benefits. Thus, increasingly, part-time employees are dropped from eligibility, and retired employees may no longer be covered under the health care plans. Retirement ages may be raised to help reduce retirement costs, at least in the short run. The opposite is true in providing incentives to retire early. The direct pay costs are reduced as long-time employees retire and are replaced by younger, lower-paid employees, but the savings may need to be shifted to the retirement system. Of course, if the system uses the defined contributions approach, the employer does not bear any increased costs for retirees.

Benefits costs also can be reduced by the use of two-tiered plans. In these plans, the generous benefits once given to employees may not be the same for new employees. The employer may reduce the level of benefits for newer employees and require them to participate more in paying for those benefits. Usually, this approach results from the legal principle that promises made to employees are considered contracts and it is difficult to change the terms of employment without sparking litigation. However, new employees can be hired under a different contract.

Summary

Position classification and compensation are two major processes in the management of human resources. *Position classification* defines jobs within an organization and organizes them according to the importance and lines of authority within it. Traditionally, classification focused on clearly defining each element of a job and then relating it to other positions. Position descriptions were very detailed, and the individual position class became the basis for many other functions within personnel administration. Classification helped to establish the value of each position, and the compensation plan became the way to differentiate pay among positions. Over time, the problems related to strict adherence to position classification have caused many organizations to change to a concept known as *broadbanding*. Broadbanding places positions in families and gives much flexibility to departmental managers in organizing the people in the organization within the job families. There also is flexibility in the levels of pay allowed the department manager in dealing with subordinates in the job families.

Compensation includes both direct pay and benefits. Levels of pay are important in competing with other employers, but benefits in the public sector traditionally have been generous and important in attracting employees. The increasing costs of benefits, especially health care coverage, developed as a major concern in the past decade. Thus, public employers have been under pressure to be creative in offering benefits to accommodate the needs of the changing workforce and in finding strategies for containing costs.

Once the classification and compensation systems are in place, jurisdictions can seek to find employees to fill positions. Chapter 5 deals with strategies for staffing the public service and for keeping the employees productive.

NOTES

1. M. M. Brown and R. G. Brown, "Strategic Planning for Human Resource Managers," in S. E. Condrey, ed., *Handbook of Human Resource Management in Government* (San Francisco: Jossey-Bass, 1998), 410–430; J. L. Perry, "Strategic Human Resource Management," *Review of Public Personnel Administration*, 13 (Fall 1993), 59–71; and J. E. Pynes, "Strategic Human Resource Management," in S. W. Hays and R. C. Kearney, eds., *Public Personnel Administration: Problems and Prospects*, 4th ed. (Upper Saddle River, N.J.: Prentice-Hall, 2003), 95–105.

2. A. T. Johnson, "Cutback Strategies and Public Personnel Management: An Analysis of Nine Maryland Counties," *Review of Public Personnel Management*, 3 (Fall 1982), 41–55.

3. Civil Service Assembly, *Position Classification in the Public Service.* (Chicago: Civil Service Assembly, 1941, reprinted in 1965 by the Public Personnel Association); and K. C. Naff, "Why Managers Hate Position Classification," in S. W. Hays and R. C. Kearney, eds., *Public Personnel Administration: Problems and Prospects*, 4th ed. (Upper Saddle River, N.J.: Prentice-Hall, 2003), 126–142.

4. M. Penner, "How Job-Based Classification Systems Promote Organizational Ineffectiveness," *Public Personnel Management*, 12 (Fall 1983), 268–276.

5. Naff, "Why Managers Hate Position Classification"; and G. A. Schulkind, "Monitoring Position Classification: Practical Problems and Possible Solutions," *Public Personnel Management*, 4 (January–February 1976), 32–37.

6. J. F. DeSanto, "Higher Pay for Good Performance—The Average Grade Approach," *Public Personnel Management*, 9 (1980), 282–284.

7. C. Ban, "The Navy Demonstration Project: An Experiment in Experimentation," in C. Ban and N. M. Riccucci, eds., *Public Personnel Management: Current Concerns, Future Challenges* (New York: Longman, 1991), 31–41; F. Cipola, "Time for the Classification System to Go," *Federal Times*, July 15, 1999, 15; National Academy of Public Administration, *Modernizing Federal Classification: An Opportunity for Excellence* (Washington, D.C.: National Academy of Public Administration, 1991); and F. J. Thompson, "Classification as Politics," in R. T. Golembiewski and M. Cohen, eds., *People in the Public Service* (Itasca, Ill.: Peacock Publishers, 1976).

8. National Academy of Public Administration, *Modernizing Federal Classification,* 1991.

9. Ibid., 44.

10. National Academy of Public Administration, *Modernizing Federal Classification: Operational Broadbanding Systems Alternatives* (Washington, D.C.: National Academy of Public Administration, 1995).

11. Ban, "The Navy Demonstration Project"; National Academy of Public Administration, *Modernizing Federal Classification,* 1991; H. Risher, "Are Public Employers Ready for a 'New Pay' Program?" *Public Personnel Management,* 28 (1999), 323–343.

12. M. Smith "Public Sector Compensation Strategies," *IPMA News,* August 2002, 7–8.

13. Fox Lawson & Associates, "Best Practices Survey Results—Changes in Pay Systems," *FLA Solutions,* 6, no. 3, 1–2; Smith, "Public Sector Compensation Strategies."

14. G. T. Gabris, "Merit Pay Mania," in S. E. Condrey, ed., *Handbook of Human Resource Management in Government* (San Francisco: Jossey-Bass, 1998), 627–657; D. K. Cohen and R. J. Murnane, "The Merits of Merit Pay," *The Public Interest,* 80 (1985), 3–30; P. W. Ingraham, "Of Pigs in Pokes and Policy Diffusion: Another Look at Pay for Performance," *Public Administration Review,* 53 (July–August 1993), 348–356; J. E. Kellough, "Employee Performance Appraisal and Pay for Performance in the Public Sector: A Critical Examination," in C. Ban and N. M. Riccucci, eds., *Public Personnel Management: Current Concerns, Future Challenges* (New York: Longman, 2002), 181–193; J. L. Perry, "Compensation, Merit Pay, and Motivation," in S. W. Hays and R. C. Kearney, eds., *Public Personnel Administration: Problems and Prospects,* 4th ed. (Upper Saddle River, N.J.: Prentice-Hall, 2003), 143–153; and G. B. Siegel, "Three Federal Demonstration Projects: Using Monetary Performance Awards," *Public Personnel Management,* 23 (Spring 1994), 153–165.

15. Fox Lawson and Associates, "Best Practices Survey Results"; R. Shareef, "Skill-Based Pay in the Public Sector: An Innovative Idea," *Review of Public Personnel Administration,* 14 (Summer 1994), 60–74.

16. R. D. Arvey, "Sex Bias in Job Evaluation Procedures," *Personnel Psychology,* 39 (Summer 1986), 315–335; E. Johansen, "Managing the Revolution: The Case of Comparable Worth," *Public Personnel Management,* 4 (Spring 1984), 14–27; and S. Neuse, "A Critical Perspective on the Comparable Worth Debate," *Review of Public Personnel Administration,* 3 (Fall 1982), 1–20.

17. M. E. Guy, "The Difference That Gender Makes," in S. W. Hays and R. C. Kearney, eds., *Public Personnel Administration: Problems and Prospects* (Upper Saddle River, N.J.: Prentice-Hall, 2003), 256–270; and National Organization for Women, *Facts about Pay Equity,* (Retrieved October 14, 2002, from http://www.now.org/issues/economic/factsheet.html).

18. *County of Washington v Gunther,* 452 U.S. 161 (1981).

19. N. J. Cayer, "Public Employee Benefits and the Changing Nature of the Workforce," in S. W. Hays and R. C. Kearney, eds., *Public Personnel Administration: Problems and Prospects* (Upper Saddle River, N.J.: Prentice-Hall, 2003), 167–179; and J. M. Rosow, "Public Sector Pay and Benefits," *Public Administration Review,* 36 (September–October 1976), 538–543.

20. B. T. Beam Jr., and J. J. McFadden, *Employee Benefits,* 6th ed. (Chicago: Dearborn Publishing, 2000); and J. J. Khavari, "Choices for a Secure Retirement," *American City and County,* 113 (1998), 41–42.

21. C. W. Gosset, "Domestic Partnership Benefits: Patterns in the Public Sector," *Review of Public Personnel Administration,* 14 (Winter 1994), 64–84; and "Lesbians and Gay Men in the Public-Sector Workforce," in C. Ban and N. M. Riccucci, eds., *Public Personnel Management: Current Concerns, Future Challenges* (New York: Longman, 2002), 95–112.

22. Human Rights Campaign, *Data on Domestic Partnership Policies. State of the Workforce* (Retrieved October 14, 2002, from http://www.hrc.org/publications/sow2002/snapshot.asp).

23. Guy, "The Difference that Gender Makes."

24. S. Fernandez, C. E. Lowman, and H. G. Rainey, "Privatization and Human Resources Management," in C. Ban and N. M. Riccucci, eds., *Public Personnel Management: Current Concerns, Future Challenges* (New York: Longman, 2002), 225–242.

25. U.S. Department of Labor, Bureau of Labor Statistics, *Employment Cost Index* (Retrieved October 14, 2002, from http://www.bls.gov/ncs/ect/home.htm).

SUGGESTED READINGS

Beam, B. T. Jr., and J. J. McFadden. *Employee Benefits,* 6th ed. Chicago: Dearborn Publishing, 2000.

Cayer, N. J. "Employee Benefits: From Health Care to Pensions." In S. E. Condrey, ed., *Handbook of Human Resource Management in Government.* San Francisco: Jossey-Bass, 658–675.

Center for Personnel Research. *Personnel Practices: Domestic Partners.* Alexandria, Va.: International Personnel Management Association, 1996.

Congressional Budget Office. *Changing the White Collar Jobs: Potential Management and Budgetary Impacts.* Washington, D.C.: Congressional Budget Office, 1991.

Epperson, L. L. "The Dynamics of Factor Comparison/Point Evaluation." *Public Personnel Management,* 4 (January–February 1975), 38–48.

H R Center. *Compensation Strategies in the Public Sector.* Alexandria, Va.: International Personnel Management Association, 2002.

_____. *Gainsharing/Goal Sharing.* Alexandria, Va.: International Personnel Management Association, 2002.

_____. *Pay for Performance: Focus on Organizational and Individual Improvement.* Alexandria, Va.: International Personnel Management Association, 2002.

Kelly, R. M., and J. Bayes, eds. *Comparable Worth, Pay Equity, and Public Policy.* Westport, Conn.: Greenwood Press, 1998.

Kettl, D. *Sharing Power: Public Governance and Private Markets.* Washington, D.C.: Brookings Institution Press, 1993.

Milkovich, G. T., and A. K. Wigdor, eds. *Pay for Performance: Evaluating Performance Appraisal and Merit Pay.* Washington, D.C.: National Academy Press, 1991.

National Academy of Public Administration. *Alternative Service Delivery: Improving the Efficiency and Effectiveness of Human Resources Services: Implementing Real Change in Human Resources Management.* Washington, D.C.: National Academy of Public Administration, 1997.

_____. *Modernizing Federal Classification: An Opportunity for Excellence.* Washington, D.C.: National Academy of Public Administration, 1991.

_____. *Modernizing Federal Classification: Operational Broadbanding Systems Alternatives.* Washington, D.C.: National Academy of Public Administration, 1995.

National Commission on Employment Policy. *Privatization and Public Employees: The Impact of City and County Contracting out on Government Workers.* Washington, D.C.: National Commission on Employment Policy.

Risher, H., and C. H. Fay, eds. *New Strategies for Public Pay.* San Francisco: Jossey-Bass, 1997.

Savas, E. *Privatization and Public-Private Partnerships.* New York: Chatham House, 2002.

Sclar, E.D. *You Don't Always Get What You Pay For: The Economics of Privatization.* Ithaca, N.Y.: Cornell University Press, 2002.

Siegel, G. B. *Public Employee Compensation and Its Role in Public Sector Strategic Management*. New York: Quorum, 1992.

SELECTED WEB SITES

Bureau of National Affairs (BNA). Publisher of reference products on personnel issues. Includes a section on employee benefits. www.bna.com

Employee Benefit Research Institute (EBRI). Nonprofit research and information dissemination organization on economic security and employee benefits. www.ebri.org

International Foundation of Employee Benefit Plans (IFEBF). Nonprofit membership organization devoted to education about benefits. www.ifebp.org

International Society of Certified Employee Benefit Specialists (ISCEBS). Organization devoted to information sharing and innovation on benefits administration. www.iscebs.org

National Association for Employee Recognition. Organization dedicated to enhanced employee performance through recognition. Shares information and sponsors conferences on strategies for and programs on recognition. www.recognition.org

U.S. Department of Labor, Bureau of Labor Statistics (BLS). Entity that publishes statistics on all aspects of labor including wages and salaries and benefits. www.bls.org

WorldatWork (formerly American Compensation Association). Nonprofit association focused on compensation, benefits, and rewards. Engages in publication of materials, networking, and certification programs. www.worldatwork.org

Exercises

1. Interview someone who works in a government job. Ask the individual to explain exactly what the job entails, focusing on specific duties. Also ask about responsibilities such as supervising others, independent decision making, and working with others in the organization. From your interview, write a job description. Then ask for a copy of the individual's position description and compare the two. What were your challenges in writing the description? What did you learn from the exercise?

2. Renee Porter has been the director of the Tech Shop for seven years and always has received excellent reviews for the shop's performance. She is very proud of her employees, who are all hard workers and take pride in their efforts. Rarely is there ever a complaint from the agencies that use the Tech Shop's services.

   Jeremy Perrill is one of the best employees at the Tech Shop. He has been a leader in keeping abreast of the latest developments in technology, especially information-processing equipment and software. He receives accolades on a regular basis from those to whom he provides services. His performance evaluations always have been the highest they can be. Porter has been concerned about losing Perrill because the organization's compensation policy does not allow her to reward him for his outstanding work. Instead, he gets the same pay increases that all other employees get.

In each of the past three years, Perrill has asked Porter to reclassify his position. Each time she has sent the request to the human resources department, and it has been denied. Perrill has requested a reclassification again. Porter is sympathetic to Perrill's request but believes it is a futile effort.

You are Renee Porter. What will you consider in deciding whether to make the request to human resources? Are there any other options? What will your final decision be, and why?

Assume that the request has been made and that you are the classification specialist from human resources assigned to this request. What will be your considerations in examining the request? Can you make any suggestions to Porter if you deny the request? If so, list and discuss them.

3. John Purcell spent twenty-five years as a police officer and retired with a full pension. During his years as a police officer, numerous disciplinary actions were taken against him. Each time they were minor enough to warrant no more than a day or two of suspension. He would go long periods with no disciplinary actions and then have two or three in a short period. The cycle was repeated throughout his career.

After three years of retirement, Purcell's colleagues were surprised to learn that he had been arrested with two others for holding up an armored car and making off with $1.5 million. As news of the arrest and Purcell's background became public, questions arose about his pension and whether he could continue to draw it after being arrested. State law allowed jurisdictions to withhold pensions in such cases and compensate the victims with those funds. However, no provision required such action.

It also was learned that Purcell's wife is unable to work and will be left without resources if the pension is taken away.

You are a benefits analyst for the pension fund and have been asked to make a recommendation to the pension board concerning whether Purcell's pension should be taken from him. What will you consider in making your recommendation? Explain the rationale for what you will consider and for the recommendation you ultimately will make.

4. Find a meeting of a legislative committee, city council, school board, county commission, or tribal council in which employee pay or benefits are on the agenda. Attend the meeting and listen to the discussion. What are the issues raised? Who participates in the discussion, and what arguments do the participants use to support their positions? What was decided? If you were voting on the issue, how would you vote? Why?

5

Staffing and Maintaining the Workforce

S taffing and maintaining the workforce in public agencies require methods for recruiting, examining, selecting, promoting, evaluating, and disciplining people so that an organization can do its work. Staffing and maintaining employees always have been a challenge for the public sector. The negative image of the public service and the inflexibility of some government personnel processes contribute to the difficulty. Until the 1970s, the processes for staffing and maintaining the workforce were fairly simple, but with the passage of the Equal Employment Opportunity Act of 1972, which brought state and local governments under the provisions of the Civil Rights Act of 1964, those processes became more complex. Over time, other legislation and policies added to the work of public personnel systems. The Americans with Disabilities Act (ADA) of 1990 established the most sweeping requirements for employers, including those in the public sector. As a result, every process in the personnel system is scrutinized for its impact on people with disabilities. Litigation based on these and other acts have complicated personnel processes as well.

Recruitment

Recruitment is the process by which an employer seeks qualified applicants for vacant or potentially vacant positions. In times of high unemployment, such as in the early 1990s and in 2002, attracting a large pool of qualified applicants posed no problems. During low-unemployment times as in the late 1990s, however, government must compete with private industry, and because of the image of the public service, it is not always easy for government to recruit. The issue will intensify as many jurisdictions face losing as much as 50 percent of their workforces by 2010 largely due to retirement. Government employees also take much abuse from elected officials, the media, and the general public. As a result, many qualified people would rather work for private industry where they are relatively insulated from such pressures. Nonetheless, many people prefer the excitement of the public spotlight and politics or have a strong commitment to public service. Generally, people in government service are as highly qualified as those in private industry. The problem lies in continuing to attract and retain highly qualified people.

Beginning in the 1970s, governments found themselves under different pressures in the recruitment process. With the passage of the Equal Employment Opportunity Act of 1972, state and local governments became subject to antidiscrimination legislation. As a result, public employers had to recruit women and minority group members for all types of government positions. Charges of discrimination could be brought against a jurisdiction by anyone who felt discriminated against in the personnel process. If the jurisdiction was found to use discriminatory practices, it could be required to make restitution to the individuals directly discriminated against and usually could be forced to develop a plan to eliminate future discrimination. Many federal grants contained stipulations permitting revocation if the jurisdictions did not follow equal employment opportunity policies.

Affirmative action is a process by which an employer makes positive efforts to recruit people representing groups underrepresented in the organization's workforce. Affirmative action plans became common features of personnel policies across the country as federal agencies often required such plans to establish eligibility for many grants and as monitoring agencies and courts ordered the development of such plans to reverse past discriminatory practices. However, the Reagan administration deemphasized affirmative action and equal opportunity during the 1980s, and the Supreme Court seemed to retreat on the issue as well; thus, state and local governments were under less pressure to maintain equal employment opportunity. Equal opportunity and affirmative action nonetheless attained enough acceptance that jurisdictions continued such efforts because it was the just and fair thing to do.

Compliance with legal requirements is still a major factor in many organizations' efforts to increase diversity of their workforces, and strategic organizations recognize that diversity has much value for them. Diversity initiatives give employers a competitive advantage in recruiting the best employees. Diverse organizations also relate better to their increasingly diverse communities. The globalization of society also demands increased diversity in organizations to be able to serve and interact with a widening array of cultures. As Audrey Mathews says: "The payback . . . will include employee retention, increased productivity, less absenteeism, better morale, an expanded market place and improved services rendered to customers."[1]

Even with the enforcement of equal employment opportunity policies, women and minority group members have had widely varying degrees of opportunities in state and local governments. They have been employed in increasing numbers, but the types of jobs and levels of positions attained suggest continuing patterns of discrimination.[2] ADA has led to additional reviews of processes to ensure nondiscrimination.[3]

Recruitment processes in themselves can be discriminatory because of the qualifications required for a position or because of the recruitment market. Public employers often exaggerate the credentials needed for a position because they believe that such requirements lead to a better quality of employee. This rationale has other implications, however. It could mean hiring an employee who is overqualified and will not be satisfied with the position. It also can prevent people who could do the job very well from being considered because they do not have the required credentials. This type of effort is often discriminatory because some groups have been systematically denied opportunity to gain certain credentials, whether educational or experiential. Equal employment opportunity policy prohibits using a qualification requirement unless it can be shown to be relevant to the position. Under ADA, qualification requirements must focus on essential job functions.

Some recent efforts to overcome discriminatory recruitment policies have included job sharing and the employment of dual-career couples. *Job sharing* permits an organization to hire two or more people to do what one person ordinarily would do. The job sharers work reduced hours and share one position. With this arrangement, the focus can be on accommodating people's unique scheduling problems (caring for children, for example) or dividing the position along the lines of the skills needed. Thus, if part of the job requires a specific highly developed skill, it is possible that one part-time employee will have that skill and that another, less skilled individual can be employed to provide the job's other functions.

Dual-career couples are another important element of the labor market. Often spouses have difficulty finding employment in their specializations in the same labor market, especially in small communities. Unless the couple live in a large urban area, chances are, for example, that two academics will have difficulty being employed in the same or even different fields. In the past, nepotism rules often prohibited married couples from being employed in the same organization. Increasingly, employers recognize that it could be to their advantage to make adjustments to accommodate the needs of such couples, including job sharing, in which the couple share one position. With two people in one position, the organization often is much more productive than it would be with one individual in that position. At the same time, the couple can pursue their professional interests together.

The recruitment process, if successful, results in a number of applicants who meet the minimum standards for a position. The next step is to select an applicant to hire. Selection is based on an assessment of the candidates' qualifications. Examinations provide one method for narrowing the field of applicants.

Examinations

Examinations were the mainstays of traditional public sector selection processes and continue to dominate in most jurisdictions. Ideally, an exam helps differentiate applicants on the basis of who is able to perform the job for which the exam is used. The exam can be either assembled or unassembled. An *unassembled exam* normally is an evaluation of an applicant's background, experience, and references. The information comes from the application and other documentation required in the application process, along with follow-ups on recommendations from former employers. These exams are most useful for managerial and professional positions, but many small jurisdictions without extensive resources also use them for most of their positions.

An *assembled exam* is employed more commonly, particularly in states and large local jurisdictions. At the federal level, the exam previously used for general entry-level recruitment (PACE, or the Professional and Administrative Careers Examination) was abandoned in 1982 after it was found to be discriminatory for entry-level positions. Office of Personnel Management (OPM) developed six different exams under the banner of Administrative Careers with America (ACWA) covering the following areas:

- Health, safety, and the environment
- Writing and public information
- Business, finance, and management
- Personnel, administration, and computers
- Benefits review, tax, and legal
- Law enforcement and investigation

ACWA proved to be unwieldy and required too much time, so most agencies now develop their own exams with assistance from OPM. Assembled exams usually are written but also can include oral interviews or problem-solving situations. In some cases, assessment center procedures are used: Applicants are placed in a highly structured situation and engage in some form of simulation exercise. Assembled exams also can require some type of performance test, such as taking shorthand or running a computer program. Many jurisdictions use combinations of any of these types of exams. The written exam commonly is used as a preliminary screening device followed by other exams as appropriate.

Ensuring that exams test the appropriate skills entails making sure they are valid. There is often a problem with regard to *relevance* (*validity*) of general knowledge on aptitude exams, although they frequently are used. There are three main types of validity: content, criterion, and construct.

Content validity means that an exam measures factors that are directly related to the duties and responsibilities of the position. Content validity is particularly useful in positions calling for a definable and measurable skill. For example, the content validity of word processing tests for word processors is easy to verify.

Criterion validity refers to whether an exam is a good predictor of performance on the job. Thus, employees are selected, and later their scores on the exam are compared with their performance evaluations or other criteria. Another way to test for criterion validity entails giving an exam to those already in these positions. If the exam is valid, those who score well on it should be successful employees whose performance is rated high by their superiors.

Construct validity is more difficult to achieve because it applies to tests that measure more elusive qualities, such as ability and flexibility. Construct validation is useful for managerial decision-making positions for which precise job content is difficult to establish.

The validity of examinations has become a major issue in the wake of equal employment opportunity. The Americans with Disabilities Act puts even more pressure on employers to ensure that exams measure factors that are relevant to performing the essential functions of a position. Furthermore, the ADA requires accommodation in the testing process so that persons with disabilities can compete for positions that they can perform. To make sure the personnel system is not discriminatory, employers must ensure that their examination procedures are valid. If examinations are found to have an adverse impact on persons with disabilities, minorities, and females, the courts can invalidate them. *Adverse impact* means that the members of such groups have a smaller chance of being selected than do others. According to federal guidelines, adverse impact is assumed if the selection rate for a protected group is less than 80 percent than the rate for the group with the greatest selection success. This selection rate is widely used, but the Supreme Court has demonstrated flexibility, indicating that the overall employment record and the particular content of the employer's actions should be considered in deciding such cases.[4] Although examinations must continue to meet the relevance criterion, it seems that the employer's total personnel system is being given increased consideration.

In the federal service, the trend since the early 1980s has been toward decentralizing the responsibility for testing potential employees. With agencies increasingly making hiring decisions, the trend is away from the use of written exams and toward promotion from within and the use of techniques such as provisional appointments and converting classified positions to exempt (not protected by civil service) status for which competitive rules do not apply.[5] Pressures for state and local decentralization of the hiring responsibility has also resulted in reforms allowing increased flexibility by agencies. Georgia, for example, permits almost complete freedom to agencies.

Selection

Most personnel offices certify applicants to the hiring unit after reviewing their applications and, when appropriate, exams. *Certified applicants* are candidates listed as eligible by the personnel office and from whom the employing unit can choose. In many jurisdictions, the *rule of three* is used, meaning that any of the top three applicants can be selected. Other jurisdictions allow choices of any one certified as eligible.

The purpose of certifying more than one applicant is to give flexibility to the hiring manager. Because of the fallibility of exams, few people rely on them exclusively. Moreover, some people do well on assembled exams but do not fit into the organization satisfactorily. Thus, a manager has the opportunity to make these judgments, but the decision rules often limit that discretion to the top candidates.

The rule of three and similar rules, however, can be unrealistic, because the interval between the administration of the exam and the certification usually is long. The top candidates often have already accepted other job offers, and the agency could be forced to go far down the list to find someone willing to accept the position. The scores also are often separated by very small differences, and differentiating among the candidates on the basis of fractions of points or even a few points is questionable, especially in jurisdictions in which exams are not regularly validated and updated. One solution is to group the examinees by natural breaking points in the scores and then select from those above the relevant breaking point.

Veterans' preference complicates the selection process. Veterans groups have been effective in persuading Congress and state legislators to enact veterans' preference as an easy way for a veteran to gain political support from an influential group. Traditionally, the federal service has given a bonus of five points to all veterans and a ten-point bonus to disabled veterans who pass the general competitive exam. Because the federal service has disbanded its general exam and allows individual departments to draw up their own exams, the regulations now apply to departmentally developed and administered exams. In some jurisdictions veterans get absolute preference; that is, they go to the top of the list if they receive a minimum passing score. The preference given to veterans thus can interfere with the appointing official's ability to select the best candidate because top scorers are pushed aside by veterans who receive bonus points. In more instances, veterans perform ably, but there is always a chance that more capable people are being turned away. The absolute preference system for disabled veterans used at some state and local levels and at the entry level in the federal service represents the most extreme problem. This inequity also is increased in some jurisdictions by giving the same preferences to the spouses and children of veterans.

Although veterans' preference laws have been under strong attack for many years, little change has been forthcoming. As part of the Civil Service Reform Act of 1978, President Carter attempted to reduce the preference and limit the time during which veterans could ask for preferential treatment. However, veterans' groups mobilized and mounted an effective lobby counter to the proposal. Ironically, instead of reducing preference, the legislation extended benefits to veterans with disabilities, allowing them appointments without competitive examinations and retention rights during reductions in force. Challenges to such policies at the state level have been taken to the courts. Helen Feeney challenged Massachusetts' absolute preference law, which put veterans who passed the exam ahead of anyone else. She had taken the civil service promotion exams three times during the twelve years she was employed by the state. Each time veterans were put ahead of her because of the absolute preference system. By a seven-to-two decision, the court upheld that state statute, noting that the law did not discriminate on the basis of gender, even though the veterans were almost always male.[6] Thus, any efforts to change such provisions have been directed to legislative bodies. The implications for public service go beyond equality because such preferential treatment remains an obstacle to women and thus to equal opportunity.

Selection procedures usually provide temporary or emergency appointments when competitive selection would be impossible. Ordinarily such appointments expire within a specific period of time. The time is provided so that examinations and other procedures can be prepared. However, if the position is a temporary one, personnel rules do not necessarily require competitive exams. Nonetheless, there is often abuse in using temporary appointments. Employers can use them to retain people who do not qualify for a permanent position. Some employers continually reappoint "temporary" employees, renewing the appointments each time they expire. The temporary employees thus become permanent employees for all intents and purposes. Of course, such employees easily can be intimidated by the threat that their appointments will not be renewed.

Selection may be made from within an agency, thus excluding outsiders from consideration. *Promotion* is the common method of filling positions from within and will be discussed later. Employee organizations often favor selection from within as a way to ensure employees an opportunity for advancement. Management could favor outside recruitment to bring in new ideas, but collective bargaining has tended to use selection from within.

Once an agency receives the list of those eligible for hire from the central personnel office, it follows procedures for making a final choice. An interview is common. The agency manager or supervisor can conduct the interview, or in some cases a panel of workers, supervisors, and managers do so. These interviews are very structured with the same questions being asked of all the candidates for the position to avoid discrimination. The equal employment office of the agency or jurisdiction should train interviewers to keep them from asking inappropriate questions that could give the appearance of discriminatory intent. Once the interviews are completed, the position supervisor or manager usually makes the final selection.

A final step in the selection process often is a probationary period during which the employee is observed on the job. A period of six months is the most common, but it can be as long as two years for some positions. During the probationary period, the employee can be terminated for any reason, and this sometimes leads to arbitrary decisions. If managers are well trained in its use and employ it correctly, the probationary period can lead to better selection decisions and provide an opportunity for on-the-job training.

Promotion

Promotion, which is a type of selection, provides an opportunity for employees to advance in the organization. Through promotion, they gain status in the organization and ordinarily improve their salary levels. Management also uses promotion to keep valuable employees and increase their input into the organization's activities. Ideally, promotions are based on the employee's merit and the organization's needs. As in all decisions in which human beings are involved, however, merit is not always the major consideration. Both management and employee organizations have an interest in the process and attempt to structure promotions to serve their interests. From management's perspective, merit is important, but so too is the employee's attitude and ability to work within the organization. Thus, promotion often is used to weed out those who challenge the organization's values and goals and to reward those who show the "proper" respect for the agency's policies and values.[7] Employee organizations such as unions usually prefer to use seniority as the basis for promotion because it is something that is easily quantifiable and leaves little to management's discretion. Promotion from within can be a motivator and morale builder for employees who see opportunity for advancement.

Promotions can hamper an organization, however, if they reward those who accept its perspective on everything. If promotions go to those who agree with management, new ideas are unlikely to be introduced, and the organization's service and productivity can suffer because its problems probably will not be resolved and new ways of doing things will not be considered. Protection of the status quo or accretion of more power could become more important than providing high-quality service to the public. To prevent such stagnation in organizations, open competition for positions by people inside and outside the organization can be used.

Except for seniority, the criteria for promotion are difficult to establish. Managers frequently promote an employee who has demonstrated good or outstanding performance in a specific job. Supervisory responsibility, however, requires skills different from those needed for the work supervised. As a result, employees often are promoted to supervisory positions for which they are not suited. Public sector agencies increasingly recognize the problem of unskilled supervisors and try to resolve it through the use of better selection processes. Assessment centers have become popular methods for evaluating employees' supervisory and managerial potential, but because they are very expensive, their use is limited. Another alternative is to have employees rated by selected associates. Because the raters are familiar with the organization and the job, the process is organization specific.

Performance Evaluation

Performance evaluation or appraisal is an essential yet difficult part of the personnel process. Performance evaluation serves different purposes, depending on whether it is viewed from the perspective of management or the employee.[8] Management or the organization is concerned about using performance evaluation to make decisions on retaining probationary employees, to improve performance, and to make decisions about compensation, training needs, promotion, and improving management. Viewed from the employee's perspective, however, performance evaluation assumes importance in regard to considerations of equity, employee growth and development, and participation and support of human resources in the organization. These sometimes conflicting perspectives can lead to a misunderstanding of the performance evaluation system and cause anxiety for the employee and the supervisor alike.[9]

The basic responsibility for performance evaluation rests with the supervisor or manager, although recent trends also have included the employee in the evaluation process. Employees' participation in the design and implementation of appraisal systems appears to increase their trust in those systems.[10] Employees often are asked to rate themselves on their performance and then discuss their evaluation with the supervisor and compare it with the supervisor's appraisal. In many cases, the employee actually sets goals and objectives with the supervisor and then is evaluated against them. The public sector has increasingly used 360-degree evaluation, in which feedback is obtained from supervisors, colleagues, clientele, and subordinates.[11] All information is used to arrive at a final evaluation.

Regardless of how evaluations are made, they tend to cause anxiety. Supervisors often have difficulty explaining exactly what is expected of their employees, and when evaluation time comes, the supervisors have difficulty measuring performance against what they see as the organization's goals. It usually is assumed that the supervisors' anxiety arises because they do not want to deliver bad news to an employee, but John Nalbandian found that supervisors are actually most uncomfortable with their subordinates' reactions to evaluation.[12] It is to be expected that employees will be defensive about their evaluations and that supervisors will be uncomfortable dealing with those reactions.

The tendency in recent years has been to formalize the evaluation process. Whereas in years past informal approaches with little record keeping sufficed, more documentation is required today. Thus, annual evaluations are common, with a formal report being kept in the employee's personnel file.

With increasing requirements from employee organizations, the law, and the courts that performance evaluation and other personnel functions be based on valid job-related criteria, supervisors must document the process and results to protect both the organization and the employee.[13]

Performance evaluations can take various forms, such as output measurements and examinations. Numerical ratings on various characteristics, such as punctuality, attitude, and ability to work with others, are common as are narrative or essay evaluations. Each of these approaches has numerous variations and negative and positive features. For example, output measurement can be effective in evaluating performance when an identifiable product is made but difficult when a service or policy is the output. Examinations are useful in measuring potential or capacity but can be ineffectual in judging actual performance.

Rating of employees on various qualities and narrative evaluations can be effective if these instruments are carefully constructed and properly used. The checkoff, or objective evaluation, assigns employees a score on qualities such as promptness, courtesy, writing ability, and initiative. The narrative approach permits supervisors to describe employees' strong and weak points. In some narrative evaluations, specific items must be discussed. These narrative evaluation techniques are not very popular because they are difficult to compare and there is little control of which qualities are evaluated. Rating people on specific qualities is easy and provides increased comparability among employees. Unfortunately, the qualities rated often have little relevance to performance, but relate to personal traits. Although personality factors could be important in some jobs, that is not the case for all or even most positions.

Governments have been shifting toward performance-based evaluation systems. The Civil Service Reform Act of 1978 requires each federal department to develop a performance-based appraisal system. Consistent with the strategic role of personnel management in organizations, performance appraisal increasingly ties performance to the organization's mission.

Several methods of evaluation incorporate elements of both the rating and the narrative approaches. The *critical incident* type of evaluation has the supervisor record specific behaviors of the employees that indicate good or poor performance and that contribute to the organization's mission. This method highlights performance-related activities and thus conforms to one of the major criteria necessary for effective evaluation. However, it tends to focus on behavioral extremes and thus may ignore overall, less visible aspects of performance that could say more about the employee's role in the organization. Thus, an employee who does well consistently but seldom does anything spectacular could be at a disadvantage.

The narrative approach has numerous variations. The supervisor could write an overall evaluation of the employee's performance or an explanation of the employee's most significant contribution to the organization and most serious weakness. This approach also can be used to describe an employee's specific factors such as quality of work, ability to get along with others, innovation, and potential for growth. As has been noted, these approaches usually are not good for comparing employees, but they offer flexibility and an opportunity for supervisors to stress individual contributions and provide a broader perspective on performance. One drawback is that supervisors vary in their ability to identify strengths and weaknesses and then write about them. The employee then benefits or suffers according to the supervisor's skills.

Forced-choice evaluation is another narrative approach that often is used when a limited number of a supervisor's subordinates can receive merit pay increases. In this method, a supervisor chooses a certain percentage of employees who deserve recognition for meritorious performance. This evaluation form usually forces the supervisor to develop specific criteria by which to evaluate the employees. It is not, however, an easy process to administer and can create morale problems.

In recent years many organizations have used group and peer appraisal. *Peer appraisal* employs any of the forms suggested previously but frequently requires a numerical rating on specific characteristics. It often also entails a simple list of individuals who should be considered good or poor workers. This method can offer illuminating perspectives on employee performance, although it can produce inflated evaluations.

In the *self-appraisal system,* employees examine their own performance relative to specified criteria. In most instances, they discuss their evaluations with the supervisor and set goals for the future. Employees tend to either over- or underestimate their contributions and cannot always see themselves in relation to the total organization; thus, their evaluations can be incorrect. Nonetheless, used in combination with other techniques, these systems can provide a useful examination of employee activities.

Performance evaluations can distort the importance of particular activities to the organization. For instance, when output is the major criterion on which employees are evaluated, it is not surprising that they neglect concerns such as coordination of effort and quality of output and focus on the activities that enable them to increase output.[14]

Perhaps the most significant problem with performance ratings is that they often are completed hurriedly and periodically. When the deadline for evaluations approaches, the supervisor does them quickly, often remembering only the exceptional or most recent occurrences. The result is a distorted view of the employee. An ongoing evaluation in which the supervisor discusses the strong and weak aspects of performance as they occur probably is the most effective approach. The employee can then make adjustments as needed rather than finding at the end of a year that she has not lived up to expectations. Adequate record keeping is also necessary. If an employee does not correct unsatisfactory performance over a reasonable period of time, disciplinary action is in order. Similarly, when an employee believes that he has been unfairly judged, a review process should be available. Most important, evaluations should have as their goal the best performance possible, and punishment to attain it should be a last resort. Typically, an evaluation interview concludes the appraisal process. This interview permits discussion of the strengths and weaknesses of employee performance and provides an opportunity to plan for improvement and set performance goals.

In recent years, performance evaluations have served to protect employees from capricious action by their superiors. A record of periodic evaluations makes it difficult for a supervisor suddenly to dismiss an employee who is out of favor. In the days when employees were not regularly evaluated, they could be told after a number of years of service that they did not meet the (often unspecified) standards of the agency. Similarly, a record of inadequate performance can be used as the basis for counseling, disciplining, and terminating employees.

Discipline

Disciplining employees is a major task of supervisors and the one they usually would rather avoid. If the organization has effective personnel policies in general, discipline should be needed only on rare occasions. Because of the spotlight in which the public service must operate, however, public employers often must judge their employees by higher standards of conduct than are used in the private sector. An effective discipline policy is clearly stated, clearly understood by employees, and uniformly applied. It also requires documentation of every action. If discipline is not timely, any delayed actions are likely to be ineffectual. In addition, unjust disciplinary actions are likely to be resented and destructive to morale. Once such actions are imposed, however, the employee should have access to an appeal process to review the action to provide protection against capricious action by supervisors.

The most commonly used forms of discipline are reprimands, suspensions with or without pay, demotion or other reassignment, and termination. Others used to a lesser degree include the loss of salary increases, seniority rights, and overtime work and the addition of demerits on the employee's personnel record. These forms of discipline once were used extensively but now are considered demeaning and not particularly productive. Reprimands, both oral and written, should be sufficient to correct most problems, particularly if there is good communication and mutual respect between the employee and the supervisor. The purpose of the reprimand should be to correct the employee's actions, not to embarrass or humiliate the person. The supervisor's training and personality are important in making this type of disciplinary action effective. A fumbling and inconsiderate use of reprimands can cause irreparable harm to employee-supervisor relations.

Suspension, demotion, and reassignment are more severe types of discipline. They should be used with care and only if reprimands are ineffective.

Suspension often leaves an employee with a loss of pay and can kindle hostility. Demotion and reassignment are appropriate when an employee has demonstrated the lack of ability in a particular position. The change of job ordinarily is made on the basis of more effectively utilizing the employee's capabilities. Using it as a disciplinary action is humiliating to employees and makes them resist the organization and its needs. Reassignment could result in sending incompetent employees to other units of the organization and thus weaken the organization as a whole.

   Termination is the most extreme form of discipline and should be used only after other efforts to correct the behavior in question have failed. Thus, the other forms of discipline normally have been applied, moving from least to the most severe, a process known as *progressive discipline*. At each step the employee is warned about the consequences of failure to correct the behavior in question. For some behaviors, such as theft, termination is the initial discipline; thus, progressive discipline does not apply in such instances. Once a decision to terminate is made, it normally is reviewed by the personnel and legal departments and by higher-level supervisors and/or managers before it is implemented. The employee usually is entitled to a pretermination hearing and can appeal the decision after it is made.

Grievances and Appeals

   When employees believe that they have been wronged, they must have available a fair and speedy system for examining and resolving their complaints. The system for resolving complaints in nonunionized settings is spelled out in personnel policies. In unionized settings, the system is spelled out in the negotiated bargaining agreement. Regardless of the system, the same general principles guide the grievance and appeals process.

   Most grievances and appeals deal with disciplinary actions, although they can apply to any personnel action the employee believes is inappropriate. Thus, employees also may appeal performance evaluations or pay increases.

   Grievance and appeals systems normally encourage informal complaint resolution. A subordinate is encouraged to try to work out the issue with the supervisor. If that does not work, the employee may appeal to the next level for relief. Depending on the type of complaint and the severity of penalty (if a discipline) issue, appeals may not go beyond a particular level in the organization. Appeals on a performance evaluation, for example, go no further than a department head in many organizations. However, a suspension can go all the way to the top executive officer such as the city manager. Terminations usually can be appealed to the top executive if they are not resolved at a lower level.

   For serious complaints such as appeals of termination, employees usually have recourse beyond the administrative hierarchy. Thus, they may appeal to a grievance board or appeals board. These boards sometimes have the power only to recommend a decision but in other cases have final authority to decide the issue, depending on the jurisdiction's policies. The appeals board holds a hearing in which each side presents its case before a decision is made.

In the unionized setting, the complaint is usually filed through the union representative or union steward. If the complaint is not resolved through discussion, it can be filed for formal grievance. Then a third party, either an arbitrator or a labor relations board, hears the case.

In situations involving charges of discrimination, the employee usually has the option to use the organization's normal grievance process or to go to the Equal Employment Opportunity Commission or a state or local government equivalent. The employee normally can use one or the other route but not both.

In the federal government, the Civil Service Reform Act (CSRA) of 1978 establishes the basic policy for appeals. For unionized employees, of course, the Federal Labor Relations Authority provides appellate opportunities under labor agreements. CSRA created the Merit Systems Protection Board (MSPB) to which employees of agencies without negotiated procedures may appeal adverse actions (removals, suspensions, reductions in grade or pay).

Employees normally may appeal to the courts if they are not satisfied with the appeals process results and have a justifiable issue. However, the courts are rarely a realistic alternative given the crowded court documents and the high cost of judicial relief. Nonetheless, the courts have been involved in ensuring due process in the grievance and appeals systems.

Managers often perceive the grievance process as an irritant that employees can use to buck the system, but the process has positive effects. One of the most important effects is that grievances often alert organizations to the need for better supervisory training. In addition, grievance procedures can help bring about solid collective bargaining procedures, correct detrimental agency practices, generate equitable methods of dealing with employees, ensure accountability, and lead to better morale and productivity.

Effective discipline is really self-discipline. A successful supervisor is one who considers discipline a form of teaching that coaches employees to perform in the most productive way possible.[15] When a problem arises, the supervisor is there to discuss the problem and suggest remedies. In the rare instances in which this approach does not work, the formal discipline process must be invoked.

Summary

To ensure adequate numbers of capable staff members, public service agencies must have a system in place for several staffing processes. In particular, it is necessary to recruit individuals to apply for positions. Historically, recruitment was a fairly simple process because the skills needed were not complicated. With the increasing complexity of government and technology, governments face the challenge of recruiting for a variety of skills; thus, the recruitment process has become more formal.

Selection procedures also have become more complex as instruments such as exams have been challenged for being inappropriate or discriminatory. Once selected, employees are given protection against discrimination in performance evaluation, promotion, and disciplinary actions. Because of various nondiscrimination laws and rules, the processes for administering the public personnel system have become highly formalized.

NOTES

1. A. Mathews, "Diversity: A Principle of Human Resource Management," *Public Personnel Management,* 27 (Summer 1998), 177.

2. M. E. Guy, "The Difference That Gender Makes," in S. W. Hays and R. C. Kearney, eds., *Public Personnel Administration: Problems and Prospects,* 4th ed. (Upper Saddle River, N.J.: Prentice-Hall, 2003), 256–270; M. Hale, "He Says, She Says: Gender and Worklife," *Public Administration Review,* 59 (September–October 1999), 410–424: and J. E. Kellough, "Equal Employment Opportunity and Affirmative Action in the Public Sector," in S. W. Hays and R. C. Kearney, eds., *Public Personnel Administration,* 209–224.

3. J. E. Kellough, "The Americans with Disabilities Act—A Note on Personnel Policy Impacts in State Government," *Public Personnel Management,* 29 (Summer 2000), 211–224; and G. M. Mani, "Disabled or Not Disabled: How Does the Americans with Disabilities Act Affect Employment Policies?" in S. W. Hays and R. C. Kearney, eds., *Public Personnel Administration: Problems and Prospects* (Upper Saddle River, N.J.: Prentice-Hall, 2003), 271–286.

4. *Albermarle Paper v Moody,* 422 U.S. 405 (1975); *Brunet v City of Columbus,* 58 F.2d 251 (1995); W. F. Cascio and H. Aguinis, "The Federal Uniform Guidelines on Employee Selection Procedures: An Update on Selected Issues," *Review of Public Personnel Administration,* 21 (Fall 2001), 200–218; *Connecticut v Teal,* 457 U.S. 440 (1982); C. Daniel, "Separating Law and Professional Practice from Politics," *Review of Public Personnel Administration,* 21 (Fall 2001), 175–184; A. I. E. Ewoh and J. S. Guseh, "The Status of the Uniform Guidelines on Employee Selection Procedures," *Review of Public Personnel Administration,* 21 (Fall 2001), 185–199; *Griggs v Duke Power Co.,* 401 U.S. 424 (1971); and *Washington (Mayor, D.C.) v Davis,* 426 U.S. 229 (1976).

5. C. Ban, "Hiring in the Federal Government: The Politics of Reform," in C. Ban and N. M. Riccucci, eds., *Public Personnel Management: Current Concerns, Future Challenges* (New York: Longman, 2002), 166–180.

6. *Personnel Administrator v Feeney,* 442 U.S. 256 (1979).

7. A. Downs, *Inside Bureaucracy* (Boston: Little, Brown, 1967); and C. Perrow, *Organizational Analysis: A Sociological View* (Belmont, Calif.: Brooks/Cole, 1970).

8. J. D. Cogburn, "Subordinate Appraisal of Managers: Lessons from a State Agency," *Review of Public Personnel Management,* 18 (Winter 1998), 68–79; P. M. Glendinning, "Performance Measurement: Pariah or Messiah?" *Public Personnel Management,* 31 (Summer 2002), 161–178; J. E. Kellough, "Employee Performance Appraisal and Pay for Performance in the Public Sector: A Critical Examination," in C. Ban and N. M. Riccucci, eds., *Public Personnel Management: Current Concerns, Future Challenges* (New York: Longman, 2002), 181–193; and G. E. Roberts, "Perspectives on Enduring and Emerging Issues in Performance Appraisal," *Public Personnel Management,* 27 (Fall 1998), 301–320.

9. J. S. Bowman, "Performance Appraisal: Varisimilitude Trumps Veracity," *Public Personnel Management*, 28 (Winter 1999), 557–576; D. McGregor, "An Uneasy Look at Performance Appraisal," *Harvard Business Review*, 35 (May–June 1957), 89–94; and D. S. Sherwin "The Job of Job Evaluation," *Harvard Business Review*, 35 (May–June 1957), 63–71.

10. B. P. Maroney and M. R. Buckly, "Does Research in Performance Appraisal Influence the Practice of Performance Appraisal? Apparently Not!" *Public Personnel Management*, 21 (Summer 1992), 185–196.

11. L. De Leon and A. J. Ewen, "Multi-Source Performance Appraisals: Employee Perceptions of Fairness," *Review of Public Personnel Administration*, 17 (Winter 1997), 22–36; M. Edwards and A. J. Ewen, *360 Degree Feedback: The Powerful New Model for Employee Appraisal and Performance Improvement* (New York: AMACOM Books, 1996); and D. M. Pollock and L. J. Pollock, "Using 360 Degree Feedback in Performance Appraisal," *Public Personnel Management*, 25 (Winter 1996), 507–528.

12. J. Nalbandian, "Performance Appraisal: If Only People Were Not Involved," *Public Administration Review*, 42 (May–June 1981), 392–396.

13. W. H. Holley and H. S. Field, "Performance Appraisal and the Law," *Labor Law Journal*, 26 (July 1975), 423–430; and D. H. Rosenbloom and M. Bailey, "What Every Public Personnel Manager Should Know about the Constitution," in S. W. Hays and R. C. Kearney, eds., *Public Personnel Administration: Problems and Prospects* (Upper Saddle River, N.J.: Prentice-Hall, 2003) 29–45.

14. P. Blau, *The Dynamics of Bureaucracy: A Study of Interpersonal Relationships in Two Government Agencies*, 2d ed. (Chicago: University of Chicago Press, 1963).

15. D. S. Lee and N. J. Cayer, *Supervision for Success in Government: A Practical Guide for First Line Supervisors* (San Francisco: Jossey-Bass, 1994).

SUGGESTED READINGS

Abramson, M. A., and N. W. Gradner, *Human Capital 2002.* Lanham, Md.: Rowman and Littlefield, 2002.

Condrey, S. E., and R. Maranto. *Radical Reform of the Civil Service.* New York: Lexington Books, 2001.

Daley, D. M. *Performance Appraisal in the Public Sector: Techniques and Applications.* Westport, Conn.: Quorum, 1992.

Edwards, M. R., and A. J. Ewen. *360 Degree Feedback: The Powerful New Model for Employee Assessment and Performance Improvement.* New York: AMACOM Books, 1996.

Gatewood, R. D., and H. S. Field. *Human Resource Selection.* Fort Worth, Tex.: Dryden Press, 1998.

HR Center. *Assessment Center Trends.* Alexandria, Va.: International Personnel Management Association, 2002.

_____. *Diversity in the Workplace.* Alexandria, Va.: International Personnel Management Association, 2000.

_____. *Recruitment Strategies.* Alexandria, Va.: International Personnel Management Association, 2001.

Light, P. *The New Public Service.* Washington, D.C.: Brookings Institution Press, 1999.

Murphy, K. R., and J. Cleveland. *Understanding Performance Appraisal: Social, Organizational, and Goal-Based Perspectives.* Thousand Oaks, Calif.: Sage, 1995.

Naff, K. C. *To Look Like America: Dismantling Barriers for Women and Minorities in Government.* Boulder, Colo.: Westview Press, 2001.

National Academy of Public Administration. *Entry Level Hiring and Development for the 21st Century: Professional and Administrative Positions.* Washington, D.C.: National Academy of Public Administration, 1999.

Rice, M., ed. *Diversity and Public Organization: Theory, Issues and Perspectives.* Dubuque, Iowa: Kendall/Hunt, 1996.

U.S. General Accounting Office. *Federal Hiring: Testing for Entry-Level Administrative Positions Falls Short of Expectations.* GAO/GGD-94-103, Washington, D.C.: 1994.

U.S. Merit Systems Protection Board. *Assessing Federal Job Seekers in a Delegated Examining Environment.* Washington, D.C.: U.S. Merit Systems Protection Board, 2001.

SELECTED WEB SITES

Bureau of National Affairs (BNA). Organization that publishes materials on all aspects of employment including federal laws and the rules and regulations implementing them. www.bna.com

Conference of Minority Public Administrators (COMPA). A section of the American Society for Public Administration (ASPA) sharing information and holding conferences on issues of concern to minority administrators in government. www.aspanet .org/sections/sectionpages/compa.html

Disability Info.gov. White House Web site featuring disability-related government resources, including employment related resources. www.disabilityinfo.gov

Human Rights Campaign. Organization that publishes reports on policies affecting employment of gays and lesbians. www.hrc.org

International Personnel Management Association Assessment Council (IPMAAC). A section within the International Personnel Management Association (IPMA) devoted to supporting professional development and publishing material concerning methodology of personnel assessment. www.ipmaac.org/

National Commission on the Public Service. Agency that studies and publishes reports on improving the public service, including how to attract the best talent. www.brookings .org/dybdocroot/volcker/commission

National Council on Disability. Advocacy organization for people with disabilities that publishes reports on their status. Also provides information and guides for accommodating people with disabilities in the workforce. www.ncd.gov

Section for Women in Public Administration (SWPA). Section of the American Society for Public Administration (ASPA) that shares information and provides networking on issues related to women in government. www.aspanet.org/sections/sectionpages/ swpa.html

U.S. Bureau of the Census. Agency that publishes statistics and reports on all aspects of U.S. society including labor force characteristics and government employment by various categories. www.census.gov

U.S. Department of Labor (DOL)
Bureau of Labor Statistics. Agency that publishes reports and statistics on all aspects of the labor force. Many focus on government. www.bls.gov
elaws Advisors. Web site containing interactive tools providing information about federal employment law. www.dol.gov/elaws

U.S. Equal Employment Opportunity Commission (EEOC). Agency that enforces nondiscriminatory and equal employment opportunity laws. Also publishes reports and statistics on the demographics of the labor force and government employment. www.eeoc.gov

U.S. General Accounting Office (GAO). Entity that publishes reports on government agencies, including their compliance with employment policies. www.gao.gov

U.S. Merit Systems Protection Board (MSPB). Organization that serves as the appeals board for federal government employees and issues regular reports on the federal merit systems. www.mspb.gov

Exercises

1. Jawana Jobe applied for a position as a police officer in the small town of High Mount. After taking the exam for police officers, she felt very optimistic but never got a call back for an interview. When she inquired about the results, she was told she had scored too high. She filed a suit alleging discrimination based on intelligence.

    The police department and city legal counsel explained that candidates who score too high on the exams tend not to be challenged by the work, become bored, and leave soon. The $25,000 spent on training at the police academy is a major cost for the city.

    You are a member of the jury in the case. How would you suggest that the jury decide? Explain why you take this position.

2. A father walks into his living room and finds his seventeen-year-old daughter and her seventeen-year-old boyfriend engaged in sexual intercourse. He slaps the boyfriend in addition to upbraiding both.

    The father is a veteran police officer who is now a sergeant. The incident comes to the attention of the police chief, who determines that the father's behavior constitutes conduct unbecoming a police officer. He suspends the father for fifteen days without pay. The father appeals to the personnel review board, saying he acted as any other father would.

    You are on the appeals board. What would you want to know? How would you vote? What public personnel issues does this situation illustrate?

3. Helen Wells was excited about having been called for an interview for a job as the liaison between the city planning department and the city council staff. The job also involved working with community-based groups interested in planning and zoning issues. Her interview was with Harry Jameson, the planning director. As the interview began, Jameson made small talk about the terrible weather and how it would be nice when it warmed up a bit. Then he turned to specific questions concerning Wells's potential employment by the city. He asked the following:

    1. Why do you think you are the person we should hire for the job?
    2. What skills do you have that would make you effective in performing the job's tasks?
    3. What is your political affiliation?
    4. When did you graduate from high school? College?
    5. Do you have small children?
    6. Have you ever been arrested?
    7. To what social and professional organizations do you belong?
    8. What is the general state of your health?
    9. How long have you lived in the city?

10. Are there any questions you would like to ask me?

After Wells asked a few questions about the planning department and its personnel policy, the interview ended and she left. She believed that the interview had gone well and that she had made a good impression. She had been uncomfortable with some of the questions she had found inappropriate. She had felt that she had to answer them, however, to have any chance of getting the job.

a. Was Wells overreacting? Explain.

b. Examine each question and indicate whether it is appropriate.

c. Even though a particular question could be inappropriate, is there legitimate information that it intended to elicit? How might the question be rephrased to get this legitimate information?

4. Jason Sanders worked for fourteen years for the City of Slippery Slope, where he advanced to a position as a division manager in the Parks and Library Department. He thoroughly enjoyed his job and colleagues. To supplement his income, he worked as a bartender in a neighborhood sports bar several nights a week. One day the bar owner asked Sanders to work a day shift two weeks later, and he agreed to do it. When the day came, Sanders called in sick to his city job and went to work at the bar.

During the day, another city employee who recognized Sanders came to the bar for lunch. He did not think much about seeing Sanders there, but later that afternoon happened to have a meeting with Sanders's supervisor and mentioned seeing him working at the bar.

When Sanders arrived at work the next day, he had a message telling him to report to his supervisor immediately. The supervisor told him that he was terminated immediately for conduct unbecoming a city employee and for defrauding the city by taking sick leave when he was not sick. The supervisor relayed information learned from the other city employee. Sanders was given a termination notice to sign indicating that he understood the action being taken and the reasons for it. He was also notified that he had the right to appeal to the Personnel Appeals Board.

You are a member of the Personnel Appeals Board. Sanders has asked the board to reinstate him with a three-day suspension after admitting that he violated city policy.

What would you want to know before you made a decision? How would the responses to what you want to know affect your decision? On the basis of the information provided, what would your decision probably be?

6

Keeping Employees Motivated and Productive

The ultimate test of the public service and its personnel system is performance. In recent years performance and its improvement have been of particular concern to public managers and citizens. Shrinking resources, inflation, and collective bargaining demands contribute to the need for top performance by public employees. This chapter examines the role of supervisors, motivation techniques, performance management, and training and development, all of which pertain to securing optimal performance. It also considers cutback management, reduction-in-force, and contracting out (privatization) as pressures on performance.

The Supervisor

Supervisors generally are considered the key to employee performance. Although some evidence suggests that supervision contributes little to the organization's productivity, it is still important in establishing the organization's smooth operation so that work can be accomplished.[1] Supervisors have a number of tasks related to the performance of those under them. They must see that the job gets done, keep work areas safe, encourage teamwork and cooperation, assist in developing employee skills, and maintain records. Because employees and work situations vary from agency to agency, the supervisory approaches must vary as well. Supervisors need training in their supervisory tasks if organizations are to avoid the pitfalls of the Peter principle, which states that "in a hierarchy, every employee tends to rise to his level of incompetence."[2] Performing well as a supervisor thus calls for many skills.

Henry Mintzberg has suggested three categories of roles for supervisors that encompass a total of ten roles.[3] The three categories are interpersonal, informational, and decisional. *Interpersonal roles* require the supervisor to be a leader, serve as a liaison for individual workers and groups, and handle symbolic and ceremonial activities. Each of these activities can help motivate workers to produce and take interest and pride in the organization.

The *informational role* involves monitoring and disseminating information and being a spokesperson for the organization. In each of these activities, the supervisor helps keep the organization productive by being aware of what is taking place and providing information to the appropriate people so that decisions can be made to maintain operations or change things when necessary.

In *decisional roles,* supervisors serve as entrepreneurs, disturbance handlers, negotiators, and resource allocators. Again, a successful supervisor must be adept in activities that help keep the organization functioning and changing as needed.

The supervisor's job requires dealing with widely varied employee needs and types. Some employees are motivated primarily by the money a job pays and work only to earn the resources needed to enjoy their desired standard of living. Such employees are not motivated by their work and need relatively structured supervision to be productive. Others are more concerned about being in a friendly workplace and enjoy the company of associates and are motivated by the organization's social norms and congeniality. Still others need to feel they have control over their careers and require significant independence to work within the constraints of their jobs. Assuming that they have the ability, these people can be given responsibility and are likely to respond favorably. Still other employees are motivated by the work itself. They are concerned with whether the work is socially meaningful or contributes to a goal to which they are committed. A particular challenge for the twenty-first century supervisor is that employees have different expectations of their work experiences.[4] Employees now anticipate changing jobs more frequently than in the past and expect employers to be flexible in accommodating their needs to a much greater extent than in the past. Supervisors face a challenge in motivating different generations of workers and workers with different personal circumstances.

In dealing with different employees, supervisors must realize that some employees need detailed instructions and others need a great deal of independence. Some need to be left alone, and others need to be stroked constantly. No two employees are exactly alike, and so supervisors must use various techniques to obtain performance from different people. Some of the resources needed for motivating employees are available to the supervisor, but others are outside her control. Certainly a supervisor can create a friendly, open, and authority-sharing work situation. However, the supervisor alone cannot determine monetary rewards, advancement, and the work situation; upper management usually has the final say in these and other matters.

The supervisor's approach depends on his knowledge of the employees and their needs. It also depends on the technology available and his authority to make changes. In addition, employee unions and organizations increasingly affect management's ability to use performance improvement techniques.

Thus, the role of the labor organization decides in part what will be done in the agency.

Approaches to Motivation

Because people are motivated by different factors, approaches to motivation must vary. Nonetheless, people generally are motivated by *extrinsic* (external) or *intrinsic* (internal) factors. Extrinsic rewards include pay and benefits; intrinsic rewards include satisfaction and psychological needs. In consideration of these factors, motivation theories usually take the form of needs theory, expectancy theory, and equity theory.

NEEDS THEORY

Needs theory posits that individuals are motivated by their needs, and every individual has different needs. Needs also vary over time for an individual. Perhaps the clearest expression of needs theory is Maslow's hierarchy of needs: physiological, safety, social, ego, and self-actualization.[5] The needs are listed in ascending order of complexity and importance. As one level of need is satisfied, it no longer motivates the individual.

- Physiological needs include food, clothing, and shelter. These needs are satisfied in the workplace primarily through compensation.
- Safety needs include security, shelter, and freedom from physical harm. The pay and benefits of a job help satisfy safety needs.
- Social needs include love, affection, and acceptance. Support from supervisors and managers provides part of the satisfaction of social needs, but informal organizations and interactions with co-workers are the primary satisfiers of social needs within an organization.
- Ego needs include a feeling of achievement, accomplishment, and self-worth. Workplaces help satisfy ego needs by offering recognition, respect, and status.
- Self-actualization needs involve the fulfillment and realization of one's potential. Self-actualization needs can be satisfied through increasing autonomy and independence in the work situation and through increasing levels of responsibility.

Approaches to motivation focus on different aspects of needs theory. Traditional theorists viewed human beings as primarily rational and motivated by economic needs. Furthermore, traditional theory based its techniques on the belief that people dislike work but do it to satisfy their material (physiological and safety) needs. According to this view, the way to increase their productivity was to raise employees' salaries. In the industrial sector, where productivity usually was more easily measured than in other sectors, the emphasis on material incentives led to the use of piece-rate forms of compensation in which an employee could earn more by producing more. Gradually, theorists learned that money motivates employees to a certain point but then loses value as an incentive.[6]

With the recognition that the appeal of monetary incentives was limited, attention turned to workers' physical environment. The Scientific Management School was at the forefront of this trend. This viewed the physical environment and monetary incentives as closely linked because morale could be improved by pleasant surroundings, thus leading to increased production, which in turn would lead to pay increases. Ironically, the concern with surroundings was responsible for the discovery of the importance of the human element in organization behavior. The well-known Hawthorne Studies at Western Electric were directed at finding the optimal physical conditions under which assembly line workers could produce. Experiments involving changing illumination levels and other aspects of the work environment led to the discovery that social and psychological factors are more important than are physical conditions in determining the level of productivity.[7]

The human relations approach to management, which focuses on people's social needs, grew out of the 1928 Hawthorne studies although Mary Parker Follett had suggested similar ideas earlier.[8] Creating a work situation in which employees believe that management cares about them is supposed to lead to increased productivity. Fostering interpersonal relationships and group dynamics became the fad in the immediate post–World War II era. Students of organization emphasized informal groups and norms in organizations and frequently ignored the formal structure.[9] Most studies in human relations concentrate on the way the requirements of the formal structure created unnatural specialization and led to the development of informal groups to overcome the tediousness of work. Little attention was given to the need for reevaluating the work process itself; managers were supposed to become the friends of workers. Industrial psychologists were employed to help design the optimum working conditions to foster increased efficiency and productivity. Such approaches led to charges that employees were being manipulated by human relations programs, and workers saw through managers whose interest was still in increasing productivity and who accomplished this using psychological rather than monetary means. Although the human relations approach certainly helped humanize the work situation, it still focused on the individual as a part of the organization's machinery.

One student of management, Chester I. Barnard, saw very early that the requirements of the individual and those of the organization had to be matched in some way.[10] Nonetheless, his focus was on motivating workers by means of effective management techniques and leadership qualities. For some time, leadership traits and styles were seen as the principal factors in gaining employees' cooperation. Particularly important were the styles of leadership used. Generally, it was concluded that the democratic style is most effective over the long run, authoritarian leadership can be effective over the short term, and laissez-faire leadership seems to be ineffective. Barnard combined his research on leadership with the reactions of employees to their leaders and was an early advocate of considering the personality of workers and managers as well as the psychological factors in workers' reactions to commands and directives. It was therefore a short step to studies on the relationship between human personality and organizations.

The organizational humanists, typified by Chris Argyris, tried to go beyond the manipulative approaches of human relations and identify the needs of individuals that affect their roles as members of organizations (ego and self-actualization needs).[11] In essence, Argyris claimed that organizations require submissive and dependent workers who do as they are told; the incongruity between personality and organizational needs increases the lower one is in the hierarchy. Argyris called for organizations to adapt to promote greater responsibility for their members.

Argyris argued that not all people react in the same way but that many needs of the mature human personality are inconsistent with the demands of organizations modeled on traditional principles, Robert Presthus, among others, pointed out that personalities differ in their adjustments to the needs of complex organizations.[12] Once the ground was broken, however, a whole new approach to maximizing individual potential was unleashed. People were no longer viewed as disliking their work per se but the way it was organized. People could be motivated to produce if they were permitted to develop themselves in the work situation. Behavioral scientists have built on these ideas to devise new approaches to human self-actualization in the workplace. The next section of this chapter summarizes some of their approaches.

The work of Presthus and others led to the recognition that different types of personalities are found at different levels of organizations. Those at the highest levels of management usually are concerned less with material rewards and the need to feel wanted by the organization than with recognition, prestige, titles, and the accumulation of the symbols of success. The relationship of the success of these persons in the organization to success or recognition in society as a whole can be much more of a driving force than it can be for those in the middle and lower levels of the bureaucracy.[13]

The behavioral approach stresses the notion that human beings enjoy and need work as much as they do recreation; therefore, ways should be found to permit employees to use their capacities to the fullest extent in the work situation. The key to effective organization became what Douglas McGregor called the *Theory Y form of organization*, which stressed people's independence, creative ability, intelligence, and willingness to perform what they view as useful tasks.[14] The realization that people do not hate work, are capable of making intelligent judgments, and are motivated to achieve objectives that they help determine has led to the advocacy by many of democratic, or participative, administration.

Behavioral scientists base their analysis on Maslow's hierarchy of needs. Frederick Herzberg suggested that most organizations do not actually build on these needs as motivators; instead, they tend to focus on "hygiene" factors—physical surroundings, status, and the like—which all members of an organization expect anyway.[15] Basing his analysis on the hierarchy of human needs, Herzberg recommended that organizations use positive growth factors as motivators because workers' motivation comes from things such as their own achievement, recognition, and increased responsibility.

EXPECTANCY THEORY

Expectancy theory is based on the idea that people expect some type of outcome from a given action or level of effort. For motivation purposes, the outcome should be a reward that is valued by the individual and results from the effort expended.[16] For managers, it is necessary to make clear linkages between effort and reward to produce motivation. Thus, employees must know exactly what is expected and what they will gain from the effort. For the expectations to motivate, the organization needs to fulfill the promised reward once the individual performs. Otherwise, the individual becomes demotivated.

EQUITY THEORY

For rewards to motivate, they also must be perceived by employees as being fair.[17] Fairness is judged on the basis of whether the reward is appropriate for the amount of effort needed to receive it. Employees also judge fairness on the basis of how the reward compares with that given to other employees. Thus, they look at other employees' levels of effort and rewards. If they are perceived as fair, the rewards can motivate, but if they are perceived as unfair, they can be demotivators.

Pay-for-performance, as discussed in Chapter 3, is an example of the use of expectancy theory. Presumably, employees will increase performance levels to earn merit/performance pay increases or bonuses. As noted in the earlier discussion, the public sector's use of pay-for-performance also usually illustrates the demotivating nature of ill-conceived use of expectancy theory. Because governments usually do not fund pay-for-performance systems adequately, employees do not realize the reward they expect for increased performance.

Motivation Techniques

Motivating employees involves using a variety of techniques, some specifically motivational in intent and others more generally concerned with humanizing and democratizing the organization. One of the most general and widely accepted behavioral conclusions is that employees are more committed and productive if they have an opportunity to participate in the organization's decisions, particularly those pertaining to the work situation.

The meaning of employee participation in the decision-making process is often vague but usually starts with the belief that individuals have the capacity and desire to assume responsibility. They are more likely to assume responsibility for achieving outcomes if they participate in deciding what the outcomes will be. Michael Smith suggests that participation also enhances the interpersonal, social, and political skills of employees, thus improving service as they interact with the public.[18] He also believes that participative management results in less resentment of those in authority, thus focusing more energy on the work to be done.

While arguments for participative management are strong, many factors also work against it. Managers are reluctant to give up their power and blur the status distinction between them and their subordinates. They also tend to try to protect the organization from the uncertainty that change brings by sticking to traditional ways of doing things.[19]

Vasu, Stewart, and Garson suggest other reasons for resistance to participative approaches.[20] They believe that traditional approaches survive because of the cozy relationship of bureaucracies to clientele and other stakeholders in the political environment. Because goals of public organizations are unclear and subject to constant change, evidence of participative management is difficult to demonstrate. Also, elected political leaders like to retain control over making policy and believe that bureaucracies are supposed to be implementing the policy, not making it.

The private sector more commonly uses participative management approaches, but many government bureaucracies do use them. Management by Objectives (MBO), for example, has been used by agencies at all levels of government. According to MBO, organization members participate in setting goals and choosing how to achieve them. It also involves participatory monitoring and evaluation of progress toward goals.[21] Most MBO in the public sector is a streamlined version focusing mostly on setting objectives. Strategic planning, now very common in government agencies, builds on basic MBO processes.

Job enrichment is a motivational technique suggested by many behavioral scientists. Job boredom seems to be a major problem in all sectors and levels of society, particularly among lower-level employees. By making the job interesting, management can increase employee commitment and motivation. Employees who have control over and responsibility for their work, see the results of their efforts, and have diversified duties are likely to identify with the job and take pride in doing it well: They also are likely to be more productive than those who perform a highly specialized task with no idea about the end product.[22] Although there are many advantages to job enrichment, managers find the principle difficult to apply because of their lack of understanding of the technique and unfounded fears of loss of status or role.

Other approaches to building organization capacity and engaging employees more fully include Organization Development (OD) and its variations. The focus in much of the literature is on adapting the organization to the changing environment and—particularly relevant to our considerations—to the changing needs of the people within the organization. The idea of OD is to break down the barriers to effective communication. The hope is that through self-awareness and the awareness of others and the organization's needs, all individuals in the organization will become more trusting of one another, more committed to the organization's goals, and more self-directed and responsible in attempting to solve organizational problems.[23] In general, this approach is based on the assumption that people will change their attitudes and behavior for the better in an open problem-solving atmosphere.

OD endeavors to help employees realize their full capacities. Many agencies use organization development techniques, but there often are limitations to its use in the public sector. Of primary concern are the political forces under which public agencies operate. Explaining the value of encounter sessions to a legislator who has received a complaint from a disgruntled employee is not easy. Few public administrators relish justifying the use of tax money for such purpose to a legislative body or to the general public; therefore, agencies are not always eager to adopt OD based programs. Because of the negative image of many organization development programs, there is an increased emphasis now on training seminars and in-house training programs in which people are asked to evaluate their organizations in open sessions in which personality factors are minimized. Still, there are problems with OD, particularly when the training sessions have little or no follow-up to continue the process.

Employees of organizations have varying values and attitudes that affect their motivation to work.[24] Some people have strong work ethics and cannot give anything less than their best effort while others are satisfied with doing the least that is necessary to get the job done. Many people have constant need of approval and ego stroking, and others desire autonomy and are motivated by their own achievements or the need to exercise responsibility. Others crave symbols of success such as titles, office accoutrements, or money. Managers need to use different approaches to motivate the various employees based on differing needs.

Managers must be adaptable and flexible in dealing with different employees. The task of accommodating differing needs of employees is a daunting one. Even if managers were capable of understanding what was important to each employee, they rarely have the capacity and resources to act on such information. There is no magic formula for success. However, research consistently suggests that managers who combine a rational goal orientation with a sincere concern and support for their employees tend to be most successful.

An addition to behavioral techniques in organizations is the quality movement, which uses many well-established behavioral principals. Total Quality Management (TQM) has been used successfully in Japan since the Japanese imported the idea from the United States shortly after World War II. After seeing its success in Japan, many U.S. companies reimported the concept during the 1970s, and the public sector experimented with it as well.

Total Quality Management focuses on improving and maintaining quality throughout the organization. The ultimate focus is on high-quality service to the customer whether the customer is external or internal to the organization. To achieve quality, processes are instituted to identify practices throughout the work of the organization that lead to errors or defects. The goal is zero defects. Catching and correcting errors as they occur enhances the quality of the end product or service. Money is saved because defective products and services should not occur, thus saving the cost of replacing them. It is less costly to correct early in the process than to go back after the fact. TQM relates to motivation by involving everyone in the organization in the analysis of work processes and efforts to improve them.

Team building is a part of TQM and represents another approach to improving employee performance. Because it deals less with individual motivation and more with the productivity of a work group or unit, team building is discussed later in this chapter.

Performance Management

Performance management encompasses numerous activities to improve the efficiency and effectiveness of organizations. Built on strategic management concepts and practices, performance management requires clarifying agency goals and adopting the actions that will achieve them. It also requires development of credible performance data to measure achievement.[25] Performance management relies on all aspects of performance, both individual and organizational. It also serves as a tool for holding organizations and management accountable.

The various incentives and behavioral techniques discussed in association with motivation are aspects of individual performance management strategies that organizations can use. Pay-for-performance and gainsharing are efforts focused on improving performance. The productivity improvement programs of the 1970s also were attempts at improving both individual and organizational performance.[26]

In the 1980s, New Public Management with an emphasis on reinventing government focused on improving government performance. Generally, it emphasized adapting private sector approaches to a market model. As a result, privatization of many government activities took place. Efficiency became the key with suggestions that government could be run like a business. Citizens were viewed as customers. The National Performance Review of the Clinton administration embodied many of the principles of reinvention and focused on making government work better while using fewer resources.[27]

Many critics of the New Public Management claim that the approach focuses on efficiency to the detriment of public service to the citizens.[28] Denhardt and Denhardt identify a different approach called "The New Public Service," the major themes of which follow:

1. Serve rather than steer—help citizens articulate and meet their shared interests.
2. Make public interest the aim, not the by-product.
3. Think strategically; act democratically.
4. Serve citizens, not customers.
5. Recognize that accountability is not simple.
6. Value people, not productivity.
7. Value citizenship and public service above entrepreneurship.[29]

These themes suggest that performance management for the public service is measured not by efficiency but by how well citizens are served including the service of the democratic values on which the system is based. Noting that accountability is not simple, Denhardt and Denhardt recognize the complexity of measuring performance according to these values.

Most government jurisdictions now use total performance measurement to cope with some of the complexities of performance management.[30] This approach uses a performance audit to examine productivity data, along with other information, to evaluate overall performance and improve productivity. Employees, clientele, and citizens can be surveyed to determine whether the organization is perceived as being productive and whether its service is effective and useful. Data on performance provided by agencies also are evaluated. Feedback to employees and managers is a central aspect of performance management. Such feedback permits everyone to understand what needs to change and encourages participation in making the changes. Performance management requires the systematic collection and reporting of data.

TRAINING AND DEVELOPMENT

In the past, governments assumed that they could acquire personnel in the labor market with the requisite skills and abilities; therefore, the training and development of public employees were not considered a high priority. However, rapid change in technology, the need for employees to constantly learn and improve, and the effects of diversity, among other factors, have required government employers to provide training and development programs.

Even truer today than in 1993 when Paul Sandwith said it, "The triple threat of most organizations today . . . are the simultaneous demands for improved quality, reduced costs, and constant innovation."[31] To meet these demands, training and development (also known as *human resource development*) are critical elements of human resources systems.[32] The recognition of the need for human resource development (HRD) stems from actions of the federal government, which passed the Government Employees Training Act in 1958 requiring federal agencies to create programs, and the Intergovernmental Personnel Act (IPA) of 1970, which funded many programs for state and local government training and development. Since the elimination of IPA during the Reagan administration, state and local governments have assumed the responsibility for HRD themselves.

When instituting a training and development program, the personnel agency and operating department usually work together, although in some government units this function is separate from the personnel agency. The personnel agency or HRD unit can provide expertise and advice, but the operating department is usually in the best position to determine the actual training need. A centralized training agency usually has the needs-assessment capabilities as well as the training competence. Many training and development programs use both central agency and operating department people and facilities.

The most elementary training program is a new-employee orientation program that can have a significant impact on behavior and productivity. Traditionally, agencies have spent a short time introducing new employees and explaining the rules, regulations, and benefits of the job. Now the orientation process often stretches over a longer period—depending on the job, of course—and employees are encouraged to discuss their problems in adjusting to and learning their duties. They also learn what resources the employer offers them to adjust to and succeed in the agency.

On-the-job training is another approach. In this case an individual without the needed skills is hired and learns the job from another employee. Often the person serves an apprenticeship. Such training also can be used to help employees move up in their organization by learning new skills.

It has become common to encourage individual employee development through a variety of programs inside and outside the organization. These programs take the form of workshops, institutes, professional conferences, university and college programs, tuition reimbursement, and sabbaticals. The national government has sponsored such programs for a long time and permits state and local government employees to participate in many of the federal programs. State and local governments also have created their own programs along the same lines.

As training and development have evolved, HRD professionals have come to recognize that different needs arise from different groups in organizations; thus, employees, supervisors, managers, and executives all have differing needs in regard to training and development programs. Consequently, these programs are specialized to focus on technical, interpersonal, or conceptual skills. While all employees need each of these types of programs, the level of need for each varies with the type of role the individual plays in the organization. Other individual variations require different approaches. For example, many employees become plateaued in the organization, meaning that they reach a level beyond which they cannot advance. Especially in today's environment in which organizational hierarchies are flat and downsizing is common, opportunities for promotion are reduced greatly. Plateaued employees need special attention if they are to remain contributing members of the organization. As with all employees, each plateaued employee will have a different reaction to the situation.

In addition to different substantive content, training and development programs employ different methods to deliver the material. Since training and development programs in the public service serve adults, they must be sensitive to how adults learn and recognize that everyone has a different learning style. Traditional lecture methods tend to be ineffective. Successful HRD programs require combinations of lecture, discussion, role-playing, and problem-solving approaches. Interactive learning increases the likelihood of comprehension and retention of the program content.

Not surprising, the national government has been a leader in many types of training programs. The Office of Personnel Management (OPM) sponsors a variety of programs and has training centers in each of its regions. Although the regional centers are primarily for middle- and upper-level federal officials, state and local personnel also can be accepted on a space-available basis. Executive Seminar Centers in various parts of the country provide opportunities for intensive programs for management personnel. The Federal Executive Institute at Charlottesville, Virginia, offers small, intensive courses for high-level administrators and demonstrates the OPM's commitment to excellence in the public service. In addition to these programs, individual departments and agencies conduct their own training and development activities.

Although state and local governments were slow to follow the national government's lead, most now have established some sort of ongoing training and development program. The Intergovernmental Personnel Act of 1970 provided the seed money for many training and development activities and demonstrated their value. Of course, training and development programs often fall victim to budget cuts, and when finances are limited, these programs suffer. Nonetheless, training and development have been recognized as essential efforts in the public service at all levels of government. The national government now mandates training for all federal employees, and many state and local governments are doing the same.

Mobility programs train employees in a broad area of activities. In the national government, for example, the Senior Executive Service (SES) is an example of a mobility program. Although its emphasis is not on training, it permits those selected to be exposed to a large part of the federal bureaucracy and thus broaden their skills and knowledge. Mobility programs were a significant part of Intergovernmental Personnel Act programs. Employees of state and local governments would often take temporary assignments in the federal bureaucracy, and federal governmental employees would do the same in state and local governments. Universities also participated in the program. Now individual federal government agencies maintain similar efforts, and the private sector sometimes becomes involved. For example, in Arizona, members of the private sector occasionally spend a specified period of time working with a public sector agency. Similarly, Arizona State University and the City of Phoenix have a loaned executive program in which a faculty member spends a year with the city and a city executive spends the year at the university. These programs help employees learn about the other organizations they deal with and offer opportunities to employees to develop new skills and expertise that can be important to their agencies. The participating organizations also benefit from the new perspectives of the people they host.

Another type of training aimed at new and prospective employees is the internship. Many institutions of higher education require public service internships as part of their undergraduate and graduate programs in public administration. Other disciplines have their own internships. Students gain experience in the practical application of what they learn in the classroom. The internship requires willingness on the part of government agencies to budget money for them and supervise the interns they host. Of course, the agencies benefit along with the student if the internship is carefully planned and executed. The Presidential Management Internship at the national level is an example of a major internship program that recruits top students from across the country to spend two years with a federal agency with the expectation that the interns will become permanent employees. Several states, including New York, Texas, and Montana, have copied this program. Dallas, Long Beach, Phoenix, and the Metropolitan Dade County government have similar programs at the local level.

Apprenticeship training is another type of training that the public sector sometimes uses. While it is common in many types of private organizations, apprenticeship training exists to a lesser extent in the public sector. This type of training combines classroom instruction with on-the-job training and normally is used in skilled crafts or trades. The U.S. Department of Defense is the largest public sector user of apprenticeship training. State and local governments use the approach mostly for fire fighters, correctional officers, and police officers, although some use it for occupations such as electricians and secretaries.

Training is costly, and the costs lead to controversy over whether it should be undertaken. The organization's long-term costs of not undertaking training may be greater than the programs themselves, however, and most governments have recognized the value of such programs. Strong support from the top political leadership is critical to getting an agency to buy in to training and development and help fend off efforts to cut programs. In this ever-changing society, a lack of training leads to employees with outmoded skills who are likely to become frustrated by the lack of growth opportunity. The end result is turnover and a need to recruit new employees, which is a costly process.

PERFORMANCE UNDER FISCAL CONSTRAINTS

Fiscal constraints are facts of life for government at all levels. Tax revolts and other spending limitations became popular nationwide in the late 1970s and continue to the present, necessitating cutback management in government. To deal with these pressures, governments have looked to the personnel function as a major concern because personnel costs are the single most expensive part of governments' operating costs. Cutback management creates many uncertainties and faces resistance from employees, their unions, interest groups, and agency managers. Attempting to accommodate the varying interests of these actors in the process and satisfy the demands of the public and politically elected officials places the personnel function in a difficult position. Reductions-in-force (RIF) and contracting out for public services are two major strategies used in cutback management.

When faced with cutbacks in funds, most governmental units attempt to achieve some form of reduction in the workforce. RIF can be accomplished through layoffs or attrition. *Layoffs* mean that positions are identified as dispensable according to criteria on which the unit agrees; *attrition* means that positions are eliminated or not filled as incumbents leave them for any reason. Each method of achieving a RIF leads to both positive and negative results for the organization.

Layoffs have the advantage of permitting an agency to reduce the size of its personnel force quickly and in the positions it identifies as dispensable. Thus, if conducted with a clear evaluation of an agency's needs and resources, layoffs can lead to a streamlined agency that is better able to use the skills and expertise of the employees it retains. Unfortunately, the task is not as easy as it sounds. Establishing the criteria for layoffs can be a very controversial process. Usually, employee unions want the decision rule for layoffs to be seniority, whereas management normally wants a criterion such as performance or contribution to the organization's needs. If the criteria depend on the evaluation of performance or the like, uncertainty is likely to develop among the employees, causing morale problems. Along with the loss of morale and the employees' insecurity, productivity is likely to decline.

Cutbacks through layoffs provide an opportunity for management to evaluate the agency and its employees and thus to find ways to use the agency's resources more efficiently in achieving the organization's goals. The evidence suggests, however, that layoffs usually do not occur as a result of such rational analysis and often lead to greater problems for the organization because of the employees' insecurity regarding the process. The public service and the citizens also do not benefit much from poorly planned and executed RIF systems.

Employees and their unions usually look on attrition more favorably than layoffs because no one loses the job involuntarily. Instead, as people leave, their positions are not filled. Attrition can ease management's job in getting the cooperation of employees in the RIF, so managers seldom oppose the process. Some managers, however, recognize that attrition can cause significant problems for the organization if it is not well planned and implemented. A basic problem is that management cannot control which positions are going to become vacant. Employees leave for a variety of reasons, and often the most valuable employees are the ones best able to acquire new jobs. As a result, the employees with the most sought-after skills or best performance records could depart, leaving management with employees with less impressive skills and performance. Obviously, the organization's productivity will suffer if this occurs.

Attrition can be an effective RIF method, however, if the organization prepares for it. Employees can be cross-trained so that if some leave, others will be able to pick up their responsibilities. Especially effective is the training of employees whose skills or operations are least valuable to the organization's work. They can be trained in more needed areas of activity and thus become more valuable to the organization. Similarly, internal training can be used to fill the gap of needed skills lost through attrition. The training also could have the advantage of giving the trainees a better perspective on the organization and could enable them to see the organization as caring about them. This could cause the employees to become more committed to its goals.

Clearly, layoffs and attrition can accomplish the objectives of reducing the number of personnel in a governmental unit. The choice of system depends on the particular situation and the speed with which reduction is necessary. Given the more humanistic nature of most personnel systems these days, attrition seems to be the most common method to achieve a RIF. The effects on the employees' performance usually loom large in the decision about which method to use.

Ironically, when governments face calls for austerity, they have to endure budget cuts at the same time demands for services increase. Budget cuts usually occur when the overall economy is in a downturn, and tax revenues decline with a downturn. As the economy weakens, people are put out of work and rely on social services for a safety net. Thus, governments often find that they need to provide more services with fewer resources. Public employees face pressures for increased service while the workforce is shrinking. The increased demand on those left can lead to stress, burnout, and morale deterioration. The human resources system then must deal with the problem of keeping the retained employees motivated and productive.

Another method of achieving cutbacks in government spending is to use contracting out for government service, often referred to as *privatization* or *outsourcing*. Contracting often is touted as a cost saver in reducing the permanent personnel of a governmental unit and giving the unit flexibility to contract for exactly the amount of service required. Thus, it is unnecessary to maintain large workforces in anticipation of a heavy workload that does not materialize or for seasonable jobs such as snow removal or swimming pool attendants. Instead, the governmental unit can contract for the job, and the private employer bears the cost of the overhead for maintaining its payroll. Having a private employer perform the service for many governments or other private organizations also can result in economy of scale, which can be reflected in the cost of the contract. It also usually is assumed that governmental jurisdictions save because they are not tied into long-term benefit programs such as retirement for the employees. The private firm handles all of that. Of course, contracting could be done with other governmental jurisdiction as well as with private firms.

Although contracting out for services seems to have many cost advantages, not everyone agrees with the proponents' rosy picture. The American Federation of State, County, and Municipal Employees (AFSCME), for instance, believes that in the long run, contracting for services is likely to cost taxpayers more.[33] AFSCME points to problems in controlling the cost and quality of the services provided and the potential for collusion between public officials and contractors. The potential abuses can cost the taxpayer, who must also bear the costs of monitoring and making the contractors accountable. Obviously, AFSCME has a special interest in protecting the jobs of public employees, but it does raise some issues that governments need to consider when they contract out for services. At any rate, contracting requires careful planning and does not guarantee efficiency or savings unless it is implemented properly and with realistic expectations.[34]

Privatization also affects the public sector and has many implications for human resources management. Privatization often is embraced as a way to reduce the public workforce and thus save money. Morale is likely to be affected negatively, and unionized employees may view the approach as a vehicle for union busting. There could be a disparity between the treatment of public sector employees and that of the employees of the private firms providing the contracted service. Public sector employees could have many procedural rights and protections that do not apply to the private sector. This leads to the issue of whether government has an obligation to ensure equitable treatment of employees who provide public services even if they work for a private firm.

As Donald Kettl points out, extensive contracting out also has implications for the nature of government work.[35] With contracting out, the government must have managers who are capable of keeping contractors accountable. Unfortunately, the resources for monitoring and assessment are not always forthcoming, and abuses have come to light frequently. These abuses waste tax money, which opponents of privatization argue would be better spent on providing services by supporting public employees.

Summary

Public employees' performance is a key concern of governments because taxpayers demand high levels of service while attempting to hold down taxes. To ensure the highest level of service possible, public employers depend on the supervisor to create an environment in which employees wish to work. In addition, organizations use various theories of motivation to persuade employees to produce at their optimum effort. In recent years, behavioral approaches to organizing the work unit and job have acquired support as ways of improving performance. Governments also use performance management programs that utilize new technology, better management, and employee participation. Evaluation systems test the performance of employees and the effects of techniques for improving performance. Performance management also helps determine the need for training and development programs to improve the skills and opportunities of employees in the organization.

Public employers are limited in their ability to use performance enhancement measures by the realities of the political environment. The political environment since the 1970s has been dominated by pressures for fiscal constraint. Thus, public employers must find ways to do the job better while having fewer resources with which to work. The result is that governments often must reduce the number of their personnel but still meet the public's demands for service. The employer therefore is caught between the demands of the employees and those of the citizens. Cutback management is accomplished through reduction-in-force methods (layoffs and attrition) and contracting out for services. Of course, some services also are eliminated and are accompanied by reductions-in-force.

NOTES

1. G. C. Homans, "Effort, Supervision, and Productivity," in R. Dulin ed., *Leadership and Productivity* (San Francisco: Chandler, 1965), 51–67; and D. S. Lee and N. J. Cayer, *Supervision for Success in Government* (San Francisco: Jossey-Bass, 1994).

2. L. J. Peter, *The Peter Prescription* (New York: Morrow, 1972).

3. H. Mintzberg, *The Nature of Managerial Work* (New York: HarperCollins, 1973).

4. M. E. Green, "Beware and Prepare," *Public Personnel Management,* 29 (Winter 2000), 435–444; P. C. Light, *The New Public Service* (Washington, D.C.: Brookings Institution Press, 1999); and A. Mir, R. Mir, and J. B. Mosca, "The New Age Employee: An Exploration of Changing Employee-Organization Relations," *Public Personnel Management,* 31 (Summer 2002), 187–200.

5. A. Maslow, *Motivation and Personality* (New York: Harper & Row, 1954).

6. A. Halachmi and T. v.d. Korgt, "The Role of the Manager in Employee Motivation," in S. E. Condrey, ed., *Handbook of Human Resource Management in Government* (San Francisco: Jossey-Bass, 1998), 563–585; and W. F. Whyte et al., *Money and Motivation* (New York: Harper & Row, 1955).

7. J. A. C. Brown, *The Social Psychology of Industry* (Baltimore, Md.: Penguin, 1962); G. C. Homans, "The Western Electric Research," in S. D. Hoslett, ed., *Human Factors in Management,* rev. ed. (New York: Harper & Row, 1951), 210–241; and H. M. Parsons, "What Happened at Hawthorne?" *Science,* March 8, 1974, 922–932.

8. M. P. Follet, *Creative Experience* (New York: Longman, Green, 1924).

9. P. Blau, *The Dynamics of Bureaucracy: A Study of Interpersonal Relationships in Two Government Agencies,* 2d ed. (Chicago: University of Chicago Press, 1963); and P. Blau and M. W. Mayer, *Bureaucracy in Modern Society,* 2d ed. (New York: Random House, 1976).

10. C. I. Barnard, *The Functions of the Executive* (Cambridge, Mass.: Harvard University Press, 1968, originally published in 1938).

11. C. Argyris, *Integrating the Individual and Organization* (New York: Wiley, 1964).

12. R. Presthus, *The Organizational Society,* rev. ed. (New York: St. Martin's Press, 1978).

13. A. Downs, *Inside Bureaucracy* (Boston: Little, Brown, 1967); C. L. Jurkiewicz and T. K. Massey Jr., "What Motivates Municipal Employees: A Comparison Study of Supervisory vs. Non-Supervisory Personnel," *Public Personnel Management,* 26 (Fall 1997), 367–377; and P. Rand, "Collecting Merit Badges: The White House Fellows," *Washington Monthly,* 6 (June 1974), 47–56.

14. D. McGregor, *The Human Side of Enterprise* (New York: McGraw-Hill, 1968).

15. F. Herzberg, *Work and the Nature of Man* (Cleveland: World Publishing, 1966).

16. V. Vroom, *Work and Motivation* (New York: Wiley, 1964).

17. J. S. Adams, "Inequity in Social Exchange," in L. Berkowitz, ed., *Advances in Experimental Social Psychology,* vol. 2 (San Diego: Academic Press, 1965).

18. M. P. Smith, "Barriers to Organizational Democracy in Public Administration," *Administration and Society,* 18 (November 1976), 275–317.

19. Ibid.

20. M. L. Vasu, D. W. Stewart, and G. D. Garson, *Organizational Behavior and Public Management* (New York: Marcel Dekker, 1998).

21. P. F. Drucker, *The Practice of Management* (New York: Harper & Row, 1954).

22. R. N. Ford, "Job Enrichment Lessons from AT&T," *Harvard Business Review,* 51 (January–February 1973), 96–106; and D. Zwerdling, "Beyond Boredom: A Look at What's New on the Assembly Line," *Washington Monthly,* 5 (July–August 1973), 80–91.

23. R. T. Golembiewski, "Organization Development in Public Agencies: Perspectives on Theory and Practice," *Public Administration Review,* 29 (July–August 1969), 367–377.

24. R. B. Denhardt, J. V. Denhardt, and M. P. Aristigueta, *Managing Human Behavior in Public Sector and Nonprofit Organizations* (Thousand Oaks, Calif.: Sage, 2002); W. B. Eddy, *Public Organization Behavior and Development* (Cambridge, Mass.: Winthrop, 1981); and M. Van Wart, *Changing Public Sector Values* (New York: Garland Publishing, 1998).

25. D. Ammons, *Accountability for Performance: Measurement and Monitoring in Local Government* (Washington, D.C.: International City/County Management Association, 1995); and J. Greiner, "Positioning Performance Measurement for the Twenty-First

Century," in A. Halachmi and G. Bouckeart, eds., *Organizational Performance Measurement in the Public Sector* (Westport, Conn.: Quorum Books, 1996), 11–50.

26. N. S. Hayward, "The Productivity Challenge," *Public Administration Review*, 36 (September–October 1976), 544–550; R. D. Horton, "Productivity and Productivity Bargaining in Government: A Critical Analysis," *Public Administration Review*, 36 (July–August 1976), 407–414; and C. A. Newland, "Personnel Concerns in Government Productivity Improvement," *Public Administration Review*, 32 (November–December 1972), 807–815.

27. National Performance Review, *From Red Tape to Results: Creating a Government That Works Better and Costs Less* (Washington, D.C.: U.S. Government Printing Office, 1993).

28. R. B. Denhardt and J. V. Denhardt, "The New Public Service: Serving Rather Than Steering," *Public Administration Review*, 60 (November–December 2000), 549–559; and C. King and C. Stivers, *Government Is Us: Public Administration in an Anti-Government Era* (Thousand Oaks, Calif.: Sage, 1998).

29. Denhardt and Denhardt, "The New Public Service."

30. The National Center for Productivity and Quality of Working Life, *Total Performance Measurement: Some Pointers for Action* (Washington, D.C.: U.S. Government Printing Office, 1978).

31. P. Sandwith, "A Hierarchy of Management Training Requirements: The Competency Domain Model," *Public Personnel Management*, 22 (Spring 1993), 43–62.

32. M. Van Wart, N. J. Cayer, and S. Cook, *Handbook of Training and Development for the Public Sector* (San Francisco: Jossey-Bass, 1993).

33. American Federation of State, County, and Municipal Employees, *Passing the Buck: The Contracting Out of Public Services* (Washington, D.C.: AFSCME, 1983); and P. J. Cooper, *Governing by Contract: Challenges and Opportunities for Public Managers* (Washington, D.C.: CQ Press, 2003).

34. K. S. Chi, and C. Jasper, *Private Practices: A Review of Privatization in State Government* (Lexington, Ky.: Council of State Governments, 1998); R. H. DeHoog, "Legal Issues in Contracting for Public Services: When Business Does Government," in P. J. Cooper and C. A. Newland, eds., *Public Law and Administration* (San Francisco: Jossey-Bass, 1997), 528–545; G. A. Hodge, *Privatization: An International Review of Performance* (Boulder, Colo.: Westview Press, 2000); and P. Seidenstat, ed., *Contracting Out Government Services* (Westport, Conn.: Praeger, 1999).

35. D. R. Kettl, "Privatization: Implications for the Public Workforce," in C. Ban and N. M. Riccucci, eds., *Public Personnel Management: Current Concerns, Future Challenges*, 2d ed. (New York: Longman, 1991), 254–264.

SUGGESTED READINGS

Ammons, D. *Benchmarking for Local Government.* Washington, D.C.: International City/County Management Association, 1995.

Berman, E. *Productivity in Public and Nonprofit Organizations.* Thousand Oaks, Calif.: Sage Publications, 1998.

Bryson, J. M. *Strategic Planning for Public and Nonprofit Organizations: A Guide to Strengthening and Sustaining Organizational Achievements.* San Francisco: Jossey-Bass, 1995.

Center for Accountability and Performance. *Performance Measurement: Concepts and Techniques.* Washington, D.C.: American Society for Public Administration, 1998.

Cooper, P. J. *Governing by Contract: Challenges and Appointments for Public Managers.* Washington, D.C.: CQ Press, 2003.

Greene, J. D. *Cities and Privatization: Prospects for the New Century.* Upper Saddle River, N.J.: Prentice-Hall, 2002.

Halachmi, A., and G. Bouckaert, eds. *Organizational Performance and Measurement in the Public Sector: Towards Service Effort and Accomplishment Reporting.* Westport, Conn.: Quorum Books, 1996.

Hodge, G. A. *Privatization: An International Review of Performance.* Boulder, Colo.: Westview Press, 2000.

Holzer, M., and K. Callahan. *Government at Work: Best Practices and Model Programs.* Thousand Oaks, Calif.: Sage Publications, 1998.

Kearney, R. C., and E. Berman. *Public Sector Performance.* Boulder, Colo.: Westview Press, 1999.

Kettl, D. F. *Sharing Power: Public Governance and Private Markets.* Washington, D.C.: Brookings Institution Press, 1993.

Lawler, E. E. III. *High-Involvement Management: Participative Strategies for Improving Organizational Performance.* San Francisco: Jossey-Bass, 1986.

Lee, D. S., and N. J. Cayer. *Supervision for Success in Government: A Practical Guide for First Line Managers.* San Francisco: Jossey-Bass, 1994.

Plunket, L., and R. Fournier. *Participative Management: Implementing Empowerment.* San Francisco: Jossey-Bass, 1991.

Robinson, D. G., and J. C. Robinson. *Moving from Training to Performance: A Practical Guidebook.* San Francisco: Berrett-Koehler, 1998.

Savas, E. S. *Privatization and Public-Private Partnerships.* New York: Chatham House, 2000.

Sclar, E. D. *You Don't Always Get What You Pay For: The Economics of Privatization.* Ithaca, NY: Cornell University Press, 2000.

Seidenstat, P., ed. *Contracting Out Government Services.* Westport, Conn.: Praeger, 1999.

Senge, P. *The Fifth Discipline: The Art and Practice of the Learning Organization.* New York: Doubleday, 1990.

Sims, R. R. *Reinventing Training and Development.* Westport, Conn.: Quorum Books, 1998.

Van Wart, M., N. J. Cayer, and S. Cook. *Handbook of Training and Development for the Public Sector.* San Francisco: Jossey-Bass, 1993.

SELECTED WEB SITES

American Society for Training and Development (ASTD). Professional association of people devoted to learning through training and development in both the public and private sectors. Publishes journals and reports furthering training and development. www.astd.org

Center for Accountability and Performance. Unit of the American Society for Public Administration (ASPA) that provides research, technical assistance, education, training, and advocacy on best practices in performance management. www.aspanet .org/cap

Government Performance Coalition. Group of researchers and organizations that makes recommendations on national government performance management issues. www.govresults.com

National Center for Public Productivity (NCPP). Research and public service organization at Rutgers University, Newark, New Jersey. Assists government at all levels to improve capacity to provide services; sponsors publications and conferences. www.andromeda .rutgers.edu/~ncpp/

National Institute for Government Innovation (NIGI). Organization that identifies and advances innovations in government through research, publications, and seminars. www.nigi.org

National Partnership for Reinventing Government. Association that provides reports on the reinvention of and benchmarking in government. http://govinfo.library.unt.edu/npr/index.html

Section for Professional and Organizational Development (SPOD). Section of the American Society for Public Administration (ASPA) that advances continuing education and training for public service organizations. www.aspanet.org/sections/sectionpages/spod.html

---

Exercises

1. Make an appointment with the director/manager of a department in a state, county, municipal, or tribal government. Ask the manager about what he or she believes is the most effective way to get people to be productive in the organization. Ask the manager to describe a situation in the organization in which there was an issue with performance of an individual or group. How did he or she handle the situation?

   From what you have heard from the manager, how would you characterize his or her assumptions about human nature? How would you describe the manager's management style?

2. Interview a leader of an employee union or association in local or state government. Ask the leader to describe the role of the union or association as it relates to participation in decision making within the organization. From the interview, what sense do you get of how much participation the group has in managing the organization? Does the relationship between the government and its employees appear to be an open, communicative one? Explain. What are the implications for how the agency operates?

3. Gary Corbett worked for five years in the Utilities Department of Milltown. He was recognized as a hard worker and appeared to work well with everyone. When an opening occurred in the directorship of the customer service division, he applied and was appointed. The customer service division had always run relatively smoothly and had a relaxed atmosphere. Gary appreciated the fact that the work got done but thought the employees could be less social and more focused on their work. On his first day he called a staff meeting in which he said:

   > I am very pleased to be joining the customer service division and look forward to working with all of you. The work of this division is very good, and with all your help we will make it even better. I want us to win the award for the most productive unit in the Utilities Department. Therefore, as time passes, there will be some changes.

Again, I am pleased to be here and encourage you to communicate your ideas and concerns to me. I will have an open door. Working together, we can become the best.

Gary then outlined some new procedures and rules, including the requirement that each supervisor document the arrival time, break time, and departure time of each supervisee. Over the next few weeks, he established more rules to tighten procedures so that all employees knew exactly how to do their jobs and to ensure accountability.

To Gary's surprise, morale in the division seemed to deteriorate, and the pleasant atmosphere that had been prevalent in the unit disappeared. People began to take more sick leave, and customer complaints about service increased. People seemed to be late in handing in reports. He also was surprised that very few people took advantage of his open-door policy to talk with him about their ideas and suggestions.

If you were called in as a consultant by Gary Corbett, what would you tell him? Could you explain the change in the behavior of employees? What was good and what was not good about the way Gary approached his new responsibilities? Do you have any suggestions for rectifying the situation?

4. Mayor Carrie Campbell was elected on a plan to make city government more productive and responsive to the citizens it serves. Just after being elected, she went to a conference associated with her private sector business and heard a motivational speaker make an inspiring presentation. The mayor was very impressed, made a point of introducing herself to the speaker, and indicated that she wanted the speaker to offer a program in her city. The mayor promised to contact the speaker later about the details.

When Mayor Campbell came back home, she called you, the director of training and development, into her office and informed you that you were to work with the conference speaker to arrange dates for her to offer her training and development program for all city employees.

How do you respond to the mayor? Is the mayor's idea a good one? Why or why not? If you were the mayor, what would you have done?

7

Rights and Duties of Public Employees

Public employees have a responsibility to perform their jobs in a manner that provides effective public service. They also have rights as citizens. Because government depends on the support of the general public, it often attempts to limit behavior that could be controversial or unpopular and infringe on the rights of employees. At the same time, public employees often enjoy more rights within the organization than do private sector employees because the due process clauses of the Fifth and Fourteenth Amendments to the U.S. Constitution apply to governments but not to private organizations. The following discussion deals with off-the-job conduct as well as the internal rights associated with public employment.

Off-the-Job Conduct

The off-the-job conduct of public employees receives more attention than does the behavior of employees in the private sector. In its eagerness to offer high-quality public service devoid of public controversy, the government often restricts the rights of those providing that service. Balancing the need for an impartial, fair, and high-quality public service with protection of employees' individual rights creates controversies and difficulties in public personnel systems. Such problems are most likely to occur in a democratic system in which individual rights are numerous and are highly valued, as in the United States.

Restrictions on public employees have stemmed from the *doctrine of privilege* as applied to public employment. The courts have long held that privileges and gratuities are not subject to the same protection as rights are.[1] Thus, if it is determined that something is a privilege, no one has a right to it, and protections such as due process do not apply in the same way they would if a right were involved. Over the years the courts have held that government employment is a privilege extended to those employed and that if people want the privilege, they must abide by the conditions imposed on it. Since the 1960s, the courts have modified their stand on this issue by dispensing with the rights/privilege distinction[2] and by recognizing that employees can have a property right in employment or in continued employment.[3] They also have liberty interests that can be affected by the employment situation.[4] As the following discussion demonstrates, legislatures and the courts continue to struggle with the balance between the constitutional rights of employees and the legitimate interests of public employers.

GENERAL EMPLOYEE CONDUCT

Administrators in the public sector usually demand a higher standard of behavior of their employees than those in the private sector do. Public employees are scrutinized by taxpayers and the media, and any misstep is likely to result in pressure for a remedy. Being less dependent on the public's goodwill and facing fewer consequences from the behavior of their employees, private sector employers can be more understanding of their employees' behavior. The support of the public, especially that of elected political leaders, is crucial to a public agency's existence. Sensitivity to potential consequences leads many public employers to take the expedient route of restricting employee rights or imposing discipline for nonwork activities that would not be a concern in the private sector.

The matter of lifestyle has become a controversial issue in public employment. The emotional fervor associated with the issue is illustrated by the controversy surrounding Colorado voters' passage in 1992 of a state constitutional amendment prohibiting the state government and local governments from adopting ordinances banning discrimination on the basis of sexual orientation. Several Colorado cities already had such ordinances. The amendment was initiated by conservatives who believed that family values do not include tolerance of homosexuality. Eventually the Colorado Supreme Court invalidated the amendment, and the U.S. Supreme Court agreed. Since that time, the groups responsible for the Colorado vote helped groups in other states attempt to put similar provisions on their ballots.

Nonetheless, jurisdictions across the country have adopted nondiscrimination policies that include sexual orientation as a protected category. As of 2002, twelve states and 130 local jurisdictions had prohibited discrimination in employment based on sexual orientation.[5] Even as gays and lesbians continue to press for protection in the hope of winning the kind of recognition given to other minorities, the controversy over the issue is not likely to abate soon. They have few political allies, although that is changing. The issue became very visible in the 1984 election campaign when the Democratic Party ticket endorsed gay rights. In 1992 the issue again attained high visibility as the presidential candidate, Bill Clinton, pledged to reverse the ban on homosexuals in the military. Bowing to political realities, President Clinton eventually backed down on his pledge and agreed to a policy of "don't ask, don't tell," which essentially maintained the ban as it is enforced by the military departments. As gay political organizations demonstrate their political clout, gays and lesbians eventually will be accorded the same consideration other groups are, and employment policies will reflect that political power. Additionally, the courts are increasingly ruling in favor of according homosexuals the same rights as other citizens.

LOYALTY AND SECURITY

Probably no aspect of public personnel administration has been more directly affected by forces in the political environment than the issues of loyalty and security. At times, officials and the public have reacted out of hysteria by restricting the activities of public employees. Loyalty and security are two separate concepts that often are perceived as one. *Loyalty* refers to an employee's support of the system, and a *loyalty risk* is one who would be likely to subvert the political system consciously. A *security risk* is someone who, without malicious intent, might divulge information or act in a way detrimental to the system. Thus, someone can be a security risk without being disloyal or can be a security risk in one position but not in another.

Loyalty and freedom are competing objectives that have created numerous problems for the political system. President George Washington demanded loyalty to the new federal system from his public servants, and President Abraham Lincoln required loyalty to the Union. However, specific tests of loyalty did not become formalized until 1939, when the Hatch Act (Section 9A) prohibited employees from being members of organizations advocating the overthrow of the government. In fact, every period of crisis in our history has produced some policies that try to ensure the loyalty of public servants. After World War II, the anticommunist frenzy led to a variety of loyalty and security programs in the public service, and a number of studies of employee loyalty were conducted. For the most part, the issue attracts much less attention today, but the events of September 11, 2001, brought attention back to the issue, and some of the discussion surrounding the creation of a Homeland Security Department raised issues about loyalty and security of its employees.

All employees of the federal government are subject to an investigation of their backgrounds to determine their suitability for the public service, although for workers in nonsensitive positions, the investigation can be conducted after placement. Those appointed to sensitive positions are investigated before appointment and are subject to in-depth investigations. At the state and local levels, the tendency has been to require employees to sign loyalty oaths as a condition of employment, but the courts have invalidated many of them for being too vague and unenforceable. A 1972 Supreme Court decision did uphold the Massachusetts loyalty oath, however; thus, loyalty oaths can still be and still are used.[6]

Although it could seem reasonable that those disloyal to the system should not be employed by the government and that security risks should not be employed in sensitive positions, there is little agreement on what constitutes a loyalty or security risk. Consequently, loyalty and security programs have been subject to much abuse. Many of them virtually ignore employees' individual rights, partly because of the privilege doctrine discussed earlier.[7] Gays and lesbians were particularly victimized by such policies during the Cold War.

The most insidious invasion of individual rights occurs among those applying for jobs. A person can be denied a position on the basis of background information acquired during the investigation. Whether the information is accurate could never be determined because unsuccessful applicants are rarely told why they are unsuccessful. Thus, people can be denied jobs in the public service on the basis of information they have no chance to see or challenge.

POLITICAL ACTIVITY RESTRICTIONS

Some restrictions on public employees date from the English canon law tradition that certain offices or activities are inconsistent with one another.[8] Conflict-of-interest statutes, orders and rulings, and legislation or constitutional provisions prohibiting holding certain public offices concurrently are the principal methods of putting this tradition into practice. The belief that politically active public servants cannot provide service free from bias led to the prohibition of certain political activities as well. In a democratic society, the rights of public employees as individuals could conflict with the right of the public to impartial service. For the most part in the United States, priority has been given to the public's right to service, and limits have been placed on the rights of public employees as a legitimate cost of the political neutrality of the public bureaucracy.

The political activity of national government employees is restricted by the 1939 Hatch Act. In 1940 the act was amended to restrict the political activities of the state and local government employees whose salaries are paid in part or in full by federal funds. The Federal Election Campaign Act amendments of 1974 repealed many of the restrictions on the state and local government employees, although the state and local levels have their own restrictions. In 1993 the act was amended again, removing many of the restrictions on federal employees.[9] Before the Hatch Act was passed, the Civil Service Commission drew up a body of rules and regulations pursuant to a 1907 executive order of President Theodore Roosevelt barring activity in "political management or in political campaigns" for those covered by the civil service.[10] In implementing its rules and regulations, the commission ruled on some three thousand cases involving restrictions on political activity before 1940. It is generally believed that Congress intended the Hatch Act to incorporate those decisions as established precedents for interpreting the act's political activity prohibitions. Thus, Congress would effectively deny the commission the authority to interpret the legislation differently. There has been some disagreement about congressional intent, but the effect was to hamper the flexibility of the commission in dealing with the issue.[11]

Regardless of Congress's intent, the Civil Service Commission administered the Hatch Act and determined that among other specific provisions, the act prohibited the following:

1. Serving as a delegate or alternate to a political party convention or as a member of a political committee
2. Soliciting or handling political contributions
3. Serving as an officer in or organizer of a political club
4. Leading or organizing political meetings or rallies or making partisan speeches at them
5. Soliciting votes or engaging in other partisan election activity
6. Being a candidate for a partisan political office.[12]

The rationale for such restrictions is that they help protect public employees from being coerced into working for particular candidates or parties, protect the beneficiaries of public services from such coercion, and prevent public officials from using public monies and positions to further their political careers. A more immediate political reason for the passage of the Hatch Act was a fear that the New Deal bureaucracy could be mobilized as a vast political machine in support of the administration. A similar concern among many legislators that the party in power could take political advantage of politically active career servants was a major factor in Congress's reluctance to liberalize the restrictions until 1993. At any rate, the Hatch Act was passed as a response to overindulgence in spoils politics.

The constitutional rights to freedom of expression, assembly, and petition were at the heart of the opposition to the Hatch Act. Because these rights were limited by the act, many public employees argued that they were doomed to second-class citizenship.[13] A number of assaults on the Hatch Act and similar state legislation surfaced in the courts. For a while it seemed that the courts would invalidate many of the restrictions—as some lower courts did—but in 1973, the Supreme Court, by a six-to-three decision, upheld the constitutionality of the Hatch Act and a similar state law reaffirming a 1947 decision.[14] In some places the coverage of the restrictions was extended, as it was in Arizona, where in 1983 the attorney general issued an opinion that the state law even prohibited participation in nonpartisan elections. Public employees focused their efforts for change on legislative bodies.

Finally, after many years of effort, supporters of liberalization of the Hatch Act persuaded Congress to revise the act in 1993. While employees in some sensitive agencies (Table 7.1) are still covered by the restrictions noted previously, other federal civil service employees have had many restrictions lifted. Now most federal employees may do the following:

1. Hold a particular party office
2. Participate in managing political campaigns while off duty
3. Distribute campaign literature and solicit votes
4. Participate in voter registration drives
5. Participate in phone banks for political parties or candidates
6. Stuff envelopes for candidates
7. Publicly endorse political candidates.

At the same time, some restrictions still exist. For example, federal employees may not do the following:

Engage in political activity while:
　　On duty
　　In any room or building occupied by federal employees
　　Wearing a federal government uniform or official insignia
　　Using a vehicle owned or leased by the federal government
Solicit contributions except:
　　From members of the same federal labor organization who are non-
　　　　subordinates of the one doing the soliciting.
　　For multicandidate political committees of the labor organization
Solicit or discourage political participation by:
　　Applicants for pending grants, contracts, rulings, licenses, permits,
　　　　or certificates
　　Participants or subjects of ongoing audits, investigations, or enforce-
　　　　ment actions by the office in which the employee works
　　Anyone using official authority to interfere with or attempt to affect
　　　　the outcome of an election
　　Anyone running for election to a partisan political office.

Collective bargaining in the public sector has numerous implications for political activity. Unions exert a great deal of pressure in the political realm when they are permitted to engage in partisan political activity. As a result, direct public employee union activity in politics usually is restricted. Nonetheless, unions support their friends by making endorsements and campaigning by their political action committees. Collective bargaining also undermines one of the justifications for prohibiting political activity in that it tends to reduce the likelihood that employees can be coerced or intimidated into engaging in the political activities desired by a supervisor. Because unions give workers leverage with management, employees have greater independence

Table 7.1 Agencies Still Covered by Original Hatch Act Prohibitions

Federal Elections Commission
Federal Bureau of Investigations
Secret Service
Central Intelligence Agency
National Security Council
Defense Intelligence Agency
Merit Systems Protection Board
Office of Special Council
Internal Revenue Service Office of Criminal Investigation
Department of Justice Criminal Division
U.S. Customs Office of Investigative Programs
Bureau of Alcohol, Tobacco, and Firearms Office of Law Enforcement

from their managers and have union support in resisting attempts by management to coerce them into political activity.

Some governments impose general restrictions on public employees' freedom of expression, privacy, residency, and personal appearance, among others. Thus, restrictions on freedom of expression are subject to the courts' determination of whether the expression is on a matter of public concern. If so, it is protected by the first amendment to the Constitution, and the court will then balance the employee's right with the interest of the employer in taking action that protects the mission of the organization.[15] Employee free speech also is protected when the employee engages in whistleblowing, the revelation of wrongdoing in the organization.[16] Although the Supreme Court seems willing to permit restrictions on various aspects of an employee's personal life, it does insist on procedural regulations in the imposition of such limitations. Another type of restriction is that placed on "moonlighting." Prohibiting the taking of a second job, especially when combined with low salaries in many jurisdictions, could create hardships for some employees or difficulty in recruiting for a jurisdiction. The employer's concern is that an employee's ability to perform a full-time job could be affected by holding another job, and if such is the case, the employer has a legitimate worry. If the second job poses no conflict, however, most employers now do not object.

Employees also enjoy constitutional protections of association, meaning that they cannot be prohibited from associating with whomever they want, nor can they be forced to associate with anyone. The issue arose when loyalty and security policies used lists of organizations that employees were prohibited from joining, such as the Communist party. The courts have been consistent since the 1960s in striking down such policies.[17]

The issue also arises with employees and labor unions. One tactic employers used to undermine labor unions was to try to prohibit employees from joining them. The courts do not permit such prohibitions.[18] At the same time, unions want all employees in an organization to pay fees to support the union's activities on behalf of the employees. The Supreme Court affirmed that fees can be collected from nonunion members in the organization who benefit from the union activities.[19] However, employees cannot be forced to pay the portion of fees that go to support political causes and candidates with whom they disagree.[20]

The courts also have been chipping away at requirements of employees in many positions to be members of a particular political party. In places where the spoils system remains, elected political leaders now have less flexibility to remove people for party affiliation reasons. To use this reason, they must be able to demonstrate that "party affiliation is an appropriate requirement for the effective performance" of the job.[21]

Liberty interests of public employees also have occasioned court review. The Fifth and Fourteenth amendments to the Constitution prohibit government from depriving individuals of life, liberty, or property without due process. Liberty pertains to a wide range of freedoms. Employers often attempt to require their employees to engage in activities such as public service projects or contribute to the United Way, and the courts have been willing to accept such requirements if they are reasonably related to the interests of the employer.[22] The Supreme Court also has ruled that school districts cannot require unpaid maternity leaves for teachers or interfere in any other way with reproductive decisions.[23]

Employers may impose residency requirements on employees.[24] Jurisdictions justify such restrictions, especially for public safety and emergency personnel, on the need to be quickly available. These employers also tend to focus on setting an example for residents and their belief that employees should pay taxes in the jurisdiction that pays their salaries. On a similar issue, some jurisdictions have policies on appearance. They justify these policies on the need to present a good image and, for public safety personnel, as a way to encourage discipline and ensure respect from those with whom they deal. The Supreme Court has allowed such rules unless the employee can demonstrate that the rule has no rational connection to the mission of the agency.[25]

On-the-Job Conduct and Rights

Public employees are expected to conduct themselves professionally on the job. To deal with instances in which public employees may be tempted to act in a nonprofessional way or in a manner contrary to public interest, many policies have been established to delimit and ensure the rights of employees in the implementation of those restrictions.

ETHICS AND PUBLIC EMPLOYEES

Ethical behavior is expected of public employees, but a problem arises when one attempts to define what *ethical behavior* means because *ethics* involves making choices among competing values. Ultimately, ethics means doing what is right. However, this depends on many factors. In the public sector, doing what is right means doing what is legal by law, rules, and regulations; doing what is in the public interest; and doing what maintains one's own integrity and the integrity of the organization. These elements of ethical actions often conflict with one another, and individuals need to balance values in making choices.

In the public sector, questions of ethics arise all the time. Any decision or action of the government has an impact on someone, and those affected will try to influence that decision or action. As a result, public employees and employers are likely to be subject to pressure or efforts to influence them. Problems often arise in regard to the appearance of being unduly influenced by those interested in the outcome of a decision or action. In the private sector decision makers usually are courted by those who are likely to benefit from a decision, but this generally is not permitted in the public sector. Thus, entertaining a decision maker or providing private benefits to a government employee can create the impression of impropriety in the public sector but is common practice in the private sector. Many scandals involving public officials occur because these officials come from the private sector and do not understand the difference in public employment. Because public officials and employees are paid from public tax money, they are subject to much more scrutiny than are their private sector counterparts.

Because of periodic scandals involving high-level public officials, people tend to think of ethical issues as involving big decisions. Such scandals go back to the beginning of government, and the United States certainly has experienced many difficulties with the behavior of employees. Efforts to develop the civil service system were traced back to the Jacksonian period earlier in this book. The abuses of that era led many people to try to develop rules for the personnel system to curb abuses. The passage of the Hatch Act of 1939 resulted in part from concerns about ethical lapses in the public business. In every presidential administration there has been some abuse that led to concern about the ethics of some of the members of the administration. These concerns extend to the type of example the officials provide for the rest of the public sector. In the 1990s ethics once again became a major issue for the public sector. The Clinton administration had difficulty governing partly because of questions of character arising from some activities of Clinton and his wife in their business dealings before he became president. Additionally, some of the activities of Clinton administration officials after the issue began to become public raised other questions of propriety. Three cabinet members were among those embarrassing the president. Secretary of Agriculture Mike Espy resigned after revelations that he had accepted substantial gifts from Tyson Foods, one of the major corporations affected by agricultural policy. Secretary of Housing and Urban Development Henry Cisneros was in the headlines when he was sued by a former mistress for breach of contract over promised cash support for her. Secretary of Commerce Ron Brown was investigated for questionable business dealings that occurred before he joined the cabinet. Of course, the impeachment charges brought against President Clinton himself for his conduct with a presidential intern raised the issue to a new high.

The George W. Bush administration has had its own ethical problems. As corporate scandals arose over accounting and executive insider trading, both Bush and Vice President Dick Cheney faced numerous questions about their dealings and windfalls as corporate executives and board members before they were elected. Several high-ranking members of the administration had been part of the Enron management team before joining the administration and got caught up in the scandal surrounding the company's collapse. Harvey Pitt, the chair of the Securities and Exchange Commission (SEC), was pressured to resign when he embarrassed the administration with numerous lapses of judgment and the appearance of being too close to those the SEC regulates. At the state level, several state legislatures (Arizona, Kentucky, Rhode Island, and South Carolina) were rocked by bribery and influence peddling scandals in the 1990s.

In 2001, one member of Congress was investigated in the disappearance of a congressional intern after it was learned he had an extramarital affair with her. The next year another member of Congress was expelled after his conviction on several charges involving fraud and corruption. Several cases involving high school teacher–student sexual relations across the country highlighted issues of inappropriate behavior among teachers. A housing official and his aide in Tampa, Florida, were investigated over the romantic relationship between them and its connection to the aide's rapid rise in the organization. Every day there are news stories about bribery of public officials, embezzlement, or harassment and sexual assault by public officials. The reality is that these cases represent a minute fraction of government officials and employees and that most often they tend to be elected or politically appointed officials. Nonetheless, these stories lead to cynicism and lack of citizen confidence in government. In response, governments adopt policies to attempt to control the aberrant behavior.

One of the reasons ethical considerations are so important to public administration is that public employees have a great deal of discretion in deciding on numerous issues that can benefit or hurt different parties. This discretion also puts public servants under pressure to act in ways that benefit the parties affected by the agency. Public employees often find themselves on the spot, and it is up to them to decide what is right and what is wrong.

Ethical behavior is influenced by both internal individual factors and external controls. The internal factors refer to the degree to which individuals perceive themselves as being responsible for their actions. Theoretically, employees who are carefully chosen and embrace democratic and professional values control their own conduct because of their dedication to the public, their professional group standards, and peer pressure.[26] Unfortunately, the pressures faced by public servants are too complex and contradictory to allow an easy formulation of right or wrong responses. It is difficult to decide when a conflict between personal values and official duties warrants resignation or protest or whether actions such as leaking or withholding information are valid. In other words, internal controls are usually not enough.

Because internal controls are inadequate, external controls become necessary.[27] Individual leaders have a responsibility for ethical behavior in their organizations and should serve as a model of behavior for their subordinates. If the supervisor has lax standards of behavior, the subordinates can hardly be expected to maintain high standards in their performance.

Codes of conduct commonly regulate behavior, but there are differences of opinion about their effectiveness. President Lyndon B. Johnson, for example, issued an executive order "Prescribing Standards of Ethical Conduct for Government Officers and Employees,"[28] but no mention of it was made during the Watergate proceedings, suggesting that no one took it very seriously. Codes of conduct provide guidelines for behavior but often are so general that they have little meaning. Without enforcement efforts, these codes are of little value—and enforcement rarely is pursued.

In addition to identifying specific prohibited behaviors, codes of conduct usually require employees to avoid even the appearance of unethical behavior. Thus, they should avoid something that might appear to be a conflict of interest; however, what constitutes the appearance of a conflict of interest poses a problem because what seems to be a conflict of interest to some people may not appear so to others. Accepting lunches or gifts from the people with whom one normally deals could influence an employee's decisions or actions even if he insists otherwise. Even though the individual resists any temptation, others may not be convinced of this. Therefore, the temptation must be avoided in order to protect the integrity of the public service. Employees who come to government from the business community often find themselves confused by these rules because behavior that is standard in private dealings is frowned on or prohibited in the public sector.

Because of these difficulties with codes of ethics, other methods of prohibiting certain practices also are used. Specific legal prohibitions on various practices are common. Most states have passed legislation on ethical behavior for public employees in recent years, and the Ethics in Government Act of 1978 cited specific legal prohibitions for federal employees. It also mandated the Office of Personnel Management to spell out specific rules and regulations to implement the act and established an Office of Government Ethics within the OPM.

The Ethics Reform Act of 1989 gave the Office of Government Ethics (OGE) statutory authority to issue ethics regulations and made OGE the sole executive branch authority for establishing ethical standards. To make them uniform, new standards were established for almost all agencies, which are not permitted to supplement those standards without permission from the OGE. Fourteen principles (Table 7.2) establish the foundation for the new standards. It is interesting to note that the last principle establishes the "reasonable person" criterion for judging whether an action is ethical, thus providing some flexibility in applying the new standards to particular situations.

Regulations under the 1989 Act apply to seven general areas of behavior:

1. *Gifts from outside sources.* Clearly, gifts from those doing business with an employee's office can create the impression of influence. Gifts such as refreshments during meetings might not create such an impression, but most other types of gifts are prohibited.
2. *Gifts between employees.* An employee may not give or solicit gifts or contributions for a superior or accept such gifts from another employee who receives less pay.
3. *Conflicting financial interest.* Employees must refrain from participating in any decision affecting a direct personal interest. In some cases, employees could be prohibited from having a personal financial interest if such an interest would lead to an appearance of a conflict of interest.
4. *Impartiality in performing official duties.* Employees must avoid the appearance of conflict by not participating in situations in which a reasonable person could question their impartiality and that involve former employers who awarded the employee highly valuable pay after deciding to take government employment.
5. *Seeking other employment.* Employees may not seek employment with employers who could be affected by the decisions or actions of those employees in their official duties.
6. *Misuse of position.* Employees are prohibited from using their positions, government property, or nonpublic information for private gain for themselves, relatives, friends, or nongovernment associates. On official time, they may not perform other than official duties or officially sanctioned activities such as doing the work of a union representative or attending professional conferences.
7. *Outside activities.* Employees may not participate in employment or volunteer activities that conflict with their official duties.

All of these provisions are subject to interpretation; thus, they are not absolute standards. They represent an effort to bring some uniformity to federal government agencies. State and local governments already tend to have statutes and rules and regulations that apply across the board.

The difficulties with this type of law illustrate the problems inherent in attempting to ensure the integrity of public employees. Obviously, government expects its employees not to use their positions for personal gain. The issue is how far government should go in controlling its employees' behavior and what serves the public interest.

To ensure ethical behavior, it is not enough to have policies to regulate employees' activities. It is necessary to provide role models and training on ethics on a regular basis. Training reminds employees what the policies are and assists them in working through situations that might pose ethical dilemmas. By being reminded of the ease with which appearances of wrong-doing arise, employees can be more cautious in their activities.

Table 7.2 General Principles of Public Service

1. Public service is a public trust, requiring employees to place loyalty to the Constitution, the laws and ethical principles above private gain.
2. Employees shall not hold financial interests that conflict with the conscientious performance of duty.
3. Employees shall not engage in financial transactions using nonpublic Government information or allow the improper use of such information to further any private interest.
4. An employee shall not, except as permitted by the Standards of Ethical Conduct, solicit or accept any gift or other item of monetary value from any person or entity seeking official action from, doing business with, or conducting activities regulated by the employee's agency, or whose interests may be substantially affected by the performance or nonperformance of the employee's duties.
5. Employees shall put forth honest effort in the performance of their duties.
6. Employees shall not knowingly make unauthorized commitments or promises of any kind purporting to bind the Government.
7. Employees shall not use public office for private gain.
8. Employees shall act impartially and not give preferential treatment to any private organization or individual.
9. Employees shall protect and conserve Federal property and shall not use it for other than authorized activities.
10. Employees shall not engage in outside employment or activities, including seeking or negotiating for employment, that conflict with official Government duties and responsibilities.
11. Employees shall disclose waste, fraud, abuse, and corruption to appropriate authorities.
12. Employees shall satisfy in good faith their obligations as citizens, including all just financial obligations, especially those—such as Federal, State, or local taxes—that are imposed by law.
13. Employees shall adhere to all laws and regulations that provide equal opportunity for all Americans regardless of race, color, religion, sex, national origin, age, or handicap.
14. Employees shall endeavor to avoid any actions creating the appearance that they are in violation of the law or the ethical standards set forth in the Standards of Ethical Conduct. Whether particular circumstances create an appearance that the law or these standards have been violated shall be determined from the perspective of a reasonable person with knowledge of the relevant facts.

Source: U.S. Office of Government Ethics (Retrieved April 5, 2003) from www.usoge.gov/pages/forms_pubs_otherdocs/fpo_files/booklets/bkdoitright_95.txt

It also is necessary to integrate ethics into all aspects of the personnel and management functions.[29] Employees need to understand the importance of ethics from the time they are hired (orientation) through the time they retire. Managers also need to be constantly reminded of the need for ethical behavior in all the decisions they make and all actions they take. Ethical values need to be part of the organizational culture if the organization is to act ethically.

HARASSMENT-FREE WORKPLACE

Harassment has been defined as "repeated and persistent attempts to torment, wear down, frustrate, or get a reaction from another. It is treatment that persistently provokes, pressures, frightens, intimidates, or otherwise discomforts another person."[30] Unfortunately, harassment has occurred and continues to occur in many, if not most, workplaces. Clearly, ethnic and racial minorities were subject to harassment as workplaces were integrated. Women have been harassed since they began participating in the workplace. Lesbians and gays suffer the same fate as do religious and other minorities.

Efforts to address harassment in the workplace stem primarily from the Civil Rights Act of 1964 and the Equal Employment Opportunity Act of 1972 (an amendment to the 1964 Civil Rights Act). Although these laws have broad impact to cover harassment of many kinds, sexual harassment has become the arena of most controversy and attention. The National Organization for Women (NOW), formed in 1966, began the effort to get public officials to recognize discrimination against women being within the scope of the Civil Rights Act. In the 1970s, women's groups began to focus on the sexual exploitation of women in the workplace and eventually succeeded in having the Equal Employment Opportunity Commission (EEOC) define sexual harassment as a violation of federal law. EEOC then published guidelines defining sexual harassment as "unwelcome advances, requests for sexual favors, and other verbal or physical conduct of a sexual nature . . . when submission to or rejection of this conduct explicitly or implicitly affects an individual's employment, unreasonably interferes with an individual's work performance or creates an intimidating, hostile or offensive work environment."[31]

Through court decisions, sexual harassment has come to be viewed as either *quid pro quo* or hostile environment harassment. *Quid pro quo* harassment involves a situation in which employment decisions depend on sexual favors. Thus, a promotion can be given or denied based on whether an individual submits to a request or demand for sex.

Hostile environment harassment refers to the situation in which the work environment is uncomfortable or intimidating because of things such as suggestive comments, touching, leering, and offensive materials on bulletin boards.

In 1986, the U.S. Supreme Court utilized these two definitions of sexual harassment in *Meritor Savings Bank v. Vinson,*[32] in which the Court for the first time found sexual harassment illegal. Lower courts had been dealing with the issue during the 1970s and had articulated many of the principles that the *Meritor* case validated. *Ellison v. Brady* (1991), a Ninth Circuit case, resulted in a ruling that the perspective of the woman claiming harassment must be considered rather than simply using the rule of a "reasonable person" to determine whether a hostile environment exists.[33] In *Harris v. Forklift Systems* (1993), the Supreme Court held that the victim's perception of a hostile and abusive environment is sufficient to establish cause for legal action.[34] In 1998, in *Oncale v. Sundowner Offshore Services, Inc.,* the Supreme Court for the first time ruled that same-sex harassment also is covered under the Civil Rights Act protection.[35]

The policy emerging from *Meritor* and subsequent cases establishes employer liability for sexual harassment. Particularly in *quid pro quo* harassment, the employer tends to be held automatically liable. In hostile environment harassment, the employer can escape liability if it can demonstrate good faith efforts to correct the behavior that led to complaints of harassment. The Civil Rights Act of 1991 allows harassed employees to sue for punitive damage up to $300,000 in addition to back pay and attorney's costs.

The extent of sexual harassment is difficult to document. Differences in understanding what constitutes sexual harassment and reluctance of employees to file sexual harassment complaints make it difficult to know the full extent of the problem.[36] Nonetheless, surveys of employees indicate that the problem is widespread with as many as 50 percent of women and nearly 40 percent of men reporting that they experienced some form of workplace sexual harassment.[37] Surveys obtain widely varying statistics, but it is clear that sexual harassment is a major problem for employers and places employees in untenable situations.

Employers can find themselves the objects of lawsuits if they do not protect their employees from sexual harassment. If employers take steps to prevent it and respond quickly to complaints of it, they can avoid liability. To prevent sexual harassment, employers need to develop a policy prohibiting it and communicate that policy clearly to all employees. Regular training to update and remind everyone about the policy also is important. Investigation of any complaints and speedy and appropriate remedial action are necessary. Retaliation against the employee making the complaint rather than correction of the action, which had been common in the past, cannot be condoned. At the same time, employers must be sensitive to the due process rights of the accused.

PRIVACY RIGHTS

Because public employers are subject to the provisions of the Fourth and Fifteenth Amendments of the U.S. Constitution, employees must be accorded protection against unreasonable searches and seizures, and due process must be followed in actions against individuals. Thus, the public sector is more limited than is the private sector in invading the privacy of individuals. For public personnel administration, the issue has particular relevance in regard to testing applicants for employment, searching employee offices, and using tests for drugs, polygraphs, and medical exams.[38]

Applicant screening exams usually are assumed to focus on individuals' skills that are relevant to the jobs for which they have applied. Thus, skill tests that demonstrate proficiency are commonly accepted. In recent years, psychological testing has become very prevalent in the private sector and is being used increasingly in parts of the public sector. Particularly in sensitive areas of employment such as public safety and in positions involving national security, psychological exams may be used. These exams test qualities such as personality characteristics, ability to deal with stress, attitudes, interpersonal skills, patterns of dealing with conflict, leadership styles, and personal preferences. Any of these qualities can be relevant to a particular position. In the private sector, these exams may be used to test most or all of these qualities, but in the public sector, only those demonstrated to be relevant to performance in the job for which they are used are likely to be permitted.

Employers also use background screening and reference checking as part of their hiring processes. Such devices can be helpful, but most employers find that reference checks provide questionable information. People generally do not use references who are not going to give positive comments. Most affirmative action policies in the public sector limit contacting references to those who are approved by the applicant. Former employers often will not provide negative information for fear of possible lawsuits by the employee. Increasingly, employers verify only dates of employment, salary, and eligibility for rehire.

Background investigations usually are relatively perfunctory except for particular types of positions. Teachers and law enforcement applicants usually are subjects of in-depth background checks. Similarly, applicants for jobs involving the handling of money or controlled substances are likely to be subject to criminal investigations. The courts have allowed background checks with little limitation for applicants.

Medical exams also have been fairly standard for people employed by most organizations, including governments. As employee health care benefit costs have increased, many employers have attempted to use medical exams and genetic tests to screen out people with or the potential for health problems. Particularly controversial has been the use by some organizations to screen out applicants with the HIV virus or those who have AIDS. Some employers also have used tests for HIV or AIDS to determine eligibility for medical insurance. The Americans with Disabilities Act (ADA) identifies AIDS as a disability for which its protections extend; thus, individuals cannot be terminated or discriminated against because they have HIV or AIDS. ADA also makes it illegal to screen for any disability unrelated to job performance.

Drug tests have evolved because of the serious drug problems in our society. Public employers pursue drug testing as a way to weed out potential employees who are drug users and current employees who can be liabilities to the employer. The standards for such tests vary with the groups subject to them. Applicants generally do not have any protections because they do not have a property right in a job. Thus, drug screening is very common for applicants for positions. When it comes to people who already are employed, however, drug testing policies must conform to the due process rights accorded to public employees.

The courts have been asked to settle disputes concerning the balancing of employee rights with the government's interest in efficient public service. Basically, the courts have ruled that blanket drug testing is not consistent with the U.S. Constitution. However, blanket testing of some employees, such as employees in positions where public safety could be affected, is constitutional. Thus, police and fire employees, transportation workers, and military personnel may be tested randomly or on a regular basis without violating their constitutional rights. General service public employees, however, usually cannot be subjected to blanket testing. Instead, such employees may be tested if there is a reasonable basis for suspicion of illegal drug use.[39]

A public employer with a drug test policy must consider several issues. The first is who should be tested: applicants, current employees, all employees, or only those suspected of using illegal drugs. Policies also must address the chain of custody of the substances tested so that all samples tested and reported on are the ones taken from the individuals identified with them. The issue of which substances to test for also must be addressed. The employer also must decide what use is to be made of the information and who will have access to it. For example, discipline can be appropriate for certain results. Additionally, employers may be required to have employee assistance plans to deal with employees who have substance abuse problems. Generally, employees cannot be terminated automatically in the public sector if they are determined to have a substance abuse problem. Instead, employers may be required to provide counseling and support, and continued employment could depend on overcoming the problem. Clearly, with the emotion surrounding drug problems in the United States, drug testing is a popular approach to dealing with the issue in the workplace, but the rights of individual employees must be weighed in public employment.

Some government agencies use polygraphs, commonly known as *lie detectors*. Generally, the polygraph cannot be used as the sole factor in making a hiring or other personnel decision. The Defense Department and Central Intelligence Agency among other agencies use the polygraph for employees with access to classified information, and state and local government law enforcement agencies routinely use it. For the public sector, the polygraph raises constitutional questions of illegal searches and seizures. The questionable reliability of the polygraph also raises issues. Because the courts allow only its limited use, employers' reasons for using it also are challenged in court trials.

In 1923, a federal appeals court ruled that polygraph results were inadmissible as evidence in a criminal trial because of the lack of agreement by the scientific community that it was accurate.[40] In 1984, the Supreme Court let stand a circuit court decision that found polygraph questions about a police department applicant's sexual relations with someone already on the department force too intrusive to be constitutional.[41] On the other hand, in a fire department case, the use of a polygraph was acceptable to a federal circuit court in a drug use investigation in the department.[42]

The Supreme Court ruled on the issue in 1993, deciding that the polygraph is admissible but that federal rules of evidence must be met, resulting in varying decisions by lower courts.[43] The court also ruled in 1998 that defendants have no constitutional right to have a polygraph admitted in evidence even if it favors their case.[44] In that decision, the court expressed doubts about the reliability of the polygraph. Public organizations continue to use the polygraph even amid questions about its appropriateness.[45] A major issue for employers is to make sure the polygraph is used fairly. Many employee organizations press to have the polygraph outlawed as a device for personnel decisions, but they have been unsuccessful so far. Litigation is likely to continue and could be the best hope for employees to rid it from public sector use.

Another privacy issue relates to the employee's office, desk, and computer files. Generally, the courts consider whether the employee has an expectation of privacy in deciding on these searches. Employees have an expectation of privacy if they have an office with a lockable door and have expectations of privacy regarding their desks and computers. However, an employer's stated policy allowing searches nullifies any expectation of privacy. Even when there is an expectation of privacy, the courts generally allow searches pursuant to an investigation of misconduct.

Summary

Employees obviously have certain duties and responsibilities as members of the public service, but they also have rights as citizens. Balancing these rights with the expectations of supervisors and the public is a difficult task. Management and the public expect public employees to be models for the rest of society. As a result, public employees often are subjected to different standards of behavior than are other citizens. Public employees often are called on to refrain from activities such as political activities that other citizens take for granted. At the same time, many pressures can be exerted on employees by their managers and supervisors; thus, protections from such coercion are also elements of public personnel policy.

Employees have the right not to be pressured to join organizations they do not want to join and the right to belong to any they do want to join. They also are protected from intimidation and harassment.

Public employees also enjoy constitutional protections against intrusion into their privacy. Thus, public employers are limited in using medical, drug, and polygraph testing.

NOTES

1. G. S. Hartman, G. W. Homer, and J. E. Menditto, "Human Resource Management Legal Issues: An Overview," in S. E. Condrey, ed., *Handbook of Human Resource Management in Government* (San Francisco: Jossey-Bass, 1998), 145–164; and D. H. Rosenbloom and M. Bailey, "What Every Personnel Manager Should Know about the Constitution," in S. W. Hays and R. C. Kearney. *Public Personnel Administration: Problems and Prospects,* 4th ed. (Upper Saddle River, N.J.: Prentice-Hall, 2003), 29–45.

2. *Pickering v Board of Education,* 391 U.S. 563 (1967).

3. *Board of Regents v Roth,* 408 U.S. 564 (1972); *Perry v Sinderman,* 408 U.S. 593 (1972); and *Cleveland Board of Education v Loudermill,* 470 U.S. 532 (1985).

4. *Board of Regents v Roth,* 480 U.S. 564 (1972).

5. Human Rights Campaign Fund, *The State of the Workplace for Lesbian, Gay, Bisexual and Transgender Americans: A Semiannual Snapshot* (Retrieved October 14, 2002, from http://www.hrc.org/publications/sow202/snapshot.asp).

6. *Cole v Richardson,* 403 U.S. 917 (1972).

7. *Bailey v Richardson,* 341 U.S. 918 (1951) and *Greene v McElroy,* 360 U.S. 474 (1959).

8. O. Kirchheimer, "The Historical and Comparative Background of the Hatch Act," *Public Policy,* 2 (1941), 341–373.

9. Public Law (P.L.) 103-94.

10. Executive Order (EO) 642, June 3, 1907.

11. H. Rose, "A Critical Look at the Hatch Act," *Harvard Law Review,* 75 (January 1962), 510–526.

12. U.S. Civil Service Commission, *Political Activities of Federal Officers and Employees,* Pamphlet No. 20 (Washington, D.C.: Government Printing Office, 1966).

13. P. L. Martin, "The Constitutionality of the Hatch Act: Second Class Citizenship for Public Employees," *University of Toledo Law Review,* 6 (Fall 1974), 78–109 and K. T. Thurber Jr., "Big, Little, Littler: Synthesizing Hatch-Act Based Political Activity Legislation Research," *Review of Public Personnel Administration,* 13 (Winter 1993), 38–51.

14. *U.S. Civil Service Commission v National Association of Letter Carriers,* 413 U.S. 548 (1973) and *United Public Workers of America v Mitchell,* 330 U.S. 75 (1947).

15. *Rankin v McPherson,* 483 U.S. 378 (1987).

16. *Pickering v Board of Education,* 391 U.S. 563 (1968).

17. *Elfbrandt v Russell,* 384 U.S. 11 (1966); *Elrod v Burns,* 427 U.S. 347 (1976); and *Sheldon v Tucker,* 364 U.S. 479.

18. *AFSCME v Woodward,* 406 F.2D 137 (1969).

19. *Abood v Detroit Board of Education,* 431 U.S. 209 (1977) and *Chicago Teachers Union v Hudson,* 475 U.S. 292 (1986).

20. *Chicago Teachers Union v Hudson.*

21. *Branti v Finkel,* 445 U.S. 507 (1980); *Elrod v Burns;* and *Rutan v Republican Party of Illinois,* 497 U.S. 62 (1990).

22. *United States v National Treasury Employees Union,* 513 U.S. 464 (1995).

23. *Cleveland Board of Education v LaFleur,* 414 U.S. 632 (1974).

24. *McCarthy v Philadelphia Civil Service Commission,* 424 U.S. 645 (1976).

25. *Kelley v Johnson,* 425 U.S. 238 (1976).

26. R. C. Chandler, "Deontological Dimensions of Administration Ethics Revisited," *Public Personnel Management,* 28 (Winter 1999), 505–514; and C. J. Friedrich, "Public Policy and the Nature of Administrative Responsibility," *Public Policy,* 1 (1940), 3–24.

27. H. Finer, "Administrative Responsibility in Democratic Government," *Public Administration Review,* 1 (1941), 335–350.

28. E.O. 11222, May 8, 1965.

29. E. K. Keller, ed., *Ethical Insight/Ethical Action Perspectives for the Local Government Manager* (Washington, D.C.: International City Management Association, 1988); J. E. Kellough, "Reinventing Public Personnel Management: Ethical Implications for Managers and Public Personnel Systems," *Public Personnel Management,* 28 (Winter 1999), 655–671; and J. P. West, "Ethics and Human Resource Management," in S. W. Hays and R. C. Kearney, eds., *Public Personnel Administration: Problems and Prospects,* 4th ed. (Upper Saddle River, N.J.: Prentice-Hall, 2003), 301–315.

30. C. M. Brodsky, *The Harassed Worker.* Lexington, Mass.: Lexington Books, 1976.

31. U.S. Equal Employment Opportunity Commission, *Final Guidelines on Sexual Harassment in the Workplace* (Washington, D.C.: U.S. Government Printing Office, 1980).

32. *Meritor Savings Bank v Vinson,* 477 U.S. 57 (1986).

33. *Ellison v Brady,* 924 F.2d 872 (1991).

34. *Harris v Forklift Systems,* 114 S. Ct. 367 (1993).

35. *Oncale v Sundowner,* 523 U.S. 75 (1998).

36. M. M. Hoyman, "Sexual Harassment in the Workplace," in S. E. Condrey, ed., *Handbook of Human Resource Management in Government* (San Francisco: Jossey-Bass, 1998), 183–198; L. A. Reese and K. E. Lindenberg, "Victimhood and the Implementation of Sexual Harassment Policy," *Review of Public Personnel Administration,* 17 (Winter 1997), 37–57; and S. C. Selden, "Sexual Harassment in the Workplace," in S. W. Hays and R. C. Kearney, eds., *Public Personnel Administration: Problems and Prospects,* 4th ed. (Upper Saddle River, N.J.: Prentice-Hall, 2003), 225–237.

37. B. A. Gutek, *Sex and the Workplace* (San Francisco: Jossey-Bass, 1985); U.S. General Accounting Office, *NIH's Handling of Alleged Sexual Harassment and Sex Discrimination Matters.* (Washington, D.C.: General Accounting Office, 1995); and U.S. Merit Systems Protection Board, *Sexual Harassment in the Federal Workplace: Trends, Progress, Continuing Challenges* (Washington, D.C.: U.S. Government Printing Office, 1995).

38. N. J. Cayer, "Privacy and Integrity Testing for Public Employees," in P. J. Cooper and C. A. Newland, *Handbook of Public Law and Administration.* (San Francisco: Jossey-Bass, 1998), 287–298; and D. E. Terpstra, R. B. Kethley, R. T. Foley, and W. Limpaphayon, "The Nature of Litigation Surrounding Five Screening Devices," *Public Personnel Management,* 29 (Spring 2000), 43–53.

39. *National Treasury Employees Union v Van Raab,* 489 U.S. 656 (1989).

40. *Frye v U.S.,* 293 F. 1013 (1923).

41. *Thorne v City of El Segundo,* 726 F. 2d 456 (9th Cir., 1983), cert. denied, 469 U.S. 979.

42. *Hester v City of Milledgeville,* 777 F. 2d 1492 (11th Cir., 1985).

43. *Daubert v Merrell Dow Pharmaceuticals, Inc.,* 509 U.S. 579 (1993).

44. *U.S. v Scheffer,* 118 S. Ct. 1261 (1198).

45. R. D. White Jr., "Ask Me No Questions, Tell Me No Lies: Examining the Uses and Misuses of the Polygraph," *Public Personnel Management,* 30 (Winter 2001), 483–493.

SUGGESTED READINGS

Baird, J., D. D. Kadue, and K. D. Sulzer. *Public Employee Privacy: A Legal and Practical Guide to Issues of Privacy Affecting the Workplace*. Chicago: American Bar Association, 1995.

Berman, E., J. P. West, and S. Bonczek. *The Ethics Edge*. Washington, D.C.: International City/County Management Association, 1998.

Brodsky, C. M. *The Harassed Worker*. Lexington, Mass.: Lexington Books, 1976.

Domino, J. C. *Sexual Harassment and the Courts*. New York: HarperCollins, 1995.

Falco, M., and W. I. Cikins, eds. *Toward a National Policy on Drug and AIDS Testing*. Washington, D.C.: Brookings Institution, 1989.

Farley, L. *Sexual Shakedown: The Harassment of Women on the Job*. New York: Warner Books, 1980.

Garofalo, C., and D. Gueras. *Ethics in the Public Service: The Moral Mind at Work*. Washington, D.C.: Georgetown University Press, 1999.

Gatewood, R. D., and H. S. Field. *Human Resource Selection*. Fort Worth: Dryden Press, 1998.

Gutek, B. A. *Sex and the Workplace*. San Francisco: Jossey-Bass, 1985.

Hauck, V. *Arbitrating Sexual Harassment Claims*. Washington, D.C.: Bureau of National Affairs, 1995.

H R Center. *Assessment Center Trends*. Washington, D.C.: International Personnel Management Association, 2002.

_____. *Ethics*. Washington, D.C.: International Personnel Management Association, 2002.

Kazman, J., and S. Bonczek. *Ethics in Action*. Washington, D.C.: International City/County Management Association, 1999.

Office of Technology Assessment, Congress of the United States. *Scientific Validity of Polygraph Testing: A Research Review and Evaluation*. Washington, D.C.: U.S. Government Printing Office, 1983.

O'Neil, R. M. *The Rights of Public Employees*, 2d ed. Carbondale: Southern Illinois University Press, 1993.

Rohr, J. A. *Public Service, Ethics, and Constitutional Practice*. Lawrence, Kan: University of Kansas Press, 1998.

Traen, T. J. *A Matter of Ethics: Facing the Fear of Doing the Right Thing*. Stamford, Conn.: JAI Press, 2000.

U.S. Merit Systems Protection Board. *Sexual Harassment in the Federal Workplace: Trends, Progress, Continuing Challenges*. Washington, D.C.: U.S. Government Printing Office, 1995.

Van Wart, M. 1998. *Changing Public Sector Values*. New York: Garland, 1998.

SELECTED WEB SITES

American Polygraph Association (APA). Professional association of polygraphers devoted to advancing the field of polygraphy. Conducts research and advances training and education to improve polygraph testing. www.apa.org

Bureau of National Affairs (BNA). Publisher of materials on legal and regulatory aspects of organizations with a particular emphasis on employment issues, including government employment. www.bna.com

Ethics Officers Association (EOA). A membership organization of ethics officers of business, government, and nonprofit organizations from around the world. Sponsors conferences and publications devoted to ethics concerns. www.eoa.org

National Organization for Women (NOW). Advocacy organization for women. Publishes reports on the status of women in employment and on harassment. www.now.org

National Partnership for Women and Families. Founded as the Women's Legal Defense Fund, the Partnership is an advocacy organization for women and families. Promotes fairness and the legal rights of women and families in employment. www.nationalpartnership.org

Section on Ethics. A section of the American Society for Public Administration that seeks to increase understanding of ethics in government and the nonprofit sectors. Publishes a journal and newsletter and sponsors presentations at conferences. www.aspanet.org/sections/sectionpages/ethics.html

Section on Public Law and Administration (SPLA). A section of the American Society for Public Administration that promotes the relationship between law and public management, including personnel-related law. Sponsors presentations at conferences and publishes periodic reports. www.aspanet.org/sections/sectionpages/spla.html

U.S. Department of Labor elaws Advisors. Agency that provides interactive tools on federal employment laws. www.dol.gov/elaws

U.S. Equal Employment Opportunity Commission (EEOC). Monitors employer compliance with nondiscrimination and equal employment law. Investigates and decides on complaints of discrimination brought to it. Also conducts studies and publishes reports on issues related to equal employment. www.eeoc.gov

U.S. Office of Government Ethics (OGE). Agency whose mission is to foster high ethical standards for national government employees and build confidence in government integrity. Helps prevent conflicts of interest. www.usoge.gov

U.S. Merit Systems Protection Board (MSPB). Monitors the federal government's merit-based employment systems and serves as the appeals board for federal employees on major personnel actions. Conducts studies and publishes reports on merit systems. www.mspb.gov

---

Exercises

1. Tanya Blackburn is a captain in the Fire Department and has been with the department for twenty years. This year, the city decided to institute random drug testing for all firefighters. In the past, testing was used only when there was a suspicion of drug use. Blackburn and many of her colleagues objected to the new policy; they believed it violated their constitutional rights against unreasonable searches and seizures. Nonetheless, all but Blackburn went along with the tests. She refused and was terminated under the new policy.

   The city believes the random testing is necessary for protection of the public. It believes the interest of safety overrides the privacy interest of the employee.

   You are a member of the Civil Service Board that will hear the appeal. What issues will you consider? How do you think the appeal should be decided? Why?

2. Min Patel applied for a position as a deputy sheriff with her county sheriff's department. She was pleased to learn that she had passed all the exams and that the department wanted to hire her. She had the job if she passed the medical exam, so she made her appointment for the exam.

As part of her medical history, Patel explained that she had lung cancer three years earlier but was in complete remission. Otherwise, everything checked out fine. The department informed her that she could not be employed because she had not passed her medical exam.

Patel filed a complaint saying that she was discriminated against based on a past medical condition that was no longer a factor. The city responded that there was a possibility the cancer could return and that as a deputy sheriff, Patel would be exposed to situations in which she could be breathing substances that could reactivate her condition.

Do you think the city is right? Does Patel have a legitimate complaint? Explain.

3. Cory Paul has been president of the state Public Labor Council for fifteen years. The 1984 gubernatorial election was a very spirited one, and the Republican incumbent eventually won. Because the incumbent had been very antilabor in her first administration, the Public Labor Council, at Paul's urging, had endorsed and worked for the election of the Democratic candidate. There was nothing unusual about the activity; the council had done the same thing during its fifty-year history in the state.

Three months after the election, Paul received a certified letter from the state personnel director informing him that he had violated the state's little "Hatch Act," which prohibits political activity by state employees. Specifically, Paul was charged with endorsing and campaigning for the election of the Democratic nominee for governor, contrary to the provisions of the law, which had been in effect for twenty-five years.

Paul was angry and confused. In his fifteen years as president of the Public Labor Council, he could not remember such a thing happening. In fact, no such case had occurred during the entire history of the little Hatch Act. His options were rather limited. The letter informed him that he would be prosecuted for violating the law and would be given a punishment ranging from suspension to termination. He was also offered the opportunity to resign, in which case the charges would be dropped.

Paul decided to fight the charges and filed an appeal with the Personnel Appeals Board, which handles disputes over personnel activities. His appeal requested that the charges be dismissed and that his record be expunged of any wrongdoing.

You are the hearing examiner. What do you want to know? What is your tentative decision? Why?

4. Cape City had a public beach with a café owned and operated by the city. Terry Talbert was employed as a food server at the café. On several occasions, two rowdy men had come to the café, and Talbert had waited on them. Each time, they had made sexually suggestive com-

ments to her and she had walked away. She had complained to the manager, who told her to ignore their comments.

One day they came in and sat in Talbert's section. She told the manager she did not want to wait on them. He told her to do so. The men started their harassing comments and she again complained to the manager, who again told her to ignore the comments. When she brought their food, one of the customers grabbed her and touched her breast. Talbert quit and walked out.

The next day her manager's supervisor called to find out what happened and offered Talbert a job in another part of the department. She declined the offer. She then filed a complaint with the EEOC, charging the manager and department with sexual harassment.

Does Talbert have a case? Explain.

8

Labor-Management Relations

Traditionally, labor-management relations for the public and private sectors have differed greatly. While private sector employees achieved full collective bargaining rights by the 1940s, not until the 1960s did many public employees achieve them. Since the 1980s, the two sectors have appeared increasingly similar in their labor-management relationships.[1] The drive by public employees to unionize and bargain produced labor-management relations modeled on private sector experience. The rapid increase in privatization since the 1980s also has blurred the distinction between public and private sector employees relative to labor relations. The term *labor-management relations* is preferred by many public managers as an indication of government's reluctant acceptance of bargaining. The term actually refers to all aspects of the interchange between labor and management, whereas *collective bargaining* refers more specifically to the process by which labor and management participate in mutual decision making regarding the work situation. In such decision making, the employees organize and select a representative to work with management on their behalf. In the absence of collective bargaining, employees are on their own and must negotiate individually with their employers.

Although much of the growth in public sector collective bargaining has occurred since the 1960s, some public employees have a long history of unionization. Craftworkers in naval installations, for example, have been organized since the early part of the nineteenth century, and the National Association of Letter Carriers came into existence in the late nineteenth century as an affiliate of the American Federation of Labor. Some state and local employees also have been unionized for a relatively long time. The International Association of Fire Fighters, an AFL-CIO affiliate, started in the 1880s as local social clubs and firefighters' benefit societies. Similarly, the American Federation of State, County and Municipal Employees (AFSCME) began in 1936 under the auspices of the American Federation of Labor (AFL). The AFL and the Congress of Industrial Organizations (CIO) were national umbrella organizations that provided financial, political, and technical support to individual affiliates and local organizations. Originally one organization, the AFL and CIO split in 1937 over internal disagreements about poachers to collective bargaining and personality conflicts among some of the leaders. After many years of spirited competition, the two groups merged again in 1955 to form the AFL-CIO.

Unionization, however, does not necessarily entail collective bargaining. Not until the 1960s did collective bargaining begin to play an important role in public personnel administration. President John Kennedy's Executive Order 10988 in 1962 was a major force in stimulating public sector bargaining activity. It granted federal employees the right to organize and engage in collective bargaining. Executive Orders 11491 (1969) and 11616 (1971) by President Richard Nixon and 11838 (1975) by President Gerald Ford clarified and formalized the bargaining process for federal employees. The Civil Service Reform Act of 1978 brought about additional changes; the most significant feature of the reform act was to spell out in a statute the right to collective bargaining so that presidents would no longer have the authority to regulate the process on their own. The process by which personnel decisions are made reflects the influence of labor organizations since the early 1960s.

Government Resistance to Unions

Several factors accounted for the lack of public sector collective bargaining in the past. Among them were an unfavorable legal environment, the legal doctrines of government sovereignty and privilege, an essentiality-of-services argument, the professional status of many public employees, the pay and fringe benefit levels of some employees, and the availability of other means by which employees could attain their objectives. In addition, the public's negative reaction to collective bargaining among government employees slowed its development.

In the current political environment, unions enjoy little public support. The 1960s and 1970s were unusual in that public opinion tended to support public employee unions and bargaining. Otherwise, the general public has been suspicious of the potential effects of bargaining activities. Many people are afraid that unions already have too much power and have disproportionate power when permitted to bargain with the government. Because unions help elect officials who are supposed to represent the public, many critics believe that public employees enjoy an undue advantage if they also have unions bargaining for them.[2]

The power of unions could be exaggerated. Public employee unions, especially at the federal level, are restricted from engaging in partisan political activity and cannot negotiate for union security agreements guaranteeing that the employees they represent will join the union or pay dues. There are also numerous restrictions as to which items can be bargained over: Pay and fringe benefits are excluded in federal bargaining and in some state and local jurisdictions. As some writers have pointed out, public employee unions are also at a disadvantage because they have no natural allies in the political process so that most organized political interests find them easy targets for attack.[3] Management often uses the fear of union power to justify denying collective bargaining to public employees.

The political climate also contributed to a legal framework in which bargaining was made difficult. Government employees were specifically exempted from the protections of the Wagner and Taft-Hartley acts, which spelled out the rights and responsibilities of parties in private sector bargaining. Also, before 1960, the courts consistently held that public employees did not have a constitutional right to join or organize unions, and public employers were under no obligation to bargain with employees. Starting in 1954, when by executive order Mayor Robert Wagner granted New York City employees the right to organize, the legal environment underwent rapid change. The collective bargaining apparatus was established in 1958, and the city began its bargaining process. In 1959, Wisconsin became the first state to authorize collective bargaining for public employees; however, only local government employees were affected, because state employees were exempted from the law. With the 1962 Kennedy order mentioned earlier, however, unionization and bargaining flourished at all levels of government.

Before the Kennedy order, collective bargaining had been nonexistent in the federal government service, although the Lloyd-LaFollette Act of 1912 granted employees the right to join labor organizations and petition Congress without fear of reprisal. Before the passage of that act, federal employees were subject to mandatory discharge and forfeiture of civil service status for union activity. Similarly, legislation in 1955 declared that a strike against the federal government is a felony and disqualifies the participants from federal employment. The Kennedy executive order, however, signaled a turning point in labor relations. As it changed federal policy on bargaining with federal government employees, it also stimulated state and local governments to reexamine and change many of their policies.

No common legal framework governs state and local government labor relations. The fifty states have their own policies or nonpolicies, and many variations exist in the approximately 80,000 local government jurisdictions across the country. Labor relations take place under policies made through common law doctrine, judicial decisions, executive orders, statutes, ordinances, and the opinions of attorneys general.

Twenty-six states and the District of Columbia extend collective bargaining to virtually all employees, and twelve more states allow some groups, such as teachers and firefighters, to bargain.[4] The remaining twelve have no collective bargaining legislation, but court decisions and decisions of attorneys general have allowed some employees to bargain.

When labor relations policies exist, they range from full-fledged collective bargaining including strikes to very restrictive policies such as meet and confer. *Meet and confer* refers to a process in which employees have the right to sit down with management and discuss issues but do not have the right to have any ensuing agreements enforced by the political or legal system. Arizona uses the meet and confer system for local governments. In that state, some jurisdictions, especially school districts, appear to engage in full-fledged negotiations, and it is politically difficult for the jurisdiction to turn its back on an agreement even though there is no legal requirement to honor it.

Traditionally, the *sovereignty of government doctrine* has been used to preclude public employees from bargaining. This doctrine holds that government is the agent of the people and cannot delegate authority to others, such as employee organizations, without violating the people's trust. In other words, the authority is not government's to delegate. This doctrine has waned in significance as governments have found it necessary to delegate power in a variety of areas and the courts have weakened the doctrine in many other decisions.

The *privilege doctrine* is another legal device that has been used to discourage public sector collective bargaining. This doctrine holds that some of the benefits governments confer are privileges, not rights, and conditions can be imposed on these privileges. For example, education, welfare, and the like have been adjudged to be privileges. Similarly, public employment was viewed as a privilege, and the prohibition of collective bargaining was one acceptable restriction that could be placed on accepting public employment. However, as with the sovereignty doctrine, the courts have essentially abandoned the privilege doctrine, and it no longer restricts bargaining in the public sector.

Services performed by governments ordinarily have been characterized as essential, and bargaining has been denied to public employees because of this essentiality of services. Particularly because collective bargaining is often equated with strikes, the prohibition of bargaining has been justified as a way to prevent the interruption of services. This argument has been weakened because many of the services government provides are not viewed as essential. In fact, many private sector services—the telephone and Internet, for example—would be more difficult to do without in the short run than would government service such as education and highway maintenance. Furthermore, experience with the loss of services such as sanitation, police protection, and education through strikes has demonstrated that people can cope with the situation for a limited time and has lessened the fears surrounding collective bargaining.

Public employees themselves often have been hesitant to engage in collective bargaining. Until the 1960s, unions and other labor organizations were not held in high esteem by public employees. Much public sector labor is white collar, and there has been a tendency for employees to think of labor organizations as typically blue collar. Teachers in particular have been split over whether it is professional to belong to a union and engage in collective bargaining. However, after finding that unions could bring them gains, public employees have been changing their view, and many professional associations are becoming bargaining agents for public employees.

Although the pay and benefits of state and local government employees are often poor, federal employees have very good benefits. Compensation, although not excessive, also has been relatively good at the starting and middle levels of the federal service. As a result, federal employees did not see as much of a need for collective bargaining as some of their counterparts did.

Finally, public employees sometimes have been slow to organize because they have other means of gaining their objectives. Because the decision makers are elected politicians, they pay attention to blocs of voters, and public employees often constitute a major bloc. Because legislative bodies often retain control over public employees' pay and benefits, lobbying is also an important method for gaining influence. The lack of centralized authority in the political system also permits interests to gain in one place what they cannot in another. Thus, if the executive does not satisfy a group, that group can go to the legislative body or a competing board or agency. Public employee groups have been effective in taking advantage of these fragmented political structures, particularly at the local level.

Politics and Bargaining

A factor that differentiates public sector and private sector collective bargaining is the political nature of the decision-making process in the public sector.[5] As Theodore Clark observed, collective bargaining is premised on the idea that the two parties to the bargaining process are adversaries who seek their own interests and that each party selects its representative without being influenced by the other party.[6] In the public sector, however, political considerations violate these premises. In particular, public employee organizations participate in the selection of management through involvement in interest group politics and through the election process. In short, employee organizations have special access to management's decision-making process, thus enhancing the organizations' power vis-à-vis management. Critics of public sector bargaining decry the special position enjoyed by public employee labor organizations and suggest that unions and the like dominate the process as a result.[7]

Summers, in contrast, believes that public employees need that special access because they face formidable opposition from all other interests in the political process.[8] Because tax revenues could have to be raised or levels of service reduced to finance public employees' demands, the political opposition to such demands can be intense. The taxpayer revolts symbolized by California's Proposition 13 in 1978 and its stimulation of similar efforts in other jurisdictions that endure to this day attest to the impact an aroused electorate can have. Similarly, public employees in San Francisco bore the brunt of taxpayer discontent with some of their gains in 1974 and 1975. In 1985, San Francisco voters rescinded an agreement establishing comparable worth. Through referenda, salaries were rolled back and limits were established regarding how to negotiate and what could be bargained. Similarly, a 1994 referendum in Oregon wiped out the state contribution to the employee retirement system. Thus, abuses by employee unions can be cited, but active citizen participation in the political process also can override the influence of public employee organizations.

The political nature of public sector bargaining also is reflected in the way management selects its representatives and decides on the policy it will bring to the bargaining table. Again, as Summers pointed out, citizens have an interest in these issues, whereas in the private sector, management makes such decisions without public involvement.[9] Because decisions on how management will select a representative and on what the bargaining position will be are matters of public concern, employee organizations can participate in them, again augmenting their influence. In contrast, management normally is prohibited from attempting to influence the employees' selection of bargaining agents and positions.

It is also difficult for management to send someone to the bargaining table who can bind public management to an agreement. There are many other decision makers to whom employee organizations can appeal if they do not get satisfaction in the bargaining process. Many times city councils or other legislative bodies need to ratify agreements but are hesitant to give up any authority to change elements of the agreement. Similarly, legislative bodies can retain control over many aspects of the work situation by either mandating or placing restrictions on personnel practices. For local governments, the issue is even more complicated by the fact that state legislation can mandate practices for all governmental bodies. If a state minimum salary or other requirement is imposed, the local jurisdiction will have little flexibility. This is the case because the costs normally must be borne by the local government even though the policy comes from above. Public employee organizations use their access to elected political leaders to influence decision-making processes and participate in the election of such officials.

Another political aspect of public sector collective bargaining is that personnel issues have larger policy implications. Personnel issues are part of the policy-making process to the extent that political representatives make the decisions that in many cases affect issues such as tax policy, budgeting, and level of services. The political representatives are influenced by what will gain them votes. Such concerns often lead to problems if a political leader does not own up to the consequences of trying to curry favor with employee organizations for the purpose of gaining elective office. Officials in some cities, such as New York City, have agreed in the past to contracts whose costs had to be borne by future officials. Pension plans in particular often were subject to such political manipulation. In the short run, the politician gains, but the taxpayers and succeeding officials must face the long-term cost. Unless the public is made fully aware of the ultimate cost, it is difficult to prevent opportunistic politicians from taking advantage of the situation. With greater public access to information since the freedom of information and open meetings laws of the 1960s and 1970s, these issues are debated publicly now, which mitigates the problem somewhat.

Because of these problems, the "fishbowl" approach to public sector bargaining developed; with this approach, the bargaining is done in public. In the private sector, closed door sessions are almost universal. The public sector, however, runs into problems when it conducts closed negotiation sessions: In a democratic society, people are supposed to know what is going on so that they can retain control over the system. If bargaining is conducted in private, the public cannot participate in the process and must relinquish control to those who participate in the negotiation. By contrast, when negotiation takes place in open meetings, participants can find themselves pushed into corners on issues. Once people state a position publicly, it becomes difficult to change it because this could be perceived as backing down. Because negotiation requires compromise, it becomes difficult to bargain effectively in public sessions. There is no easy way to reconcile the need for openness in a democratic government and the need for frankness and compromise in collective bargaining.

Elements of a Labor Relations System

A public labor-management relations system is created by public policy in the form of legislation, an executive order, a court decision, or a legal opinion. The policy normally spells out who has authority for labor-management relations and the basic rules and steps in the bargaining process. Of course, the question of whether the right to bargain is to exist is the system's most basic element.

ADMINISTRATION OF LABOR-MANAGEMENT RELATIONS

If the right to bargain is granted, there must be a way to administer the process; thus, most policies assign the responsibility to an existing agency or create a new one. The national government, under the Civil Service Reform act of 1978, created the Federal Labor Relations Authority (FLRA) to oversee bargaining unit determination, supervise elections, and coordinate agency labor-management activities. The FLRA consists of three bipartisan presidential appointees, with one designated as the chairperson. Also appointed is a general counsel who investigates unfair labor practices, and the Federal Service Impasses Panel resolves impasses in negotiation.

At the state and local levels, the supervision of the collective bargaining process varies. Some states create an agency whose sole purpose is to supervise public employee labor relations, usually including local governments. Maine, New York, and Hawaii are examples of such states. Another approach is to assign the responsibility to personnel departments, departments of labor, or personnel boards, as is done in Alaska, Massachusetts, Montana, and Wisconsin. A combination of approaches also may be used in which a state board may oversee collective bargaining generally but individual departments have the specific responsibility for bargaining in their areas. Thus, it is common to see departments of education and local boards of education supervising their own bargaining.

UNIT DETERMINATION

Unit determination refers to those employees who are considered a unit for bargaining purposes. The criteria for making such a decision are community of interest, desires of the employees and employer, history of experience, efficiency of management, and limiting fragmentation. *Community of interest* pertains to the similarities of the people in the proposed unit. Similarity of duties, skills, working conditions, job classifications, employee benefits, promotional ladders, and supervision are some of the factors considered. In addition, employees may be grouped because of the amount of interchange, integration of physical operations, or centralization of administrative and managerial functions. The main concern is having a bargaining unit consisting of employees who have similar interests so they can work together. Employees often like to have many units because the narrower a group's interests are, the greater its solidarity is likely to be. Sometimes that concern is sacrificed for size, however, because an overly narrow focus could lead to very small numbers of eligible employees for the unit. Management usually prefers larger units because there are likely to be disagreements within the unit that management can exploit and because when units are large, management must deal with fewer employee representatives.

The two main types of unit are agency and occupational units. *Agency units* are those in which a particular department or agency forms the basis for organizing the bargaining process. The Treasury Department at the national level and police and fire departments at the local levels are examples of agency units. The state of Minnesota uses agency units throughout the state service. An advantage for management is that the channels of communication are already in place in the agencies. However, problems with inequity among similar employees in different units can exist, and consensus is often difficult to achieve because an agency employs many types of employees.

Occupational units are based on the type of work done. Thus, all clerical staff may be in one unit, all lab technicians in another, and so on. Clearly, each group is likely to have well-defined interests, and similar work in different agencies is covered under similar policies. Managers often have difficulty with this approach because it centralizes authority on bargained issues, thus weakening departmental control over employees.

Some jurisdictions use a combination of the two approaches. New York City, for example, bargains over some issues (overtime, reduction-in-force policies, grievance procedures) citywide. Other issues, such as caseloads, may be negotiated at the departmental level, and still others related to items such as the salary for a particular job title may be bargained at yet another designated level. Such a system is said to have *multilevel units.*

An issue that comes up in the public sector but not in the private sector is whether supervisors should be in the same unit as the people they supervise. In the private sector, supervisors generally are not permitted to bargain, but if they are, they are in separate units. In the public sector, it is not uncommon to find supervisors in the same units with their subordinates. Police and fire departments often have everyone except the chief in the bargaining unit. Conflicts can arise because the bargaining unit's representative has to represent the employees in grievances. If the supervisor against whom a grievance is filed is also a member of the unit, a conflict of interest occurs. The shop steward or union representative is supposed to represent everyone in the unit and certainly cannot represent both sides at the same time. Being in the bargaining unit with subordinates also compromises the supervisor's role as a member of the management team. In the public sector, these problems arise because the role of supervisors is not as clear as it is in the private sector. Supervisors in the public sector often are considered lead workers in their units but are not considered part of management. Thus, there is confusion over whether they should be part of the bargaining unit.

BARGAINING REPRESENTATIVES

Management often has difficulty organizing for bargaining because of the fragmentation of political authority in government units. Nonetheless, as bargaining activity has increased, most jurisdictions involved in bargaining have hired labor relations experts to lead negotiations and administer the overall labor-management relations program. Representatives of personnel, legal counsel, and representatives of the department or unit to which negotiations pertain usually work with the labor relations expert.

Employees choose representatives to bargain for them. The selection process usually requires an election in which the employees decide whether to adopt collective bargaining and determine who will bargain for them. The election of the unit's representatives is known as the *certification election,* and, like the election on whether to bargain at all, it is supervised by the agency responsible for administering the labor-management relations program. The two actions may be taken at the same election or in separate elections. Representatives of employees fall into three categories: union, employee associations, and professional associations.

Unions, of course, are the most readily recognized participants in collective bargaining because they have been the traditional agents of employees in the private sector. Unions in the public sector can have only public employee members or can have mixed membership, that is, have members from both the public and private sectors. As union membership in the private sector has declined, unions have increasingly opened to public employee membership to maintain their strength. The largest public sector union is the American Federation of State, County, and Municipal Employees (AFSCME), with a membership of approximately 1.3 million.[10] Membership tells only part of the story, however. Unions in the public sector represent everyone in the bargaining unit, even though they cannot require all employees in the unit to be dues-paying members. Thus, AFSCME represents well over 1.5 million employees at the local, state, and national levels. The National Association of Government Employees with about 60,000 members represents 150,000 workers at all levels of government.[11]

Representing mostly federal government employees are three other relatively large unions. The American Federation of Government Employees (AFGE) represents approximately 600,000 employees and has about 218,000 members, and the National Federation of Federal Employees (NFFE) represents 120,000 employees and has about 35,000 members.[12] The National Treasury Employees Union (NTEU) represents about 155,000 employees and has about 70,000 members.[13] Many public employee unions, like their private sector counterparts, are having difficulty retaining members. Fiscal stress in governments has weakened union ability to do much about wages and benefits. Additionally, working conditions have improved to the point where many employees no longer see the need for unions to protect their interests. Taken for granted are relatively safe working conditions and programs to protect employees' security in times of illness and injury. Without a strong perceived need for their services, unions must convince employees of their benefits, and with unions' current image, that is not always easy.

The uniformed services are among the most highly unionized and are represented by unions with almost exclusively public sector membership. Police officers are represented by two major organizations, the Fraternal Order of Police (FOP) with 300,000 members and the International Brotherhood of Police Officers (IBPO).[14] Some other unions, such as AFSCME and the Teamsters, also represent the police in some jurisdictions. Because police protection is one of the essential services people fear losing, these unions usually have been successful in obtaining their demands. Police unions usually play up the professional nature of their work and organizations rather than the union image that normally goes with such employee organizations.

Sick-ins and slowdowns are common techniques used by police employee unions. When strikes occur, the current political climate dampens the public's enthusiasm for them. Also, strikes are not always successful, as the experience of the New Orleans police demonstrated in 1979. The strike, timed to occur during Mardi Gras, the city's busiest tourist season, was calculated to bring pressure from business and the community to bear on public officials. The union expected that such pressure would make management settle quickly to the benefit of the police. The actual result was that much of the Mardi Gras celebration was curtailed, the police union lost its credibility with and the support of the community, and management held out for its original offer until the police were willing to settle. The New Orleans experience demonstrates the taxpayer's growing frustration and shows that unions do not always get what they want. Similarly, President Reagan's firing of 11,500 air traffic controllers who went out on strike in 1981 was a dramatic message to public employees that strikes could be broken. This action encouraged many public employers to take harder lines with their employees' representatives.

Firefighters also have a long tradition of collective bargaining in an essential service. They are almost unique among public employees because the International Association of Fire Fighters (IAFF) exercises virtually exclusive jurisdiction over them. In contrast with the police organization, the 250,000-member IAFF traditionally has stressed its union image in association with the AFL-CIO.[15] Although the international union does not officially sanction strikes, it provides assistance to striking locals.

As was noted earlier, some unions consist of membership from both the public and private sectors. During the late 1950s, many private sector unions lost members and looked to the growing public sector to increase their rolls. These unions usually seek members from all levels of government rather than from just one level. The AFL-CIO now has a department devoted entirely to public sector collective bargaining. Reflecting the private sector's tradition, these unions tend to be more occupationally segregated and more likely to favor strikes. Among these mixed-memberships unions are the Service Employees International Union (SEIU) with a membership of more than 1.5 million of whom more than 500,000 are public employees;[16] the International Brotherhood of Teamsters with approximately 170,000 public employee members;[17] and the Amalgamated Transit Union with approximately 90,000 public employee members.[18] Many other unions have mixed memberships. Interests in mixed-membership unions are divided between public and private sector contingents, leading to some concern about how strongly they can represent public employees' interests. However, they have the vast resources of the parent union behind them and are effective in marshaling support in the political process.

Public employee associations are the second type of representative in public sector collective bargaining. Some associations on the state and local levels have existed for many years. Although originally organized to improve employee opportunities and the status of public employees, many associations have redirected their activities toward collective bargaining. Because of their original purposes, they tend to favor strikes less and instead rely heavily on public relations and lobbying. They are becoming increasingly militant, however, as the competition for membership grows between them and the unions. Many have merged with unions, and others have joined the Assembly of Government Employees (AGE) to strengthen their clout.

Professional associations, the third category, also have been organized for a long time to better the status of their professions and members. However, their membership is much more limited than that of public employee associations in that educational or occupational criteria are imposed for membership. They generally have resisted joining the bargaining movement because they have viewed bargaining as unprofessional behavior. However, the success of unions and employee associations in recruiting and gaining benefits for their members has stimulated professional groups to organize for collective bargaining. Among the more active professional associations in bargaining are the American Nurses Association (ANA), the National Association of Social Workers (NASW), and the American Association of University Professors (AAUP). The National Education Association (NEA) is the largest, with a membership of more than 2.7 million and is one of the most active in the bargaining process.[19] Its state affiliates decide how deeply involved they wish to be in bargaining. The NEA and its affiliates provide some of the clearest evidence of the conflict in professional organizations over the collective bargaining issue. It has been pushed further into the bargaining process by the success of the American Federation of Teachers (AFT) in recruiting members and winning benefits. To retain its membership, the NEA feels the necessity for bargaining. The rivalry between NEA and AFT led them to propose a merger, but it never occurred. Instead, they created the NEAFT Partnership to work together on common interests while allowing each organization to act separately as it sees fit. The American Association of University Professors (AAUP) has faced a similar conflict as the representative of college and university faculties.

The variety of employee organizations in the bargaining process creates numerous approaches to issues in labor-management relations. Unions tend to be most militant, although they vary greatly from one to another. Unions associated with both private and public sector employees usually are more likely to support the right to strike, but police and fire fighter unions certainly also have done so in recent years. Employee and professional associations usually prefer to use public relations and lobbying to accomplish their objectives but have been pushed into more militant positions by unions' success in their bargaining efforts. Similarly, some organizations, particularly employee associations, stress the independence of their affiliates, and the unions stress the resources their national organizations provide. All in all, approximately 37 percent of eligible public employees are union members, with local workers leading with

43.2 percent of workers unionized. The percentage of state workers unionized is 30 percent and of federal employees is 32.5 percent. Among occupational groups, public safety workers (police and fire) led at 38 percent unionized.[20]

SCOPE OF BARGAINING

The labor relations policy also addresses the scope of bargaining or what can be bargained. The policy may make bargaining on issues either mandatory or permissive. Mandatory issues are those that must be bargained, and permissive issues are those that may be bargained if both parties wish. There are also prohibited issues, that is, issues that cannot be bargained over according to policy. In the national government, for example, wages and salaries cannot be negotiated, and in many state and local governments, negotiators may be prohibited from bargaining on items such as assignment of personnel and decisions about the nature of the service to be delivered. Discriminatory provisions cannot be included in agreements in any jurisdiction.

A conflict arises over the scope of bargaining because management wishes to maintain as much of its prerogative as possible in decisions, and labor wishes to share in that responsibility. This conflict usually leads to a definition of the items that can and cannot be negotiated. Generally, it is assumed that management rights exist independently of the collective bargaining relationship until modified by that relationship. As with most other aspects of labor relations policy, the scope of bargaining varies greatly by jurisdiction.

Labor relations policy defines the basic rules under which labor relations take place. The policy addresses issues other than those just noted, and they will be treated separately because of their significance in the bargaining process. Those issues include impasse resolution procedures, strikes, and contract administration. They will be examined after the next section, which deals with the negotiations themselves.

The Negotiating Process

Once it has been determined what can be negotiated and the employees have decided to use collective bargaining procedures and have selected a representative, the process begins. Ordinarily, the employees express their desire to bargain on an issue or issues by presenting proposals covering the items they wish to consider. In recent years, it has been common for management also to draw up a list of demands to be considered at the negotiating table. Thus, management now sees the process as proactive rather than reactive. Once the proposals have been exchanged, the two sides meet to determine what procedures or ground rules will govern the negotiations. The proposals may be exchanged before the first meeting or at the meeting, depending on the particular case.

After both sides make and explain their proposals, each studies the other's position so that reactions and counterproposals can be made. These reactions and counterproposals become the focus of the negotiating process. Before the actual negotiations, however, each side spends considerable time in preparation. To be prepared, each side must be well versed in personnel rules and regulations and the way they are implemented as well as in the legal limitations imposed on personnel practices. Each side also will review the previous agreement and any problems that have occurred under it. Of particular interest will be any grievances filed under the current agreement. In addition, each party normally costs out its proposals and collects data on economic indicators, productivity, budget and revenue projections, and wages and salaries in similar and surrounding jurisdictions. Armed with these data, the negotiators are ready to begin negotiating over their proposals.

The behavior of the parties in the negotiations is extremely important, and posturing is common. One party or the other could decide to take an aggressive, challenging, hard-line approach on every item, hoping to wear down the other side. Alternatively, the strategy can be to focus on a few issues that are of particular importance and make concessions on other issues. Another approach is to appear conciliatory in order to establish goodwill. Often participants attempt to impress their own constituents as much as their adversaries in the negotiations. The strategy chosen normally depends on how far apart the parties are and how important the issues are. Relative political power also is a factor in the public sector, as was illustrated by some of the examples cited earlier, particularly in New York City, where employee organizations can bring other political forces into play. The Professional Air Traffic Controllers Organization (PATCO), however, miscalculated its power to influence management through appeals to citizens and the business community.

Most collective bargaining ends in an agreement at the negotiating table. Then each side must take the agreement back to its constituency for approval. The members of the employee organization vote on ratification of the agreement. If they vote no, more negotiation is necessary. If they vote yes, management usually must go to the relevant legislative body for approval and funding. Occasionally, a city council or school board rejects an agreement, in which case the negotiations must be restarted, but the agreement ordinarily wins approval. At the state and national levels, specific legislative approval usually is not required, but in states in which salary and fringe benefits are bargained over, funding for the provisions requires legislative appropriations and thus indirect approval.

Impasse Resolution Procedures

If the parties do not reach an agreement at the negotiating table, several alternatives are available to help them resolve the impasse. These alternatives are called *impasse procedures* and include mediation, fact finding, arbitration, and referendum. All use outside parties, usually called *third parties*. There are many types of third parties. At the national level, the Federal Mediation and Conciliation Service (FMCS), an independent agency, provides mediation services to the private sector and state and local governments. The Federal Service Impasses Panel (FSIP), which is part of the Federal Labor Relations Authority, also provides service to federal agencies. State and local governments sometimes have their own services for impasse resolution, but more commonly they seek federal help or the services of consultants who specialize in such work. The American Arbitration Association also has trained people to provide impasse resolution services under contract. In small jurisdictions, respected members of the community can be asked to perform this function as a public service.

FACT FINDING

Fact finding is a variation of the mediation process. In fact finding, a neutral third party works with both parties to the dispute and conducts a formal investigation of the issues separating them. The fact finder then issues a formal report stating the "facts" of the situation. The idea here is that by formally pinpointing the differences, the report will put pressure on the parties to resolve their differences. The reports usually must be made public in the hope that public opinion and pressure will cause the parties to settle.

MEDIATION

Most jurisdictions that permit bargaining use mediation, in which a neutral individual—usually trained in labor relations—tries to get the two parties to resolve their differences through compromise. Although they cannot impose decisions on the parties, the mediators meet with each party and discuss points of disagreements and how they could be reconciled. Then the mediators recommend solutions to the parties in the hope that the parties will work out the differences themselves.

ARBITRATION

If fact finding and/or mediation fail, the next step is more controversial. Because public jurisdictions generally prohibit strikes, some form of final, binding decision becomes attractive. The alternative normally available is *arbitration*. In arbitration, a neutral third party has the authority to impose a settlement or, in the case of advisory arbitration, is asked to recommend a solution. Conventional arbitration is binding in the sense that if parties go to arbitration, they are bound to accept the arbitrator's decision. The arbitrator does much the same work a mediator or fact finder does: evaluates the situation and then decides on an equitable solution. The difference is that the decision is binding.

In some instances final-offer arbitration is used. Each party presents the arbitrator its final offer for settlement, and the arbitrator then selects the better of the two. The logic behind this approach is that the parties can be expected to offer the most reasonable solution out of fear that the arbitrator could choose the settlement proposed by the other party, which could be worse. Connecticut and Indiana use forms of final-offer arbitration.

Arbitration also often is differentiated as voluntary or compulsory. *Voluntary arbitration* means that the parties voluntarily choose to go to arbitration. In *compulsory arbitration,* the parties have no choice but to go to arbitration at some specified point. Thus, the law may require arbitration if mediation has been attempted and has failed or after a certain number of days of impasse. The difference between these two types of arbitration lies only in how the parties arrive at arbitration; once the process starts, it is the same.

A combination form of impasse resolution is the *med-arb* approach used in Wisconsin municipalities and school districts. With the med-arb, a mediator attempts to resolve the impasse. If this is unsuccessful, the mediator then becomes an arbitrator. This system is supposed to be more efficient because the mediator already knows the situation and so, as an arbitrator, does not have to spend time becoming familiar with it. Knowing that the same person is going to arbitrate if mediation is unsuccessful also may encourage the two parties to work out their differences along the lines of the mediator's suggestions. This approach has not been used very commonly in the United States.

REFERENDUM

The fourth impasse procedure is the voter *referendum,* in which the contested issues may be taken to the public for a vote. Colorado permits municipalities to use this method. As with final-offer arbitration, the referendum approach can bring pressure to get the decision made through the negotiating process to avoid potentially harsher agreements from the outside. However, complex bargaining issues do not lend themselves very well to an election campaign that requires gaining voters' short attention spans.

The impasse procedures outlined here progress from the least to the most coercive in terms of the ability of outside parties to impose settlement. However, there is interaction among the processes. The developments in mediation and fact finding provide part of the basis for the arbitration process if it progresses that far. Variations in each of the procedures also can combine elements from one or more of the "pure" impasse procedures described. The availability of any or all of the procedures varies among jurisdictions. When more than one is available, the mildest form usually is used first and then the process moves through the more coercive choices.

Strikes

If these procedures are not available or do not resolve the impasse, employees can decide that they have no alternative but to strike. Although most jurisdictions prohibit strikes by public employees, there has been no dearth of strikes in the public sector (Table 8.1). Since 1980, however, the number of public sector strikes has dropped. The PATCO experience, high unemployment, and the public's disaffection with labor unions all probably contributed to less militance by employee organizations. Opposition to strikes is evident to the extent that all but ten states prohibit them, and where they are permitted, they generally are limited in that only certain types of employees may engage in them. Police, fire, hospital, and corrections personnel usually are excluded.

Thirteen states—Alaska, California, Hawaii, Idaho, Illinois, Michigan, Minnesota, Montana, Ohio, Oregon, Pennsylvania, Vermont, and Wisconsin— give public employees limited rights to strike through legislation or court decisions, but strict prohibitions are more common. Even where prohibited, however, strikes are numerous. The beginning of every school year is marked by teachers' strikes across the country. In 2001, 22,000 Minnesota state workers went on strike. Teachers in Denver and the Washington cities of Bremerton and Federal Way went on strike in the fall of 1994. Strikes of Denver transit workers in 1982 and of police in Corona, California, in 1983 were illegal. However, implementing legislation banning strikes is not easy. Officials, including judges, often are reluctant to enforce no-strike legislation by jailing strikers because of the possible martyr effect. The people jailed become heroes to other employees willing to go to such lengths for their cause.

Table 8.1 Work Stoppages Involving a Thousand or More Employees

Year	Number
1960	222
1970	381
1980	187
1990	44
2000	40
2001	30
2002	20

Source: U.S. Bureau of Labor Studies, retrieved from http://data.bls.gov/cgi-bin/ surveymost, April 6, 2003.

As noted earlier, however, some jurisdictions have been very effective in handling strikes. The firing of the PATCO strikers broke that strike and has been used as a symbol of management's tougher stance. However, even though successful in the short run, such tactics damage the morale of other employees and the credibility of management with its workforce. The long-term impact is not clear. When labor regains its political clout, management could face militant employee organizations.

Contract Administration

Once an agreement is reached, it must be implemented; the process for doing this is *contract administration*. This process gives meaning to the agreement and thus is an important part of collective bargaining. Implementation is generally management's responsibility, but the employees will react to what they perceive to be management's misinterpretations of the agreement. Many provisions in a contract may be vague, causing problems in interpretation, or the parties can disagree on what is meant by terms such as *reasonable time, just cause,* and *normal practices.* Similarly, unanticipated situations develop and must be dealt with under the contract's terms.

Although the labor relations office has the overall responsibility for implementing the agreement, the first-line supervisor is the key person for management in contract administration. She has continuous contact with the employees and thus effectively carries out the agreement's provisions. To ensure that supervisors understand the contract and implement it consistently, they are given training on the contract. It's provisions are interpreted for the supervisors, who also are instructed carefully about all the contract's contents.

Sometimes employees complain about the way part of the agreement is or is not implemented, and normally one individual is chosen as the *shop steward* or *union representative.* This person represents the employees and tries to resolve their complaints. The steward also monitors the contract's implementation to ensure compliance with the agreement and raises objections as appropriate. Most of management's contact with the employees concerning the contract's administration is through the steward.

Despite efforts to implement the agreement correctly, problems often develop, and the parties could be unable to resolve disagreements over specific provisions. In most bargaining agreements, this eventuality is provided for by *grievance arbitration.* The process normally calls for an employee with a complaint to file a written grievance with his or her immediate supervisor. The complaint can be settled at that level, but usually it can be appealed for resolution up through top management. If the parties still are unable to resolve the issue, arbitration will be invoked. The process is essentially the same as the arbitration procedure for resolving negotiation impasses. If the collective bargaining agreement has no grievance arbitration clause, personnel or civil service rules will provide a mechanism for dealing with complaints involving the agreement's implementation.

Unfair Labor Practices

Both management and labor are prohibited from engaging in unfair labor practices, which usually are defined by statute. At the national level, the 1978 Civil Service Reform Act spells out unfair labor practices, and most state statutes do the same by drawing on the national legislation or guidelines developed by the National Labor Relations Board for the private sector. Unfair management labor practices include the following:

1. Failing to bargain in good faith
2. Interfering with the right to organize
3. Attempting to influence the outcome of a bargaining election or the selection of a representative
4. Retaliating against individuals who exercise their right to organize.

Unfair union labor practices include these:

1. Coercion of employees in their exercise of the choice to bargain or in selecting a representative
2. Unfair work stoppages
3. Failure to bargain in good faith
4. Collusion with management in discriminating against nonunion workers.

Statutes, rules, and regulations define many more unfair labor practices, and the agencies that implement labor relations policies specify still more in response to complaints brought by management or labor. Statutory provisions are often vague; thus, it is up to the responsible agencies to give specificity to issues such as bargaining in good faith.

Charges of unfair labor practices are adjudicated by the Federal Labor Relations Authority at the national level. States provide for the resolution of such charges in their own way, with most giving the Public Labor Relations Board (PLRB) or a comparable authority the responsibility for resolving complaints. They normally have the authority to order the offending party to cease its actions.

Impact of Public Sector Bargaining

The effects of collective bargaining are experienced in all areas of management and service delivery. Collective bargaining has clear implications for financial management, budgeting, personnel and planning, and the roles of employees and managers in the system.

In the area of financial management and budgeting, collective bargaining agreements often lock a jurisdiction into positions from which it cannot easily extricate itself. As the effects of taxpayers' demands clearly illustrate, voters believe that collective bargaining adds to the cost of government. The empirical evidence continues to be confusing, however. Recent studies suggest that the impact has been to increase the cost to government but that overall increases have been relatively small. Specifically, collective bargaining now increases public sector wages on salaries about an average of 3.5 percent.[21] The advantage varies by occupation and jurisdiction. Because personnel costs typically make up as much as 80 percent of a jurisdiction's budget, it is inevitable that increased personnel costs will affect the cost of government unless they are accompanied by a reduction in personnel and services. As a result, jurisdictions try to offset personnel costs by increasing productivity or reducing the number of people employed. The sustained fiscal stress that governments have faced since the 1980s have caused them to make trade-offs. Clearly, the bargaining process puts costs under constant scrutiny, providing the potential for containment and the elimination of questionable spending.

Budgeting processes also are affected by bargaining. Negotiation and agreement typically take place before the budget is drawn up; thus, flexibility in budgeting can be diminished. If management or the legislative body refuses to provide funds to cover the agreement's costs, including salaries and wages, problems with the employee organization are certain to arise. Although legislative bodies have the power to adopt governmental budgets, the bargaining process actually affects that authority as the decision makers need to consider what will happen in negotiations. Budgeting and planning thus become more difficult.

The personnel function is affected greatly by the bargaining process because it is difficult to limit the scope of bargaining. Because many states permit bargaining on all aspects of the employment situation, all elements of the personnel system can be negotiated. It seems clear that merit system principles and personnel rules and regulations will increasingly become the subject of negotiation and will change in the process, although in many states two separate systems seem to be emerging: the civil service and collective bargaining systems.

Collective bargaining affects management in many ways. Traditionally, management has taken the position that bargaining is detrimental to its ability to manage. There is no question that with collective bargaining, management must share its power to govern and thus has much less discretion. However, management can and does reap the benefits from the bargaining process if it is willing to do so. Lanning S. Mosher pointed out that management can be improved through the bargaining process because the bargaining focuses attention on it as a team. By identifying management's weaknesses and training needs, the bargaining process provides leverage for obtaining the resources necessary to prepare for negotiating and working with labor organizations.[22] Management also is under pressure to do a good job when it knows its activities will be under scrutiny in the bargaining process.

Collective bargaining has the potential to create a wide variety of types of working conditions as each group of employees bargains with management. However, with a standard general policy under which agreements are bargained, the process can produce decisions that reflect a general perspective rather than the particular concerns of the moment or situation. In other words, collective bargaining can help establish a general policy within which decisions can be made.

Bargaining also has many effects for employees, not the least of which is the ability to help decide what the working conditions are to be. Workers often find that unionization and bargaining help them develop a consciousness of the importance of their work; this has been particularly true of employees in jobs such as sanitation and garbage collection. During the 1960s, racial minorities who dominated these positions found unionization to be both a way to gain dignity as human beings and a force for racial and social justice. Generally, employees believe that collective bargaining protects them against the arbitrariness in personnel and managerial decisions. Also, because employees participate in the decision-making processes, they are likely to be more committed to the organization than is the case when management unilaterally dictates policy. In fact, management often has an ally in the employee representative in presenting its policies. Employees are much more receptive to decisions that are explained by one of their own; otherwise, employees may be obstacles to change and accommodation to management's desires. Some studies also indicate that unionized organizations are more productive than nonunion ones.[23]

The Evolving Bargaining System

The politics of the 1990s and 2000s, with continuous pressure for cutting government and privatizing many government functions, placed the labor movement in a difficult situation. The election of politicians who promise to downsize government has hit labor hard because downsizing usually means cutting employees. Decreasing revenues ensures that cuts will be necessary. Management relations and labor leaders understand that new approaches are necessary. In many places, labor relations has evolved into a more cooperative approach. The new style of labor relations is seen at all levels of government.[24]

This cooperative approach has labor and management work together rather than as adversaries. Both sides recognize that the ultimate aim is the same, public service. Thus, in this era of fiscal stress, labor is sitting down with management to determine ways to get the work done. In places where labor and management are not cooperating, the old acrimony in the relationship results in losses for everyone, including the public. In the federal service, the Ogden, Utah, Internal Revenue Service Center represents an effort to reengineer a labor-management partnership. There a partnership council oversees initiatives such as the attendance of union representatives at meetings of directors and division staff at meetings on budgets, joint instructorship at training sessions for all employees, and creation of a conflict resolution council to attempt to resolve complaints about unfair labor practices in an informal process. The IRS developed a successful reengineering of the whole service following the Ogden Office success using the cooperative approach. Some of the success at the federal level appears to be threatened by President George W. Bush's antiunion initiatives. Systems vary greatly at state and local levels but cooperative approaches, such as the long-standing Phoenix Fire Department cooperative process, are being cited as models for successful labor-management relations.

Summary

Public sector collective bargaining was one of the most visible elements of public personnel management in the 1960s and 1970s. During the 1980s, the growth in the movement leveled off considerably as the political and economic environments became less supportive. Facing financial and political constraints, public employee unions were forced to reconsider their strategies. They therefore have become less militant and seem more conciliatory toward management. Management in the public sector, however, became more strident as it saw the opportunity to use its new clout to retrieve some of the things it gave up in the earlier days. Currently, collective bargaining is not a prominent issue in most of the public sector. Despite the reduced popularity of collective bargaining and unions, public managers still must deal with the process. Thus, public policy provides a variety of ways to recognize unions and bargain with them. There are also many alternatives for dealing with impasses. Although it is illegal in most places, public employees strike frequently.

Clearly, management must continue to bargain with employees, but the nature of the bargaining relationship is always evolving. New issues arise that provide the basis for continued efforts by unions. Certainly, unions have encroached on management flexibility, but they also have been effective in improving many policies and practices. Thus, their effects for personnel administration have been both positive and negative.

NOTES

1. R. C. Kearney, *Labor Relations in the Public Sector,* 3d ed. (New York: Marcel Dekker, 2001); and G. T. Sulzner, "Revisiting the Reinvented Union," in C. Ban and N. M. Riccucci, eds., *Public Personnel Management: Current Concerns, Future Challenges,* 3d ed. (New York: Longman, 2002), 113–133.

2. C. Ball, "Union Donations to Congressional Candidates," *Review of Public Personnel Administration,* 13 (Summer 1993), 8–18; S. Silbiger, "The Missing Public: Collective Bargaining and Employment," *Public Personnel Management,* 4 (September–October 1975), 290–299; and C. W. Summers, "Public Bargaining: A Political Perspective," *Yale Law Journal,* 83 (May 1974), 1156–2000.

3. Summers, "Public Bargaining: A Political Perspective."

4. U.S. General Accounting Office, *Collective Bargaining Rights: Information on Number of Workers with and without Bargaining Rights* (Washington, D.C.: U.S. General Accounting Office, 2002).

5. R. T. Clark, Jr., "Politics and Public Employee Unionism: Some Recommendations for an Emerging Problem," *Cincinnati Law Review,* 44 (1975), 680–689; and Summers, "Public Bargaining: A Political Perspective.

6. Clark, "Politics and Public Employee Unionism."

7. G. Bennett, "The Elusive Public Interest in Labor Disputes," *Labor Law Journal,* 25 (1974), 678–681; R. D. Horton, *Municipal Labor Relations in New York City* (New York: Praeger, 1973); and Silbiger, "The Missing Public: Collective Bargaining and Employment."

8. Summers, "Public Bargaining: A Political Perspective."

9. Ibid.

10. American Federation of State, County, and Municipal Employees, *About AFSCME* (Retrieved November 15, 2002, from http://www.afscme.org/about/index.html).

11. L. Mao, *Federal Employee Unions History* (Retrieved November 16, 2002, from http://www.nage.org/aboutnage.html).

12. Ibid.

13. National Treasury Employees Union. (Retrieved November 16, 2002, from http://www.nteu.org/).

14. Fraternal Order of Police, *A Brief History of the Fraternal Order of Police* (Retrieved from http://www.grandlodgefop.org/history/index.html); Brotherhood of Police Officers (IBPO), *IBPO History* (Retrieved from http://www.ibpo.org/history.html).

15. International Association of Fire Fighters, *Across the IAFF* (Retrieved November 15, 2002, from http://www.iaff.org/across).

16. Service Employees International Union, *Who We Are* (Retrieved from http://www.seiu.org/who/, April 6, 2003).

17. International Brotherhood of Teamsters, *About IBT* (Retrieved from http://www.teamsters/org/about/about.htm, April 6, 2003).

18. Amalgamated Transit Union, *Amalgamated Transit Union: Moving America and Canada Safely* (Retrieved from http://www.atu.org/, April 6, 2003).

19. National Education Association, *About NEA* (Retrieved from http://www.nea.org/aboutnea.html, April 6, 2003)

20. U.S. Bureau of Labor Statistics, *Union Membership Summary* (Retrieved November 16, 2002, from http://stats.bls.gov/news.release/union2.rr0.htm).

21. J. Ashraf, "The Effects of Unions on Professors' Salaries: The Evidence over Twenty Years." *Journal of Labor Research,* 23 (Spring 1997), 339–449; H. G. Lewis, *Union Relative Wage Effects: A Survey* (Chicago: University of Chicago Press, 1986); W. J. Moore and J. Raisian, "Union-Nonunion Wage Differentials in the Public Administration, Educational, and Private Sectors: 1970–1983," *The Review of Economics and Statistics,* 69 (November 1987), 608–616; and U.S. Bureau of Labor Statistics, *Monthly Labor Review* (Retrieved from http://www.dol.gov).

22. L. S. Mosher, "Facing the Realities of Public Employee Bargaining," *Public Personnel Management,* 7 (July–August 1978), 243–248.

23. R. B. Freeman and J. L. Medoff, *What Do Unions Do?* (New York: Basic Books, 1984); M. E. R. Kelly and B. Harrison, "Unions, Technology, and Labor-Management Cooperation, in L. Mishel and P. B. Voos, eds., *Unions and Economic Competitiveness* (New York: M. E. Sharpe, Inc., 1992); M. Roberts and W. E. Bittle, "The Union Contract: A Solid Investment," *Federationist*, 88 (1981), 8–10; and Sulzner, "Revisiting the Reinvented Union."

24. Sulzner, "Revisiting the Reinvented Union"; and R. Kirkner and S. Sharfstein, "Aligning Traditional Collective Bargaining with Nontraditional Labor Relations," *The Public Manager*, 30, No. 4 (2001–2002), 27–30, 35.

SUGGESTED READINGS

AFL-CIO. *Public Employers Bargain for Excellence.* Washington, D.C.: AFL-CIO, 1997.

Bowers, M. H. *Contract Administration in the Public Sector.* Chicago: International Personnel Management Association, 1976.

Freeman, R. B., and C. Ichniowski, eds. *When Public Workers Unionize.* Chicago: University of Chicago Press, 1988.

Freeman, R. B., and J. L. Medoff, *What Do Union Do?* New York: Basic Books, 1984.

Goldfield, M. *The Decline of Organized Labor in the United States.* Chicago: University of Chicago Press, 1987.

Government Employee Relations Report (GERR). *Special Report: Employee-Management Cooperation in the Federal Service: A Selective Look.* Washington, D.C.: The Bureau of National Affairs, 1990.

HR Center. *Alternative Dispute Resolution.* Washington, D.C.: International Personnel Management Association, 1995.

HR Center. *Collective Bargaining.* Washington, D.C.: International Personnel Management Association, 2002.

Johnston, P. *Success While Others Fail: Social Movement Unionism and the Public Workplace.* Ithaca, N.Y.: ILR Press, 1994.

Kaufman, B. E., and M. M. Kleiner. *Employee Representation: Alternatives and Future Directions.* Madison, Wisc.: Industrial Relations Research Association, 1993.

Kearney, R. C., with D. G. Carnevale. *Labor Relations in the Public Sector,* 3d ed. New York: Marcel Dekker, 2001.

Leibig, M. T., and W. L. Kahn. *Public Employee Organizing and the Law.* Washington, D.C.: Bureau of National Affairs, 1987.

Levine, D. I. *Reinventing the Workplace: How Business and Employees Can Both Win.* Washington, D.C.: The Brookings Institution Press, 1995.

National Partnership Council. *A New Vision for Labor-Management Relations: A Report to the President on Progress in Labor-Management Partnerships.* Washington, D.C.: National Partnership Council, 1995.

Rabin, J., T. Vocino, W. B. Hildreth, and G. J. Miller, eds. *Handbook of Public Labor Relations.* New York: Marcel Dekker, 1994.

Riccucci, N. M. *Women, Minorities and Unions in the Public Sector.* New York: Greenwood, 1990.

U.S. Department of Labor. *Working Together for Public Service.* Washington, D.C.: U.S. Department of Labor, 1996.

SELECTED WEB SITES

Bureau of National Affairs (BNA). A publisher of information on legal and regulatory policy and actions on management and labor. Publishes extensively on labor relations as well as other employment issues. www.bna.com

Federal Labor Relations Authority (FLRA). Oversees labor management relations in the federal service and publishes information regarding labor relations. www.flra.gov

Industrial Relations Research Association (IRRA). Membership organization of people interested in Human resources and labor relations. Holds conferences and publishes research on labor topics. www.irra.uiuc.edu

National Public Employee Relations Association (NPELRA). A membership organization of employees and others interested in labor-management relations. Conducts research and publishes on all aspects of labor relations. Also conducts conferences on labor issues. www.npelra.org

Section on Personnel and Labor Relations (SPALR). Section of the American Society for Public Administration, which sponsors panels and workshops promoting a wider recognition of the role of human resources in government and nonprofits, including labor relations. www.aspanet.org/sections/sectionpages/spalr.html

U.S. Department of Labor Bureau of Labor Statistics (BLS). Collects and publishes data on all aspects of employment and labor relations. www.bls.gov

elaws Advisors (elaws). Provides interactive tools with information on federal employment laws. www.dol.gov/elaws

Working for America Institute (WAI). An AFL-CIO organization that provides technical assistance and support to improve work organizations through research, information dissemination, and technical assistance to labor leaders, community activists, and public officials. www.workingforamerica.org

Each union and employee association has its own web site that provides information about it and other labor topics.

Exercises

1. Interview an officer of a public employee union or employee association. Find out what the organization's mission is and how it attempts to accomplish its mission. Ask about the relationship that the union or association has with the public employer. Write a report on your findings. In your report, also discuss what effect you believe the political environment has on this particular union or association and the approach it uses.

2. Contact a Public Employee Relations Board or comparable organization. Find out when it will be having a hearing on a case brought before it and attend the hearing if it is open. Describe the nature of the issues raised in the hearing. What is your impression of the hearing process? Is it what you expected? Why or why not?

3. Form an even number of groups of four or five, each representing either management or labor. Then have each management group meet with a labor group. Assume that the groups are going to negotiate a labor agreement. During this meeting, negotiate the bargaining rules that will be used in the negotiations.

4. The city has a policy that prohibits strikes by public employees. Over the past two years, the city budget has been cut, and many jobs were eliminated. The Public Works Department lost twenty positions, or ten percent, of its original numbers. Because of the age of the city's infra-

structure, the work load actually increased. Employee morale dropped to the point that people lost their sense of commitment. For the last two weeks, about 20 percent of the employees called in sick each day.

Management believes that the union is staging a job action or sick out that it considers an illegal strike. It filed an unfair labor practice complaint. You are the hearing officer hearing the complaint.

a. What information do you need?
b. What do you lean toward recommending?
c. What is your reasoning?

9

Social Equity and Diversity in the Workplace

Public organizations of the twenty-first century are vastly more diverse than ever before. More public employees are women, people of color, people with disabilities, foreign-born people, and part-timers. They also are older. Public policy supports enhancing opportunities for people previously discriminated against in employment to have chances to become employed even though many of the programs directed at increasing opportunity have faced serious challenges.

Volunteers provide a good deal of service to organizations, although managers often resist using them for fear of not being able to manage them very effectively because volunteers do not depend on the organization for their livelihood.[1] The personnel challenge is to develop strategies for effectively integrating volunteers into the organization. Employers need to review and adjust their risk management plans to accommodate the issues posed by volunteers. Volunteers are likely to become more significant participants in public organizations.

Public personnel systems increasingly face challenges surrounding the diverse workplace as do the managers, supervisors, and employees in the line departments. For the personnel manager, the challenges are to manage and monitor the diversity programs, provide training and assistance on diversity to managers, supervisors, and employees, and to assess the attempted efforts. The main challenges are in creating a diverse workforce, managing it, and establishing and assuring accountability for diversity. This chapter deals with the challenges to the public service resulting from diversity and other social changes.

Creation of a Diverse Workplace

Diversity in public employment has been increased through nondiscrimination, equal employment, and affirmative action programs, and other policies that deal with discrimination in employment. The objective of these poli-

174

cies is in part to make the public service representative of society as a whole. The policies also require that nonjob-related factors not be considered in personnel decisions.

REPRESENTATIVE BUREAUCRACY

Representative bureaucracy is a concept that has been important in public personnel management since the beginning of our government. As was noted earlier, President George Washington and his successors were concerned with representing influential political groups in their administrations, and the Jeffersonians and Jacksonians made clear that government offices should be held by people supportive of the president. Political leaders at all levels have used appointments to public office as a means of rewarding supporters or consolidating the support of others. Thus, a form of representativeness always has been a major part of personnel decisions. Since the 1960s, the concept has been refined and now includes a concern for the representation of all elements of society, whether or not they have political power. Of course, if people have political clout, their concerns are likely to be considered more quickly.

Representative bureaucracy is characterized as active or passive representation, as suggested by Mosher.[2] In *active representation,* a representative is expected to act in the interest of all sectors of society regardless of the group to which the representative belongs. In *passive representation,* a person is assumed to represent the interests of the group from which he comes. Thus, in passive representation, the representatives' personal characteristics and social background are important, and advocates of such representation believe the bureaucracy should be a mirror image of society as a whole. Passive representation is exemplified by the goals and timetables affirmative action plans use to make the public service reflect the population accurately.

There are major differences, though, in the ways people perceive the linkage between active and passive representation. The assumption underlying equal employment opportunity and affirmative action programs is that passive representation eventually will lead to the active representation of groups that are becoming members of the bureaucracy. That assumption is the subject of much study and disagreement.[3] Despite these differences of opinion, government has acted on the premise that all groups in society should be represented and will influence the public service in its actions. Another important consideration is that individuals are more likely to feel comfortable in dealing with bureaucrats from their own groups. Thus, these policies have as one of their intended effects making bureaucracies and their programs more accessible to groups previously denied such access. Thus, as Rosenbloom and Kinnard observed, representative bureaucracy is advocated for two reasons: (1) to provide distributive justice and equal opportunity and (2) to allow for input from all social and economic groups.[4] Research tends to suggest as well that a representative bureaucracy is a more responsive bureaucracy.[5]

Development of an Unrepresentative Bureaucracy.   Although the Jeffersonians and Jacksonians "democratized" the public service in many ways, the U.S. public service never has been really representative of society as a whole. Among the many reasons for this are political considerations and traditions. Some also argue that the bureaucracy, by its nature, requires skills that are not distributed equally throughout the population.[6] As a result, bureaucracies often discriminate in favor of middle-class people who have the necessary skills. The reasons many people do not acquire such skills are often political and social.

Jacksonian Democracy opened the public service to the common man, but the new participants were still exclusively white males. The reign of the spoils system entrenched white males in the public service because friends and relatives of those already holding political power reaped the rewards. By the time minority group members and women achieved some political influence, the spoils system had been fairly well destroyed as a means of staffing the federal bureaucracy and was on the way out in many state and local jurisdictions as well. With the blanketing-in procedures used to extend civil service protection, white males were more or less ensured of control over the bureaucracy and the selection of new members. Consequently, newly emerging groups had few opportunities to enter the system.

Although the Civil War emancipated the slaves, the political power of the African-American population was minimal until after the middle of the twentieth century. The Fourteenth Amendment required implementation, but many barriers developed to restrict its effect. A gradual process of judicial and legislative extension of rights to minority groups and women took place during the late nineteenth and early twentieth centuries. The Nineteenth Amendment to the Constitution was supposed to open the doors to women, but they, like African-Americans, found that constitutionally guaranteed rights do not automatically translate into rights in practice. Instead, much effort is required to realize those rights.

A concern for the rights of minorities and individuals alike developed in the middle of the twentieth century. The Warren Supreme Court and its libertarian and civil rights orientation jolted the consciences of citizens and political leaders, resulting in many court decisions and much legislation prohibiting discrimination against minorities and eventually women. The Civil Rights Act of 1964 and Equal Employment Opportunity Act of 1972 made it illegal to discriminate in employment on the basis of race, religion, sex, and so on. Toward the latter part of the twentieth century, two other groups began to achieve equality in the system. People with disabilities gained legislative protections, including employment protection, through the Americans with Disabilities Act of 1990. Gays and lesbians began to have some success in their battle to be accorded the same rights as other citizens through court victories and policies adopted by the federal government executive branch as well as some state legislatures and local governing bodies. Although these nondiscrimination policies helped, they fell far short of providing equality of opportunity, particularly in high-level positions.

From Nondiscrimination to Affirmative Action.   Because nondiscrimination laws and regulations failed to achieve the expected results, government leaders instituted new approaches. President John F. Kennedy, a recipient of strong minority group support, emphasized positive action to promote the well-being of those who had been discriminated against. African-Americans in particular were brought into prominent positions in the public service. President Lyndon Johnson, eager to shed his Texas and southern identification for a national constituency, increased the pressure to employ African-Americans. Minority group support also concerned President Richard Nixon, who took a special interest in Hispanics, as did President Ronald Reagan in his 1984 reelection campaign. As women developed greater political consciousness in the late 1960s and 1970s, the leaders of both parties at all levels of government began to demonstrate concern for women's rights (and votes) by trying to increase the public employment of women. In the 1984 presidential election, the gender gap became a major issue as the Democratic party nominated a female vice presidential candidate to attempt to exploit its perception of the Reagan administration's lack of concern for women's issues. The Reagan administration explained that it did not talk about women's issues; it just employed women in prominent positions. However, one of the complaints of minorities and women was that the Reagan administration did not emphasize equal employment and affirmative action issues and had in fact made efforts to weaken agencies such as the Civil Rights Commission and the Equal Employment Opportunity Commission. The 1992 election featured a sharp distinction, with President George Bush's campaign appealing to white middle-class males and the Clinton campaign promising the inclusion of all segments of society in government. The 1994 elections, however, resulted in a congressional majority seemingly bent on dismantling affirmative action requirements. The administration of George W. Bush, elected in 2000, points to its appointment of women in its cabinet and other high-level positions as evidence of its support for women in employment.

Equal employment opportunity and affirmative action have been the two main approaches to expanding employment opportunities for women and minority group members. Equal employment opportunity does not necessarily result in increased employment; it merely requires that all groups have the same chance to compete for positions and are treated equally once employed. Of particular concern is that personnel decisions be made on the basis of criteria that are pertinent to the work. Equal opportunity requires neutrality on issues other than merit and ability in the personnel process. The Civil Rights Act of 1964 provides the basic requirements for equality of opportunity. Because that act applies to private sector employers only, the 1972 Equal

Employment Opportunity Act was passed to extend the policy to state and local governments. Passage of the Americans with Disabilities Act of 1990 and the Civil Rights Act of 1991 reaffirmed nondiscrimination as national policy and provided strong enforcement tools, as will be explained later.

Although guarantees of equal employment opportunity are important, they do not take effect on their own. Enforcement agencies and monitoring mechanisms therefore have been created to ensure that the acts are implemented. The Equal Employment Opportunity Commission and the Civil Rights Commission are the principal agencies at the national level that have enforcement responsibilities. Each department or agency that distributes grants or services or has contracts with other employers, including state and local governments, has some type of compliance office to ensure that equal employment opportunity exists. Monitoring agencies have difficulty gaining compliance because they usually are staffed inadequately and often are on functional agencies' periphery. Standards for what constitutes equal opportunity also tend to be vague and difficult to enforce. As a result of these problems, the concept of affirmative action developed.

Affirmative action requires employers to make a conscious effort to eliminate from their personnel systems intended and unintended discrimination as well as the effects of past discrimination. Thus, it calls for an examination of all personnel functions to identify possible barriers to equal employment opportunity so that they can be removed. The key to determining whether discrimination exists is to be found not in the policy's intent but in what occurs as a result of that policy. In *Griggs v. Duke Power Co.*,[7] the Supreme Court established the doctrine that prohibited discrimination can be unintentional, occurring as a result of personnel practices. Once a plaintiff establishes "disparate impact," meaning that the practice had a disproportional impact on protected groups, the burden shifts to the employer to demonstrate "business necessity" to avoid liability for the discrimination. In *Wards Cove v. Antonio*,[8] the Supreme Court reversed itself and shifted the burden back to the plaintiff to prove that the discrimination was intentional, making it much more difficult for complainants to win their cases.

In the 1980s, the concept of affirmative action became a major public issue and was challenged in the courts and through electoral politics. Critics of affirmative action equate it with quotas and reverse discrimination. By 1989, Supreme Court decisions limited or undermined affirmative action efforts. Congress decided to counter with a new Civil Rights Act in 1990, but it was vetoed by President George Bush. Many viewed the conflict as political posturing. Congress passed the Civil Rights Act of 1991 and President Bush signed it, presumably with an eye on the 1992 presidential election. In 1992, Bill Clinton, a supporter of affirmative action, was elected.

In the 1990s, the Supreme Court did not rule directly on affirmative action but allowed numerous lower court decisions to stand. At the appellate court level, cases have varied in outcome; thus making a Supreme Court test almost inevitable. The Court did take the position that racial classifications in federal set-aside programs require strict scrutiny analysis, meaning that the policy must satisfy a compelling governmental interest and must be construed narrowly to meet its specific goals.[9] It also let stand an Eleventh Circuit Court decision invalidating a promotion plan favoring African-American firefighters.[10] Similarly, it declined to review an award of $425,000 to a white engineer who claimed he was passed over so that an African-American could be promoted.[11]

In *Hopgood v. State of Texas* (1996), the Supreme Court let stand a Fifth Circuit decision striking down an affirmative action admissions program at the University of Texas Law School.[12] Without ruling on the substance of affirmative action, it ruled in 1999 in *Lesage v. Texas* that the appellate court erred in not considering whether the University of Texas doctoral program in education would have reached the same admission decision if there had been no affirmative action.[13] There are Circuit Court decisions upholding race-based admission policies in Washington State and in Michigan.[14] In 2003, the Supreme Court accepted the Michigan case for review.

The politicization of affirmative action has led to efforts at the state and local levels to prohibit affirmative action programs. In 1996, California voters approved Proposition 209 forbidding use of affirmative action in public employment, education, and contracting. A similar initiative passed in the state of Washington in 1998, and efforts have been successful in some but unsuccessful in other jurisdictions. In some states, governors have addressed the issue through executive order. The result is that public employers have no clear guidance on what to do. As Riccucci notes, public employers tend to hold on to affirmative action as a way to increase diversity in their workforces and to avoid costly litigation.[15]

Enforcement or compliance agencies avoid using the term *quotas* and argue that goals are different. Theoretically, these goals are targets that the employer attempts to attain. However, circumstances can prevent reaching the goals, in which case the employer normally must explain why. Therefore, many employers feel constrained to achieve them, regardless of how they do so. However, affirmative action does not require such reverse discrimination. Compliance agencies frequently are at fault for their single-minded concern with meeting goals, but most compliance agencies recognize that circumstances do not always permit employers to meet all anticipated goals and thus make their judgments on the basis of good-faith efforts.

Critics of affirmative action argue that merit and competence are sacrificed to meet goals and timetables. Most critics believe that the quality of public service suffers from affirmative action efforts and accordingly base their opposition on that belief. In fact, research indicates that these arguments are not true. In reviewing 200 studies of affirmative action, economists Holzer and Neumark found little evidence that affirmative action affected overall performance. They also found that supervisors rank affirmative action hires the same as everyone else.[16]

Certainly, some critics have an interest in maintaining the status quo and preventing the opening of the workplace. Many employees and employee groups have been in the forefront of battles to protect their turf from intrusion by minorities and women. However, as employee associations and unions have seen their memberships level off or decline, their stances have changed, and now they are often among the strongest advocates of minority and women's causes. They see support for minorities and women as an issue of workplace justice and a way to attract new members.

The record so far does not indicate that the critics' fears are well founded. Although minorities and women are increasingly evident in government employment, they are not represented at all levels of employment in proportion to their percentage in the general population. The higher levels of management are still essentially the preserve of white males, although changes are occurring.[17] This phenomenon is referred to as a *glass ceiling* because it presents a barrier to the advancement of women and minority group members. Because of the disproportionate representation of females and minorities at the low levels of public bureaucracies, there is now more emphasis on upward mobility programs and eliminating discrimination in promotion policies.

The ultimate goal of affirmative action is to make sure that factors irrelevant to the performance of duties are not considered in the employment process. In the short run, however, it could be necessary to consider sex and race in order to equalize the balance and redress past discrimination. The concept of affirmative action has developed a negative connotation. As Riccucci notes, it often is viewed as leading to "preferential treatment," "quotas," and "reverse discrimination."[18] Because of this negative image, employers increasingly focus on diversity in the workplace to avoid using the term *affirmative action*. In many cases, employers simply rename old practices.

While race, ethnicity, and gender are the major dimensions of diversity, other forms also impact personnel activities. For example, the Age Discrimination in Employment Act of 1967 prohibits discrimination on the basis of age. In 1974, it was amended to include state and local governments within its purview. However, the Supreme Court ruled that Congress did not have the power to give individuals the right to sue states to enforce federal law.[19] Consistent with the Court's other decisions strengthening states rights under the Constitution since the mid-1990s, the decision raises serious questions about Congress legislating social justice in the workplace. People will have to turn to state legislatures and courts for help. The age of employees in organizations today is much more diverse.[20] The aging of the workforce and the differences in attitudes toward work by younger employees present challenges to employers.

Family situations vary greatly across employees as well. Younger workers often require flexibility to deal with their children's needs. Single-parent families can present special challenges. Other employees have elder care issues as they become responsible for elderly relatives. Many people, called the *sandwich generation,* have both child care and elder care responsibilities. Nontraditional families such as same-sex couples, sometimes with children, add to differing family needs calling for understanding by supervisors and colleagues.

The introduction of policies against discrimination on the basis of sexual orientation also has an impact. Lesbians and gays in the workforce can produce tensions because the efforts to ensure acceptance run counter to the strongly held beliefs of some employees.

The requirements of the Americans with Disabilities Act of 1990 bring another element of diversity to organizations. Besides accommodating people with disabilities, organizations need to deal with the attitudes of other employees toward people with disabilities and managers' and supervisors' attitudes about their abilities. ADA has generated a great deal of litigation about what constitutes disability and what accommodations are reasonable. Definitive definitions are unlikely for some time.

In the wake of the September 11, 2001, terrorist attacks in New York and Washington, D.C., employers also have had to deal with prejudices against people of Middle East origin and of the Islamic faith. Dealing with religious diversity has been an ongoing challenge for employers, but the September 11 attacks raised the level of tension with a specific focus on Muslims.

All of the tensions surrounding diversity call for attention to managing the diverse workforce. The challenges for public managers are to capitalize on the opportunities that diversity presents.

Management of Diversity

If organizations are to be productive, provide high-quality service, and relate to their environments, they must be able to manage a diverse workforce. Ignoring the tensions that inevitably develop in a diverse workplace will lead only to wasted resources focused on constantly addressing problems. If potential tensions are not addressed in a positive fashion, they also are likely to lead to low morale and a hostile work environment. These conditions, in turn, can lead to disgruntled employees, turnover, and litigation. Management can use numerous strategies to ensure that diversity is valued throughout the organization.[21]

Leadership by top management is essential to establishing and maintaining an effective diverse workforce. That means top managers must become personally involved and commit the resources to ensure that diversity exists and is valued. Nothing works better than management modeling the desired behavior in its own activities.

One of the basic efforts of management must be constant training addressing the meaning of diversity and why valuing it is important for the organization and all of its employees. Training also needs to address how to work in the diverse environment, including how to understand and work with people of different cultures and backgrounds. Strategies for including everyone are important as well.

Diversity programs do not work if accountability for success is ignored. Thus, managers, supervisors, and all employees need to be held accountable. It starts with involving all of them in the development of diversity programs and policies so that employees start with commitment to the program's success. Then performance evaluation must include a diversity component to ensure that everyone recognizes it as being a serious commitment. Of course, accountability has different dimensions and becomes much more focused for supervisors and managers who do the hiring and training.

Other successful strategies might include mentoring programs, monitors, advocates, and managers and supervisors willing to be flexible so that they can accommodate different needs of people in their organizations.

Impacts of Diversity

The development of diverse workplaces has had impacts on organizations far beyond making them more representative of society. Diversity has caused organizations to be more sensitive to issues such as harassment as discussed in Chapter 7 and to policy changes needed to better accommodate employees' differing needs. Nowhere has the effect been more pronounced than in benefit programs.

With dual career couples, the sandwich generation, unmarried couples, and all the other variations being a reality of the workforce, traditional benefit programs no longer meet the needs of employees. Thus, employee benefit packages have been adapted to meet the changing demographics of the workplace.[22] Called *family-friendly* or *work-life benefits,* they include such things as flexible work hours, dependent care, telecommuting, domestic partner benefits, professional development, employee assistance, and financial planning. Many organizations roll their traditional benefits into their work-life benefits programs. An important feature of the plans is giving employees flexibility to choose the benefits important to them rather than having the same benefits for everyone. Such features are known as *cafeteria-style benefit plans.*

Another issue of equity involves relatives working in the same organization. Employers often have nepotism policies ranging from prohibiting family members from being employed to policies to ensure that family members do not supervise one another. What constitutes a family member or relative is less than clear in today's society. Do same-sex couples fall under nepotism policies? What about people who are romantically involved? Should they be covered under nepotism policies? The answers to these questions have implications for employees' perceptions of fairness and equity.

Summary

The public service in a democracy usually is considered to be the servant of the general public, and as such, it should be responsive to that public. In recent years, efforts to make the public service responsive have included making the public service representative of society. Thus, equal employment opportunity and affirmative action programs try to ensure that all segments of society have the opportunity to compete for public jobs, and, once employed, are treated fairly in the personnel processes. Through affirmative action and equal employment opportunity, the public service can become more sensitive to all interests and thus accomplish the goal of being democratically responsive. As controversy surrounds the concept of affirmative action, employers increasingly label their efforts *diversity programs.* As the workplace becomes more diverse, challenges emerge for managing them.

NOTES

1. J. L. Brudney, "Supplementing Common Myths with Uncommon Management: The Effective Involvement of Volunteers in Delivering Public Services," in S. W. Hays and R. C. Kearney, eds., *Public Personnel Administration: Problems and Prospects* 4th ed. (Upper Saddle River, N.J.: Prentice-Hall, 2003), 287–300.

2. F. C. Mosher, *Democracy and the Public Service,* 2d ed. (New York: Oxford University Press, 1982); and D. H. Rosenbloom and J. G. Featherstonhough, "Passive and Active Representation in the Federal Service: A Comparison of Blacks and Whites," *Social Science Quarterly,* 57 (March 1977), 873–882.

3. Rosenbloom and Featherstonhough, "Passive and Active Representation in the Federal Service"; D. H. Rosenbloom and J. G. Featherstonhough, "Response to Sigelman and Carter," *Social Science Quarterly,* 58 (March 1978), 726–728; and L. Sigelman and R. L. Carter, "Passive and Active Representation in the Federal Service: A Reanalysis," *Social Science Quarterly,* 58 (March 1978), 724–726.

4. D. H. Rosenbloom and D. Kinnard, "Bureaucratic Representation and Bureaucratic Behavior: An Exploratory Analysis," *Midwest Review of Public Administration* 11 (March 1977), 35–42.

5. K. J. Meier, "Representative Bureaucracy: A Theoretical and Empirical Exposition," in J. L. Perry, ed., *Research in Public Administration.* New Greenwich, Conn.: JAI Press (1993); K. J. Meier and J. Stewart Jr., "The Impact of Representative Bureaucracies: Educational Systems and Public Policies," *The American Review of Public Administration,* 22 (1992), 157–171; S. C. Selden, *The Promise of Representative Bureaucracy: Diversity and Responsiveness in a Government Agency* (Armonk, N.Y.: M. E. Sharpe, 1997); and S. C. Selden, J. L. Brudney, and J. E. Kellough, "Bureaucracy as a Representative Institution: Toward a Reconciliation of Bureaucratic Government and Democratic Theory," *American Journal of Political Science,* 42 (1998), 717–744.

6. J. Gardner, *Excellence: Can We Be Equal and Excellent Too?* (New York: Harper & Row, 1961); N. Glazer, *Affirmative Discrimination: Ethnic Inequity and Public Policy* (New York: Basic Books, 1975); and S. Koslov and D. H. Rosenbloom, *Representative Bureaucracy,* 2d ed. (Englewood Cliffs, N.J.: Prentice-Hall, 1984).

7. 401 U.S. 424 (1971).

8. 109 U.S. 2115 (1989).

9. *Aderand v Pena,* 115 S. Ct. 2097 (1995).

10. *In re Birmingham Reverse Discrimination Employment Litigation (BRDEL)*, 20 F.3d 1525 (11th Cir. 1996); cert. denied.

11. *Claus v Duquesne Light Company*, 46 F.3d 1115 (3rd Cir. 1994), cert. denied, 1155 S. Ct. 1700 (1995).

12. *Hopgood v State of Texas*, 78 F.3d 932 cert. denied (1996).

13. *Lesage v Texas*, 120 S. Ct. 467 (1999).

14. *Smith v University of Washington*, 233 F.3d 1888 (2000); and *Gratz and Hamacher v Bollinger, Duderstadt, and the Board of Regents of the University of Michigan* (2000).

15. N. M. Riccucci, "The Immortality of Affirmative Action," in C. Ban and N. M. Riccucci, eds., *Public Personnel Management: Current Concerns, Future Challenges*, 3rd ed. (New York: Longman, 2002), 72–84.

16. H. Holzer and D. Neumark, "Assessing Affirmative Action," *Journal of Economic Literature*, 38 (March 2000), 483–568.

17. M. E. Guy, "The Difference That Gender Makes," in S. W. Hays and R. C. Kearney, eds., *Public Personnel Administration: Problems and Prospects*, 4th ed. (Upper Saddle River, N.J.: Prentice-Hall, 2003), 256–270; and K. C. Naff, *To Look Like America: Dismantling Barriers for Women and Minorities in Government* (Boulder, Colo.: Westview, 2001).

18. N. M. Riccucci, "Affirmative Action in the Twenty-First Century: New Approaches and Developments," in C. Ban and N. M. Riccucci, eds., *Public Personnel Management: Current Concerns, Future Challenges* (New York: Longman, 1991), 88–99.

19. *Kimel v Florida Board of Regents* (2000).

20. T. Chambers and N. M. Riccucci, "Models of Excellence in Workplace Diversity," in C. Ban and N. M. Riccucci, eds., *Public Personnel Management: Current Concerns, Future Challenges*, 2nd ed. (New York: Longman, 1997), 73–90.

21. T. Cox Jr., *Creating the Multi-Cultural Organization: A Strategy for Capturing the Power of Diversity* (San Francisco: Jossey-Bass, 2001); K. C. Naff, *To Look Like America: Dismantling Barriers for Women and Minorities in Government* (Boulder, Colo.: Westview, 2001); and N. M. Riccucci, *Managing Diversity in Public Sector Workforces* (Boulder, Colo.: Westview, 2002).

22. N. J. Cayer, "Employee Benefits: From Health Care to Pensions," in S. E. Condrey, ed., *Handbook of Human Resource Management in Government* (San Francisco: Jossey-Bass, 1998), 658–75; and N. J. Cayer, "Public Employee Benefits and the Changing Nature of the Workforce," in S. W. Hays and R. C. Kearney, *Public Personnel Administration: Problems and Prospects*, 4th ed. (Upper Saddle River, N.J.: Prentice-Hall, 2003), 167–179.

SUGGESTED READINGS

Brudney, J. L. *Fostering Volunteer Programs in the Public Sector.* San Francisco: Jossey-Bass, 1990.

Cox, T., Jr. *Creating the Multicultural Organization: A Strategy for Capturing the Power of Diversity.* San Francisco: Jossey-Bass, 2001.

Edley, C., Jr. *Not all Black and White: Affirmative Action, Race, and American Values.* New York: Hill and Wang, 1996.

Farley, L. *The Sexual Harassment of Women on the Job.* New York: Warner Books, 1980.

Goldin, C. *Understanding the Gender Gap: An Economic History of American Women.* New York: Oxford University Press, 1990.

Graham, H. D. *The Civil Rights Era: Origins and Development of National Policy, 1960–1972.* New York: Oxford University Press, 1990.

Gutek, B. A. *Sex and the Workplace.* San Francisco: Jossey-Bass, 1985.

HR Center. *Diversity in the Workplace.* Washington, D.C.: International Personnel Management Association, 2002.

Naff, K. C. *To Look Like America: Dismantling Barriers for Women and Minorities in Government.* Boulder, Colo.: Westview, 2001.

Nelen, S., and A. Hondeghem, eds. *Equality Oriented Personnel Policy in the Public Sector.* Amsterdam: IOS Press, 2002.

Riccucci, N. M. *Managing Diversity in Public Sector Workforces.* Boulder, Colo.: Westview, 2002.

Rosenbloom, D. H. *Federal Equal Employment Opportunity: Politics and Public Personnel Administration.* New York: Praeger, 1977.

Selden, S. C. *The Promise of Bureaucracy: Diversity and Responsiveness in a Government Agency.* New York: M.E. Sharpe, 1997.

Stivers, C. *Gender Images in Public Administration.* Thousand Oaks, Calif.: Sage Publications, 2002.

U.S. Merit Systems Protection Board. *Sexual Harassment in the Federal Workplace: Trends, Progress, Continuing Challenges.* Washington, D.C.: U.S. Government Printing Office, 1995.

Zuckerman, A. J., and Simons, G. F. *Sexual Orientation in the Workplace.* Thousand Oaks, Calif.: Sage Publications, 1996.

SELECTED WEB SITES

Conference of Minority Public Administrators (COMPA). Section of the American Society for Public Administration that is an advocacy group for minorities in public administration. Recognizes contributions of minorities through publications, conferences, and awards. www.aspanet.org

Human Rights Campaign (HRC). Advocacy group for interests of lesbians and gays. Tracks policies dealing with gays and lesbians and publishes reports on progress, including in employment. www.hrc.org

Job Accommodation Network (JAN). A free consulting service that provides information relating to the Americans with Disabilities Act (ADA) and job accommodations. http://janweb.icdi.wvu.edu

National Organization for Women (NOW). Advocacy organization for women. Collects and publishes information on the status of women in the workforce. www.now.org

Section on Women in Public Administration (SWPA). A section of the American Society for Public Administration that provides networking for and information on women in public administration. Recognizes contributions of women through awards and conference panels and is an advocacy group. www.aspanet.org

U.S. Department of Labor. Publishes information on all aspects of the labor force. Publishes *Monthly Labor Review,* which updates statistics monthly. www.dol.gov

U.S. Department of Labor, Bureau of Labor Statistics (BLS). Collects and disseminates statistics on labor-related issues including employment patterns. www.bls.gov

U.S. Equal Employment Opportunity Commission (EEOC). Has responsibility for enforcing nondiscrimination and equal employment laws and policies. Also publishes data on employment of minorities and women. www.eeoc.gov

Exercises

1. Interview the director of the office responsible for equal employment opportunity for a public agency or jurisdiction (a public college or university might be a good choice). Find out what the office does. What are its biggest challenges? Its biggest successes? Write a report on what you have found. What sense do you have of how successful the office has been?

2. Access historical information about the employment of women or minorities in government on the Internet. From the information you retrieve, write an assessment of how much progress has been made. How do you account for the current situation regarding public employment of minorities or women?

3. Carrie Southern supervises the clerical division of the public works department. The department is made up of several divisions, some of which focus on management support and others that provide direct public works services such as street maintenance and repair. Southern found that she makes approximately 30 percent less than three male supervisors in the department. In examining the situation with four other female supervisors, she noticed that each receives 20 to 30 percent less than the male supervisors.

   Southern talked with her female colleagues and all agreed that the pay structure seemed discriminatory. They asked for a meeting with the department director and asked him to rectify the situation. He denied the request saying that the pay structure was within his discretion to establish and he believed it was fair. Southern and her colleagues appealed to the next level, the assistant city manager. Normally, the assistant city manager would ask the personnel department to investigate, but the personnel director and the public works director are spouses. You are called in as a consultant to investigate the situation and prepare a report and recommendations for the assistant city manager.

   Prepare a request for information on which you will base your report and recommendations. Indicate what you will need to examine and why you need the particular information you are requesting.

4. The water district has a nepotism policy stating that spouses cannot be employed at the same time in the district. The policy also says that if unmarried employees subsequently marry, one must quit.

   Candace Wilson and Enrique Partune have both worked for the water district for six years and met on the job. A romance bloomed, and they decided to marry. Upon learning of the impending marriage, the district manager reminded them of the policy and requested a resignation of one of them. Both declined to resign. After they were married, they were told again that one would have to resign. They again declined, and each was suspended for 15 days without pay and informed that if one had not resigned by the end of suspensions, they both would be terminated.

   They appealed their suspensions, claiming that the policy was discriminatory. They noted that at least one same-sex couple and two heterosexual couples had lived together without marriage and continued employment with the district.

   You are the hearing the appeal. What do you do?

10

Continuing Challenges for Public Personnel

Public administration has been characterized as being like life in the swamp where the ground is not firm, the path is unclear, and mean and hungry alligators are ready to strike.[1] For the personnel administrator in the public sector, the challenges of the administrative swamp are legion. This book has examined the role of public personnel administration in the context of continuing challenges in the public sector's efforts to deliver high-quality, efficient, and responsive service. As we look to the future, new challenges and opportunities arise. The major challenges for public sector personnel relate to the competitive edge, resource limitations, technology, litigation, privatization/outsourcing, violence, changing demographics in the workplace, and continuing reform.

Competitiveness

The immediate future for public personnel administration includes being competitive in an ever-changing job market. Because of the economic downturn, the availability of strong applicants was good in 2002. As the economy improves, however, the situation will change. In addition, one-third of federal employees have been predicted to retire by 2005 and one-half by 2010. Similar projections are made for state and local employees. Thus, all employers will face strong competition for qualified candidates.

To be attractive to good applicants, the public sector will have to develop recruitment strategies to address the concerns of the "new age employee"[2] who tends to be committed to a career but not necessarily to an organization. On average, people are likely to work in six or seven organizations over their careers rather than having a long career in a single organization as in the past. Thus, employees will be more interested in professional growth and responsibility than in loyalty to the organization. Personnel systems and managers need to adapt to this reality by providing opportunity for growth and independence.

Because of decreasing loyalty to the organization, if it does not accommodate the needs of employees, they are less likely to remain. Thus, personnel policies need to be flexible to meet employees' needs and still do their work. Studies have indicated that nearly 60 percent of university students preparing to enter the job market rate the balance between work and personal life needs as important in their consideration of jobs.[3] Flexibility in time off or leave is an important consideration. Increasingly, people want time off when they want it, not when it is convenient to the organization. If the organization wants to attract and retain employees, it needs to scrap rigid rules on advance requests and timing of leave. As the economy and job market improve again, employees will be more likely to quit if they do not get what they want, confident that they can find another job.

Competitiveness requires attention to compensation as well. Budget constraints in the public sector have left many employers at a disadvantage in pay. Increasing benefit costs, especially in health care benefits, also constrain the state and local public sector employers. Thus, public personnel administration faces a serious challenge in providing benefits. Innovative methods for providing benefits will continue to require attention.

Resource Limitations

A theme of governments for the past several decades has been that of doing more with less. The politics of cutting government and taxes has been constant since the late 1970s. Economic downturns that occurred in 2001 and 2002 exacerbate the situation as tax revenues decline. At the same time, demands for services rise as more people are out of work and need help. The challenge for public managers is to deliver those needed services with fewer resources.

Fewer resources mean agencies need to find ways to reduce costs. The easiest target is personnel because this area is by far the largest expense of governments. As jobs are cut, tensions develop in the organization. What criteria are to be used for deciding who is cut? How is the work to be done with fewer employees? When cuts are made, expectations are not. Cuts also lead to declining morale and stress. People who retain their jobs often feel guilty about the fate of those laid off and feel stressed as the workload increases for them. Personnel managers then are faced with handling employee stress, burnout, and emotional problems. Productivity of the organization is likely to suffer.

Resource limits also conflict with keeping benefits competitive. As benefits costs continue to increase, more costs are shifted to the employee. Public employees have gone from having benefits that cover the entire cost to sharing responsibility for such costs. Thus, most public employers now require employees to pay part of the premiums on health care benefits and to contribute to their retirement programs. At the same time, the level of benefits is being reduced. For example, employees who once had full coverage for many health care services now pay co-pays, which seem to increase every year. Deductibles also are increasing regularly.

Technology

It is impossible to predict what technological advances will occur, but it is certain that there will be advances and that public personnel management will be affected by them. With new technology come new expertise and new ways to solve old problems. The introduction of the computer after World War II, accentuated in the 1970s by the advent of the minicomputer and the personal computer, is among the most significant changes in technology. Because of computers, personnel offices have been able to operate more efficiently while personnel functions have changed. Employees throughout the organization are affected by changes in technology.

Technology allows employees to do their work much more quickly and with increasing accuracy. Efficiency usually increases with the introduction of technology. The challenge for personnel management is to manage the integration of technology into the organization. Resistance to any change often occurs because employees fear learning new things and the impact of the change on job security or other interests. Computers are now found throughout public organizations, but there still are challenges in dealing with them.

On the technical side, various parts of an organization do not always have compatible systems. In these cases, introduction of computers can actually increase work and lead to inefficiency. Turf battles can erupt over what system or software to use.

Access to information is a major benefit of computer use to organizations. Employees can access information relevant to their jobs from around the world almost instantaneously. They can communicate very quickly and with many people at once. The communication capacity also can create problems. Managers have had to create policies on appropriate use of the technology and discipline policies for inappropriate use. Email access is an important tool for managers and employees, but it also can lead to problems. People sometimes send email messages that should be communicated selectively to a wide group. Such intentional or inadvertent mailings can result in embarrassment, hurt feelings, and conflict within the organization.

Innovations in technology also enhance opportunities for telework. Employees can do their work from home or from dispersed locations, thus reducing dependence on centralized facilities. Telework presents general advantages to the community because of the decreased commuting and therefore reduced pollution from automobiles. For people with dependent care responsibilities or other constraints, telework can help them avoid having to spend the day at the office. The challenge for managers is to focus on completion of work rather than the presence of employees on the job. Telework also can diminish the sense of cohesiveness of the work organization because interpersonal contact decreases.

Technology also affects personnel organizations and functions, including the possibility of moving to virtual human resources management.[4] Although the development has been gradual, public employers now recruit online, accept online applications, use computer-based testing, and even conduct preliminary interviews on line or via telecommunication. E-learning is an increasingly common method of training employees. Employees can select and process benefits without ever seeing or talking to a benefits specialist. Payroll and benefits management lend themselves well to computerization. It is difficult to imagine any personnel function that cannot be conducted, at least in part, online or through computer software. Workforce planning utilizes sophisticated software.

Cooperative programs among jurisdictions also are likely to continue to expand as a way to limit costs. Such agreements for recruiting, examining, and certifying are certain to attract more attention in the future. These programs can improve the ability of small jurisdictions to perform personnel functions without adding greatly to their costs. Although the initial benefit to large jurisdictions will not always be apparent, the large jurisdictions will be able to save resources by sharing the costs of such operations with other units of government that use the services.

Privatization/Outsourcing

Privatization and outsourcing of services and functions have become very popular as advocates of reducing the size of government have succeeded in elections across the country. *Privatization*, sometimes called outsourcing, involves the delivery of governmental services or functions by nongovernmental entities. The entities may be private for-profit enterprises or nonprofits. A variation is contracting with other governmental jurisdictions.

Advocates of privatization normally suggest that contracting for services leads to their more efficient, less costly provision. Small jurisdictions often find that large capital investments are needed to offer many services and that they can contract at a lower price with private firms or other jurisdictions for the services. Some cities, for example, have found that they can contract with private water companies or fire protection services more cheaply that they can provide the services on their own. Contracting with other jurisdictions for water, health, and computer services also is common among small local governments. Not the least of the savings are benefits. Governmental jurisdictions find that they can avoid costly health care and retirement programs by contracting out rather than employing their own people to provide a service.

Privatization requires much adaptation and change for personnel administration.[5] It requires careful assessment of exactly what is being contracted for and expertise in advertising, obtaining and assessing proposals (bids), and drawing up agreements to ensure the services will be provided. Then the contract or agreement must be monitored, enforced, and evaluated. For the personnel function, these activities require the recruitment and/or training of employees with the requisite expertise.

Once privatization occurs, employers need to address the needs of public employees who are displaced. Employers also need to deal with remaining employees who feel threats to their job security and work situation. Privatization inevitably affects relationships with employee unions or associations as well, resulting in the need to be attentive to them.

Outsourcing personnel functions is one of the newest forms of privatization.[6] A governmental jurisdiction may contract out any or all personnel functions. Many human resources services have traditionally used private vendors. Thus, health care benefits typically are provided under contract with private insurance vendors. Use of head hunters for some recruitment also is common. What is relatively new is the employment of outside vendors to operate recruitment, testing, evaluation, and other day-to-day human resource functions.

Litigation

Taking issues to court seems to be the way to resolve the problems in U.S. society, and personnel managers constantly find themselves objects of litigation. Discrimination and equal employment opportunity issues have spawned considerable litigation.[7] The Americans with Disabilities Act of 1990 resulted in a large amount of litigation to challenge every aspect of personnel management.

The increasing number of lawsuits necessitates new expertise in the personnel field. Personnel managers have not been noted for their legal training, but legal staffs well trained in the public personnel field now are common. Personnel offices need people to represent them in all aspects of employee relations. Human resource professionals also realize that the best protection against litigation is the preparation of managers and supervisors throughout the organization so that problems are avoided in the first place. There is a need for training in constantly changing laws, regulations, and judicial interpretations of policy that affect personnel management and for taking a proactive position to ensure that violations of these complex policies do not occur.

Violence in the Workplace

Workplace violence now claims more than two million victims and costs employers in the United States more than $40 billion annually.[8] Reports of homicides in the workplace have become common on the evening news. The causes of such violence are many, including the stressful economic situation in which people find themselves, domestic problems, drug abuse, and other personal problems. Personnel decisions such as termination often provide the immediate spark for the violent action. For employers and personnel systems, workplace violence requires a number of actions. It is impossible to anticipate violent acts by employees, former employees, spouses of employees, and clientele, but employers can develop programs and policies to help avoid such acts.[9]

Employers need to assess the climate and attitudes in their organizations to determine the potential for violence and what steps could be taken to prevent it. Employers also should educate employees, supervisors, and managers to understand the signs that contribute to violent situations and how to deal with people who are exhibiting signs of stress or domestic abuse. A policy to address violence is needed in all aspects of the workplace. This must include dealing with the aftermath of a violent incident.

Applicant screening poses particular problems because it relates to assessing the potential for violence. Violence in the workplace has caused many employers to conduct more thorough background checks, but former employers often are reluctant to disclose information pertinent to assessing the potential for violence. They fear being sued by former employees. The irony is that they could be sued for negligence if they fail to disclose pertinent information and the individual commits violence at a new place of employment. Because of these concerns, most states now have reference immunity laws that protect them from providing information as long as the information is complete, accurate, and without malice. The courts have adopted the same principles. Once employed, individuals need to be observed during the probationary period for any signs of trouble.

The Employee Assistance Plan (EAP) mentioned earlier is important in dealing with troubled employees. Having access to counseling and other services of the EAP allows an employee to release built-up tension and anger that could lead to violence. It also can refer employees to other resources to help resolve whatever problems they have. The EAP also typically provides training for supervisors to help them identify and deal with stressed employees. If an incident occurs, counseling for employees also is an important service of the EAP. Such incidents, especially those that result in death, leave employees of the organization traumatized and in need of help in grieving and overcoming the trauma. The EAP or other counseling intervention is very important in helping everyone to cope.

Another concern for employers is providing security in the first place. Without becoming fortresses, organizations cannot completely prevent incidents of violence, but precautions can be taken, especially by offices that deal with disgruntled individuals. Employers need a plan to deal with the unavoidable violent situation; thus, crisis management and intervention plans are part of the human resources management agenda of the 2000s.

Changing Demographics

As noted throughout this book, the demographic changes in the work-place are constant. Workplaces will continue to change. The challenge of managing diverse organizations already has been addressed. However, some of the other changes in the workplace are creating the need for adjustments. Because of revenue limitations and efforts to avoid future costs, many public employers are using part-time and/or temporary employees and volunteers. These categories of employees present their own challenges.

Issues of equity and fairness for the part-time and temporary employees often arise. Frequently, these employees cannot participate in benefits programs or are ineligible for pay increases. Some employers use temporaries or part-timers precisely to avoid increased benefits commitments. The practice raises concerns of social equity. Temporaries and part-timers can also feel less connection and commitment to the organization, especially if their employment is on a short-term basis, which can raise issues of motivation and compliance with organization policy and norms.

Continuing Reform

With change always occurring in the political environment, there also are continuing pressures for reform of personnel management systems. Every president brings to office some views for changing public bureaucracy. President George W. Bush continues the tradition. "Strategic Management of Human Capital" is part of his agenda. The human capital initiative of the administration focuses on recruiting high-quality employees and developing strategies for motivation and performance. While the administration is working out the details, some clues about what it means are emerging. Clearly, the administration would like to eliminate many of the rules and regulations that protect federal employees so that they would be more responsive to the elected and politically appointed leadership. The president's success in getting the Department of Homeland Security created without those protections is one example of the effort.

Another clue to the administration's plans is the push for privatizing more activities. The president has said that half the jobs performed by federal employees could be privatized. Ironically, the push comes as one private workforce, airport security screeners, was federalized because of the problems arising from performance of those jobs by the private sector.

These changes are consistent with continuing efforts at the state and local levels for the reform of personnel systems. There is a strong effort to eliminate civil service protections as has been done in Georgia and Florida. A spirited debate about returning to a spoils system in the public sector also is taking place. While no one suggests that governments go back to prereform spoils as was known in the nineteenth century, many do argue that managers should have greater control over personnel decisions and that incompetent employees should not be protected by personnel department rules and regulations.[10]

As noted at the beginning of this book, the changing environment brings pressure for changes in what personnel administration does and how it does it. The constant is that change continues.

Summary

Many forces will change the field of public personnel management. The same changes that affect the rest of society will be important to managers of public personnel. What will not change is the fact that public personnel management is a product of the political environment in which it operates and that environment is ever changing.

NOTES

1. N. J. Cayer and L. F. Weschler, *Public Administration: Social Change and Adaptive Management.* 2d ed. (San Diego: Birkdale Publishers, 2003).

2. A. Mir, R. Mir, and J. B. Mosca, "The New Age Employee: An Exploration of Changing Employee-Organization Relations," *Public Personnel Management,* 31 (Summer 2002), 187–200.

3. G. O'Bannon, "Managing Our Future," *IPMA News,* July 18–20, 2001.

4. J. P. West and E. Berman, "From Traditional to Virtual HR," *Review of Public Personnel Administration,* 21 (Spring 2001), 38–64.

5. S. Fernandez, C. E. Lowman, and H. G. Rainey, "Privatization and Human Resources Management," in C. Ban and N. M. Riccucci, eds., *Public Personnel Management: Current Concerns, Future Challenges,* 3rd ed. (New York: Longman, 2002), 225–242; and Lawther, "Privatizing Personnel: Outsourcing Public Sector Functions," in S. W. Hays and R. C. Kearney, eds., *Public Personnel Administration: Problems and Prospects,* 4th ed. (Upper Saddle River, N.J.: Prentice-Hall, 2000), 196–208.

6. W. G. Lawther, "Privatizing Personnel"; G. Siegel, "Outsourcing Personnel Functions," *Public Personnel Management,* 29 (Fall 2000), 225–236.

7. D. Jaegal and N. J. Cayer, "Public Personnel Administration by Lawsuit: The Impact of Supreme Court Decisions on Public Employee Litigiousness," *Public Administration Review,* 51 (May/June 1991), 211–221; D. H. Rosenbloom and M. Bailey, "What Every Personnel Manager Should Know about the Constitution," in S. W. Hays and R. C. Kearney, eds., *Public Personnel Administration: Problems and Prospects,* 4th ed. (Upper Saddle River, N.J.: Prentice-Hall, 2003), 28–45.

8. Injury Prevention Research Center, 2001. "Workplace Violence: A Report to the Nation," University of Iowa (Retrieved November 23, 2002, from http://www.public-health.uiowa.edu/iprc/nation.pdf); and "Workplace Violence Costs U.S. Employers Nearly $40 Billion Annually," *IPMA News,* November 25, 1999.

9. J. S. Bowman and C. J. Zigmond, "State Government Response to Violence," *Public Personnel Management,* 26 (Summer 1997), 289–300; E. Chenier, "The Workplace: A Battleground for Violence," *Public Personnel Management,* 27 (1998), 557–568.

10. S. E. Condrey and R. Maranto, eds., *Radical Reform of the Civil Service* (New York: Lexington Books, 2001).

SUGGESTED READINGS

Abramson, M.A., and N. W. Gardner. *Human Capital 2002.* Lanham, Md.: Rowman and Littlefield Publishers, 2002.

Brudney, J. L. *Fostering Volunteer Programs in the Public Sector: Planning, Initiating, and Managing Voluntary Activities.* San Francisco: Jossey-Bass, 1990.

Condrey, S. E., and R. Maranto, eds. *Radical Reform of the Civil Service.* New York: Lexington Books, 2001.

HR Center. *Internet/Computer.* Washington D.C.: International Personnel Management Association, 2002.

HR Center. *Workplace Violence III.* Washington, D.C.: International Personnel Management Association, 2000.

Injury Prevention Research Center. *Workplace Violence: A Report to the Nation.* Iowa City, Iowa: University of Iowa, 2001.

International Personnel Management Association. *Technology Trends and the Impact on Human Resources Management.* Washington, D.C.: International Personnel Management Association, 2001.

Jones, J. W. *Virtual HR: Human Resources Management in the Information Age.* Menlo Park, Calif.: Crisp, 1998.

Kettl, D. F. *Sharing Power: Public Governance and Private Markets.* Washington, D.C.: The Brookings Institution Press, 1993.

Light, P. C. *The New Public Service.* Washington, D.C.: The Brookings Institution Press, 1999.

Marcella, A. *Outsourcing, Downsizing and Reengineering.* Chicago: Institute of Internal Auditors, 1995.

McNaught, B. *Gay Issues in the Workplace.* New York: St. Martin's Press, 1993.

National Academy of Public Administration. *The Case for Transforming Public Sector Human Resources Management.* Washington, D.C.: National Academy of Public Administration, 2000.

National Academy of Public Administration. *Work/Life Programs: Helping Managers, Helping Employees.* Washington, D.C.: National Academy of Public Administration, 1998.

National Organization for Women Legal Defense and Education Fund. *Creating Solutions—Creating Change: The Impact of Violence in the Lives of Working Women.* Washington, D.C.: National Organization for Women, 2002.

Rothwell, W. J., R. K. Prescott, and M. W. Taylor. *Strategic Human Resource Management: How to Prepare Your Organization for the Six Key Trends Shaping the Future.* Palo Alto, Calif.: Davies-Black Publishing, 2000.

Sims, R. R., and J. G. Veres, III, eds. *Keys to Employee Success in Coming Decades.* Westport, Conn.: Quorum Books, 1999.

U.S. Department of Labor, Bureau of Labor Statistics. *Violence in the Workplace.* Washington, D.C.: Bureau of Labor Statistics, 1995.

SELECTED WEB SITES

Center for Digital Government. National research and advisory institute that provides support, research, and education to government and industry on integrating technology into organizations. www.centerdigitalgov.com

E-governance Institute. Institute within Rutgers University's National Center for Public
   Productivity; collects and shares information to enhance understanding and use of the
   Internet and information technologies and their relationship to the performance of
   government. www.andromeda.rutgers.edu/~nccp/
Family Violence Prevention Fund. Nonprofit institution that works to prevent domestic
   violence. Publishes data and sponsors educational efforts. Includes material on the
   relationship between domestic and workplace violence. http://endabuse.org
International Personnel Management Association for Human Resources (IPMA-HR).
   Membership organization that disseminates information and holds conferences on all
   aspects of human resources including trends and innovations. www.ipma-hr.org
National Association of State Personnel Executives (NASPE). Organization of state personnel directors that publishes a newsletter and reports on innovations in state personnel practices. www.naspe.net
National Center for Injury Prevention and Control. Agency that provides research and
   assistance on workplace injuries and how to prevent them. www.cdc.gov/ncipc
National Commission on the Public Service. Established to conduct research on the federal
   service and to make recommendations for reform. www.brookings.org/dybdocroot/
   volcker/commissionmembers.htm
National Institute for Government Innovation (NIGI). Organization that promotes innovations in the public service. Includes information on technology, e-government, and
   contracting/privatization. www.nigi.org
U.S. Department of Labor, Occupational Safety and Health Administration (OSHA).
   Agency with responsibility to ensure safety in the workplace, including workplace violence. Collects and publishes information on the issue. www.osha.gov

Appendix:
Journals That Regularly Publish Articles on Public Personnel

The following list includes journals that publish materials on public personnel administration on a regular basis. Because other journals also publish on the topic, readers should not regard this list as inclusive.

Administrative Science Quarterly
Advances in Developing Human Resources
The American Review of Public Administration
CRS Review
Compensation and Benefits Review
Disability and Society
Disability, Handicap and Society
Disability Compliance Bulletin
Employee Assistance Quarterly
Employee Benefit Plan Review
Employee Benefits Journal
Employee Relations Law Journal
Governing
Government Executive
Government Union Review
Harvard Business Review
Human Relations
Human Resources Abstracts
Human Resources Development Review
Industrial Relations
Industrial and Labor Relations Review
IPMA News
Journal of ASTD
Journal of Collective Negotiations in the Public Sector
Journal of Labor Research
Journal of Public Administration Research and Theory
Labor Law Journal
Management

Mental and Physical Law Reporter
Monthly Labor Review
National Disability Law Reporter
Personnel
Personnel Psychology
Proceedings of the Annual Meeting of the Industrial Relations Research
  Association
Public Administration Quarterly
Public Administration Review
Public Integrity
Public Management
The Public Manager
Public Personnel Management
Public Productivity and Management Review
Review of Public Personnel Administration
State and Local Government Review
Work and Occupations

INDEX